LITTLE HOUSE IN THE SUBURBS

LITTLE HOUSE IN THE SUBURBS
BACKYARD FARMING AND HOME SKILLS FOR SELF-SUFFICIENT LIVING

DEANNA CASWELL AND DAISY SISKIN

BETTERWAY HOME
CINCINNATI, OHIO
WWW.BETTERWAYBOOKS.COM

CONTENTS

INTRODUCTION

SELF-SUFFICIENCY SUBURBAN STYLE

Most people think that to live a simple life, you have to quit your job, sell your house, and move to the boonies.

That's a bunch of hooey.

When you reminisce about the "simpler" times, before the industrial revolution heralded in the age of convenience and consumerism, remember that not everyone lived on a farm. Consider the village blacksmith, the schoolteacher, and the general-store owner. Maybe some had a garden or some had chickens, but they lived in town and had jobs. The town cobbler wasn't saying, "Boy, I need to get back to basics and quit making shoes. I need to move to the country and start farming so I can sustain myself." These people lived simple, self-reliant lives within city limits.

And so can you.

Plenty of books out there will tell you how to thrive in the boonies: building cabins, digging wells, slaughtering your own meat, and growing grain. This book is not one of those. This book is about those simple-living behaviors that fit easily into a typical suburban neighborhood.

Humans are *makers*. We always have been. We look at our environment and build, mix, or cobble what we need. But presently we don't need to make much, and when we do make something, it's as a hobby not a necessity. We've lost touch with that take-care-of-yourself-ness that people had before discount megamarts.

Make one batch of lotion or soap and see how good you feel. It's like having superpowers. That sense of confidence and accomplishment is what years of comfort have taken away from us.

Again, there are plenty of books out there about remaking your universe from little more than tree sap, birch bark, and a can-do attitude. That lifestyle will certainly give you back your sense of self-reliance, and make no mistake, we think those books are *cool*, but this just isn't one of them.

Remember the village schoolteacher we talked about? There's plenty of empowerment to be had within the town limits. We're not advocating going whole hog, but we are advocating filling that little need we all have to stay in touch with our resourceful side. It's about finding what we've lost, having fun, and stopping when you've had enough.

Page through this book and learn how things are made. Then try your hand at a few. Don't worry about screwing it up. We sure have. And none of this stuff is carved in stone. Sure, we tested and re-tested the recipes for you, but we don't know *everything*, yet. So, jump in! If something doesn't work out, blame us and try something else.

You don't have to go as far as we have, raising plants and egg-laying hens, but try making a fruit roll-up or some mayo. You'll never get over the sense of accomplishment you get when you make something with your own two hands out of stuff around the house. Did you know that you can *make* a Pop-Tart?

There's a good, wholesome sense of empowerment and grown-up-ness that comes with being able to create from scratch something you previously thought was hatched in a store.

Deanna found a recipe online just the other day. Amazing!

We sincerely hope that this book does several things for you:

- First, that you, like us, have that wonderful, "you-can-really-make-that-stuff?" experience. There's a childlike joy in finding out that things aren't born in boxes.
- Second, that you find at least three things in here that can become part of your life and give you the satisfaction of having made something yourself.
- And finally, most of all, we hope this book gives you a greater sense of power and control over your world.

There's something comforting in knowing that we've equipped ourselves to look at our environment and, out of it, make something we want or need. That training reassures us that if we were in a crisis or dropped on a desert island—or that zombie apocalypse Deanna's husband keeps practicing for on the Xbox ever happens—we'd be better prepared to function.

So why go self-sufficient suburban style? Superpowers.

Fine. Family health and superpowers.

1

WHY SIMPLE LIVING IN THE SUBURBS?

Getting back to basics is just plain good for you! In this chapter, we'll outline some of the million reasons why you should try it, and we'll address some of the most common objections. We'll tell you why it's great for your body, your soul, and your planet, and why it's all possible right in the middle of the burbs.

It's Good for the Body

HOMEGROWN PRODUCE IS HIGH IN NUTRITION AND FLAVOR

DAISY My five-year-old and her faithful two-year-old shadow (her sister) stood at the edge of the fall mesclun bed, eyeballing it hesitantly.

I confess, I can be a tiny bit, shall we say . . . *maniacal* when it comes to children in the vegetable garden. Give 'em an inch and they take a mile. Or, more accurately, they will plow in the dirt like giant groundhogs and decimate an entire crop. I've had to lay down ground rules, so the older one knows to ask first.

"Can we have some?" she inquired politely.

This is a normal suburban child, not some alien wunderkind from Planet Whole Foods.

I'm saying this kid knows how to pry open a SnackPak and how to pop open a bag of chips.

"Of course," I answered. "Have as much as you like." How many mixed salad greens could people whose combined age is lower than my ring size possibly eat? I reminded them how to pick leaves without pulling up the entire plant (a hard-won lesson), and went about my business.

The next day, as I prepared to water the garden, I stared in alarm at an entire four-foot row of arugula, mixed mustards, oakleaf lettuce, and kale. It was nibbled down to stubs. Rabbits? Ravenous caterpillars?

Then I remembered. Rug rats.

My babies ate about a pound of fresh-as-it-gets, organically grown leafy greens straight up.

I shouldn't have been surprised. They're fascinated by the vegetable garden. It has so

much of their favorite things: dirt, dirt, more dirt, blossoms, bugs, watering wands, and stuff growing in it that you can eat! Who cares that it's vegetables? It's out there in the yard! You pick it yourself!

It's not just *my* kids. Experts have compared the eating habits of children receiving garden-based nutrition education with that of kids getting classroom-only nutrition education. The group who got the hands-on learning increased their fruit, vegetable, fiber, and vitamins A and C intake significantly compared to the classroom-only group.

Seeing it, feeling it, smelling it, tasting it—that's how you get comfortable with something and learn to accept it as a part of your life. This is so important because the habits children pick up early on impact their eating patterns throughout their lives.

Another reason my kids will plow through the garden, metaphorical fork in hand, is that the food tastes so good. Homegrown, particularly organically homegrown, produce is fresher, sweeter, and more delicious than much of what ends up in the supermarket. The varieties of veggies and fruits available in supermarkets are selected for their ability to withstand shipping and handling over long distances, and not for their taste or texture. Heirloom vegetables and fruit are famously delectable while having a shorter shelf life, so you'll have a hard time finding them in your major-chain grocery store.

When you grow your own, you can choose from a breathtaking breadth of succulent, colorful, and even whimsical cultivars, no matter how poorly they perform when packed into eighteen-wheelers and shipped across the country. When you grow them yourself, they'll only need to travel from your backyard to your kitchen, or from the little chubby hand of a toddler to his mouth.

DIRT IS GOOD FOR YOU

I heard the noise first. It sounded like a road grader was scraping the asphalt off the driveway. I looked out the kitchen window and saw that it was my kids, pulling each other across the rough pavement in one of the recycling bins to which I've attached a rope.

Cute, right?

Until you know it's the same recycling bin that doubles as a tote I use to haul horse manure from a nearby horse stable to my compost pile.

This started me thinking about the unconventional twist on my family's suburban lifestyle. On the surface, our home is a normal house on a normal street in a suburban bedroom community. Scratch that surface, though, and you'll find some differences. In the backyard, every jot and tittle of sun space

is taken up by a raised-bed vegetable-and-herb garden. Beyond the garden, eight fluffy-bottomed hens peck and scratch and make addictively relaxing cooing sounds as they search for treasure (bugs) in the chicken yard. In the far corner, behind a shed, about forty thousand honeybees conduct their mysterious apian business in a homemade beehive. Fig and peach trees push and shove the blueberry and blackberry bushes for the last of the sunny spots. I haul manure in recycling bins in the back of my car. And, apparently, I let my kids play in the bins.

As I watched them through the window I had a brief thought of putting an end to their fun, but then I got over it. While I won't go so far as to say a little horse poop never hurt anybody, it, well, it never hurt anybody.

I had, of course, rinsed it out—I think—but if the scientists are right, I shouldn't have. The number of people with allergies and autoimmune disorders is going up, and some point the finger of blame at our overly scrubbed and sanitized lives.

Our immune systems aren't getting the same early training they once received when

consortium on perfect parenting decreed that permitting my two-year-old to sit on the kitchen counter and eat leftover gorgonzola cheese dressing out of a bowl with her hands is the apex of responsible child rearing.

Dirt is good for people? Yep, especially kids, and the younger they get dirty, the better. When I heard about these studies, in addition to the excitement described above, I felt confusion. I'd always been warned to wash my hands clear down to the nub fifty times a day. I've watched disinfectant commercials with germy animations that made me want to seal my family up in a bubble. I've been told to bleach this and boil that, to wrap my infants in cocoons of sterility until their early twenties, at least.

Now they say early exposure to dirt promotes a robust immune system and gives protection against allergies, Type 1 diabetes, multiple sclerosis, irritable bowel syndrome, Crohn's disease, asthma, and even heart disease and Alzheimer's. Farm kids exposed to rural dust, including manure, were less allergic than their non-farm counterparts. Holy mackerel.

I may be doing my kids a favor by letting them play in the manure/recycling bin. I'm relieved. And not just because I won't be subjected to their tortured howls if I have to tell them to get out of it. It means my off-the-beaten-path lifestyle as a suburban homesteading pioneer has one more thing to recommend it.

REAL WORK KEEPS DAISY FROM BICYCLING IN CIRCLES

An acquaintance once told me, "The biggest result of the Industrial Revolution is that we all got fat. Machines do for us what we used to do for ourselves, and oddly, for us to remain healthy, all of that effort and sweat we no longer use to feed, clothe, and shelter ourselves

we were all "down on the farm," and now our bodies don't know how to act. Early exposure to germs and allergens teaches our immune reactions how best to protect us from actual germs while ignoring dust, pollen and other harmless irritants.

In short, dirt can be good for you. As a parent of small children, let me tell you how that makes me feel. It's like the authorities have declared that eating a pint of Häagen-Dazs dulce de leche ice cream while spending all day in your pajamas is the secret to a long and prosperous life. It's like the international

tangible purpose. You can work for hours and then stand back and look at what you've done.

Gathering manure in those recycling bins is not a shabby way to spend an afternoon (contrary to how it sounds), and it gives you a heck of a work out. The horses watch me dubiously as I make my way around the pasture, pulling my bin behind me from patty to patty, scooping with a flat-bladed shovel. I collect all I can, so the bins are impossibly heavy by the time I'm ready to lift them into the car.

I could get this good of a workout at the gym, but it wouldn't have the side effect of gargantuan organic Swiss chard and tomatoes the size of cantaloupes. And, I can't pay a fitness center in jars of homemade pickles, which is how I compensate the owner of the horses for use of their manure.

Deanna doesn't share my manure obsession, but you'll never catch her in a gym either. Her most common form of exercise is animal chasing. She has wonderful fences, but curious children, so the animals get released—often. She's forever chasing chickens around the yard to get them back in the coop, pinning reluctant goats between her knees to file their hooves, and chronically moving her hay pile from here to there, to there, and to there (she's yet to find a permanent spot she likes).

She's a dirt-mover, too, and constantly changing her mind about where she wants things in her yard. She digs up the flowerbeds and replaces them with strawberry patches. When the Bermuda grass invades the strawberries to the point that she can't weed them in a week of Sundays, she mows it all down and replants something shrubby.

And she's never had the same garden twice. One year it was four boxes here; the next year twelve boxes over there; then the next year she dug it all up for a 40' × 40' (12m × 12m) row garden. She burns a lot of calories that way.

must be replaced. So we go to the gym." I have to agree.

The gym is one solution. The other is turning back the clock a bit, here and there, to pre-Industrial-Revolution practices so you can skip the gym membership entirely.

I am not a fan of regimented exercise. Put me on a workout schedule and I rebel. I refuse to stay on the schedule, and the guilt over broken promises to myself and to my cardio-vascular system is crippling. However, give me some hard labor that involves composting, weeding, or animal care, and I have to be dragged away from it. It has an immediate,

Now we're not saying that our bodies couldn't use a few good walks around the neighborhood each week, but back-to-basics living certainly isn't your typical sedentary American lifestyle.

Good for the Soul

GARDENING + ANIMAL CARE = HEALTH AND WELL-BEING

I wish I had a blood pressure cuff to capture empirically what I know instinctively to be true: Gardening chills me out.

When I walk into the garden, the rest of the world hops back. Even if I've been feeling just a skosh homicidal, I can let it go amongst the vegetation. All that matters is the fresh, wee sprouts, standing at attention in the rich soil as if impressed by their own greenness. All I can think about is which plant is looking gorgeous today, which one looks like it could use a drink, and which one just had half its peppers eaten off by a hornworm.

I examine each bed, every plant, amazed. One of the things that astounds me most is how much time I can waste staring at the same doggone plants day after day, month after month. It's phenomenal. What is going on with me? Just about everything else bores me eventually.

If you haven't started growing food yet, but are about to, consider this your fair warning. Start buying presentable pajamas and house shoes with hard-wearing soles. The vegetables will whisper to you while you are enjoying your morning tea, "We've been growing all night. Remember that water you gave us yesterday? Mmm, it was so good we're extra plump and green and our blossoms are all bursting open."

Before you know it, you're out there pawing though the cucumber vines to count the bristly baby cukes with mulch clinging to your fuzzy slippers and your robe waving open to your neighbors in the morning breeze.

It's magic. So what if your arms are itchy and the neighbors now know your unseemly affinity for SpongeBob SquarePants night wear? The okra is in bloom and their blossoms outshine the most fanciful gowns ever to grace a red carpet. There are white eggplants suspended like giant pearl earrings beneath broad, velvety leaves damp with dew. The air smells like dill and humus and the gardener's aphrodisiac: tomato leaves.

Leave it to the scientists, not content with poetic hyperbole like me, to conduct research on man's relationship with his bit of ground.

No surprise here, gardening correlates with emotional well-being, stress relief, resilience, and a sense of achievement. The benefits of the physical activity of gardening as well as its mental and emotional advantages form a whole greater than the sum of its parts. Add to this garden a few hens to fuss over or a pair of busybody goats and you've got something else entirely to focus on other than your own navel.

It's enough to make the most type-A personality take it down a notch. I'm not promising you can toss all your mood prescriptions in the bin, but maybe, just maybe, the FBI can slide you down a little lower on its watch list.

BACK-TO-BASICS BRING THE FAMILY TOGETHER

DEANNA Every summer, when I was a child, my siblings and I spent a week at my Pop and Gran's house while my parents attended the annual conference for my father's job. In those days, Pop and Gran still grew a great deal of their own food. They hunted, fished, and made all kinds of things from scratch.

One of my fondest memories is of sitting around with them snapping pole beans for canning. It wasn't an activity Gran had made up for us to do together; it was necessary work—just a part of having a bountiful garden. The beans all came in at the same time, so there were bags and bags of them to string and snap.

I also loved collecting squash with Pop and pulling up peanuts and picking blackberries together. These weren't idle five-minute (or even fifteen-minute) activities. It took ages.

And when my parents came back on Friday, there was always a fish fry, so during the week, there was plenty of fishing to be done. We had to help prepare the meal simply because we were there. Pop cleaned, cut, and battered the fish we caught. Gran fried the fillets. And the children made the hush puppies.

My grandparents passed away years ago, but I've never once thought, *I wish I'd spent some "quality time" with them.* All the time we spent together was quality time. Turning back the dial a bit on the "progress" meter eliminates the need for scheduled family time. Family time is what happens when Mom is up to her eyeballs in zucchini and everyone has to pitch in.

At my house, the same thing happens when we dig the sweet potatoes, pick the strawberries, take the goats out to "pasture" in the front yard or when it's time to trim hooves and clip the chickens' wings. It's a big job, so we do it together.

Way back in the days before big-box stores, our lives revolved around food, clothing, and shelter. The entire family worked together to meet these needs, taking care of family quality time along the way. Whether it was tearing up scraps for the next quilt or shucking a field of corn, the family worked together to get it done.

It sounds silly to say that it's time our lives got back to revolving around food (that's exactly what the talk shows are telling us not to do, right?), but that seems to be what humans are made for. I can hear you say, "But, we're Americans! Aren't we meant for something more important?"

True, taking the long way around to provide our basic needs may not be the flashiest deal on the planet, but lots of really important things happen during those chores. On his deathbed, no one says, "I wish I'd kept up more with current events." People always wish for more time with family. If you want to go to sleep each night thinking, *If I were told I'd die tonight, I wouldn't change anything about this day,* try getting back to basics. Simple living is family togetherness.

BUILD YOUR SELF-RELIANCE
I used to think that pretty much everything delicious or useful was born in a factory. These things were closely guarded magic formulas, like the Colonel's eleven herbs and spices. You couldn't *make* shampoo or croutons! And even if you did, homemade couldn't be as good, or why would anyone buy it from a store?

The truth is, there's an unconscious, uncomfortable helplessness that comes with relying on corporations and factories for everything. And when you figure out a way not to rely on the system to survive, something deep inside you is nourished. I've yet to met anyone who didn't get a power high from eating green beans they grew themselves or from scrubbing up with homemade soap.

Let me illustrate: Back in the Civil War, Daisy's great-great grandmother's farm was burnt to the ground, and she and her family lived under an oak tree for several months. Grammy Siskin wasn't specially trained in survival skills, but she knew how to survive nonetheless. She and her eldest son walked twenty-two miles to get wheat from one of the few fields that hadn't been destroyed by the war. They harvested it by hand, and threshed out two bushels of grain by beating it against a rail. To make the boiled wheat palatable, she managed to get salt by boiling the dirt floor of the destroyed smokehouse.

In 2002, we had a storm of straight-line winds in our area. Locals called it Hurricane Elvis. We were without electricity for two weeks. After the panic settled, I felt a general irritation at our helplessness. Lots of folks went to the big-box hardware stores and bought generators. But, I kept thinking about Daisy's great-great grandmother. I had ten times more than she had under that oak tree: a home, running water, plumbing, a car, stores full of food—but somehow I was helpless. I was more educated, but somehow much less able to take care of myself. I did cook dinner in the fireplace while my neighbors went out to eat every day, so I knew that I wasn't quite as helpless as some. But Great-great-grandma would have been ashamed of me!

Now, we're not advocating becoming like Daisy's great-great-grandmother (if that's what you're looking for, you'll need to contact our friends the Survivalists), but it appeals to something at a primal level in all of us suburbanites to be able to make something out of our environment with our own two hands.

SIMPLE LIVING REALLY IS EASIER
People think back to basics is so much work! Right now, when you're in lazy mode, you probably say something like this: "I don't feel like cooking from scratch. Let's buy a frozen pizza."

As you get back to basics, you'll discover your idea of cutting corners, or being lazy, shifts. You'll be able to say, "I don't feel like going to the store today. We're having fresh eggs and broccoli from the garden." You won't need to go to the store because you'll have fresh food from your garden on hand.

When you become less dependent on big-box stores, you find that visiting them is so tiresome that you'll put off that trip as long as possible. You'll start thinking, *What do I have around the house that will do the trick so I don't have to deal with all those lines?* Making something from scratch or "making do" with something less convenient is so much easier!

Good for the Planet

There's nothing like simple living to reduce your trash-day contribution to the landfill. The goats and chickens eat every leftover, every vegetable end, every banana peel. The only thing we don't feed the chickens is chicken. Not that they won't eat it—it just grosses me out. But if it doesn't bother you, every single food item can disappear and turn into eggs.

Even if you don't choose to have animals, all your vegetable ends and banana peels will be in the compost pile or the garden. Every lawn clipping and fallen leaf (I don't have these because of the goats) goes, too. All your paper and pizza boxes can go in as well. Or it can all go in your mulch beds as fertilizer and weed blankets. I think every box from last Christmas ended up in the front flowerbeds, and with three kids and three sets of grandparents, that's a lot of cardboard.

Once you start cooking real food from scratch more often, you'll encounter less packaging of every kind. Flour sacks and fruit peels? It's just not the same as the mountain of cardboard, layers of plastic wrap, and unrecyclable little foil bags that conventional snacking and pre-made meals create.

And heaven forbid you start canning! No more rinsing for the recycling man? No peeling labels? No BPA? It's mind-boggling.

When you're used to being self-reliant, you'll realize that you don't need to replace every convenience item you own. You'll find substitutions. My slow cooker died, so now I use a big pot. My teapot died, so I boil water in a small cooking pot. My yogurt maker died, so I use a bowl on a heating pad. My bread maker and dehydrator died, so I use the oven. My microwave died, so I use my toaster oven

(which I will totally replace when it dies. It's the most useful gadget I own).

So not only is there no packaging or far-flung shipping for my bread, yogurt, dried fruit, and more, there's also no packaging or future disposal for all the convenience contraptions.

Maybe you won't be as crazy as we are, but just remember, the simpler you live, the greener you get.

SIMPLE LIVING: COMING TO A TOWN NEAR YOU

The town of Mouscron, Belgium, population 53,000, had a problem. Their community received a bill for $15,000 for going over their landfill waste allowance for 2004—not good for an already tight budget. Residents put their heads together and devised a plan for reducing the average amount of household waste. Part of that plan involved, of all things, chickens.

The city offered a pair of hens to each household that would agree to keep them for a minimum of two years and feed them kitchen and yard waste.

It's estimated that one chicken can consume about 330 pounds of green waste in a year. This waste is converted into about two hundred eggs and, of course, manure, about forty-pounds worth that can be used to fertilize garden soil.

To date, residents of Mouscron have adopted 150 pairs of chickens. That's three hundred chickens with the combined potential of consuming up to 100,000 pounds of waste. That's also sixty thousand eggs and twelve thousand pounds of fertilizer.

Chebeague Island, Maine, had a similar problem. As an island, removing the community's waste uses up a large chunk of the local budget. In this case, a private, grassroots effort arose to help free up part of the budgeted waste-removal money to better spend it on the island's residents and businesses. Using a five hundred dollar grant, salvaged materials, and volunteer labor, residents built compost bins and located them on donated land. The organizers have a common drop-off point for donations of waste and also visit participating residents twice a week for pickups. They plan to expand the program in the future by conducting composting education workshops and by spreading the success of their program to other area islands.

The small town of Collierville, Tennessee, has a reputation as a prosperous suburban community. But like most places, many of its residents have been hard-hit by tough economic circumstances. The local free-food pantry was doing a brisk business, but something was missing: fresh produce. Local master gardeners decided to meet this need by beginning the Collierville Victory Garden to serve as a source for fresh vegetables for the pantry as well as a site for community gardening education. Located behind a church, the garden is operated by teams of volunteers. To date, the garden has yielded almost ten thousand pounds of fresh produce for donation to those in need, and served as an example of urban gardening for area schoolchildren.

These are just three small examples. Whether city-organized and subsidized or privately funded and run, diverse sustainable programs are taking root across the world. From the micro level (composting your own kitchen waste, starting a small garden) or a community level (city-wide composting and gardening education, for example), it's worth the effort.

If you're thinking, *My neighborhood tells me what colors I can paint my shutters. There's no way they're going to sit still while I get all sustainable over here*, you may be right. It depends in good measure on how you do it, what you choose to do, and how progressive the powers that be are willing to be.

There's a delicate balance to these issues, and that's where we want to help: Balance.

Seriously, In the Suburbs? Yes!

DEANNA You may agree with everything you've read so far, but you still may be thinking there's no way you can pull off this simple, sustainable life where you currently live. You think you need land! That's what everyone said. Get out of the burbs! You need acres! Like we were the reverse Beverly Hillbillies.

Our answer is *no*! We like it here. We like being surrounded by people. We like that when the toddler escapes, we know he's in the neighbor's garage. We like our postage-stamp-sized front yards and our privacy fences and our police departments with under-two-minute response times. We like that we can be as weird as we want and still get to Chili's in under five minutes. I'll make roast chicken and gravy and biscuits and fried green tomatoes for dinner . . . oh, shoot. Let's just have a pizza delivered! See? That's awesome.

We don't dig wells, and we're not reclaiming acres of land. But we get back to the land—it's just tiny, well-groomed, two-minutes-from-Target land. And it still counts! Don't let the naysayers fool you. You can totally be back-to-basics and drive a pimped-out minivan. We do.

SIMPLE LIVING WON'T TAKE OVER YOUR LIFE

DAISY I promise you, readers, there is no law that says you have to give up your fine-tuned grooming habits to hang with the simple-living lifestyle. Gentlemen, you don't have to grow Grizzly Adams beards.

Ladies, you don't need to stop shaving your underarms.

You don't have to forswear impractical shoes, except while actually gardening. You don't have to convert your wardrobe to 100 percent hemp. You don't have to look any different at all. Your house and yard don't need to undergo any extreme upheavals. The neighbors won't have any concerns about lowered property values or wonder if you've joined a cult.

While we're not talking about a complete lifestyle change, here are some of the things we are talking about:

- You can grow a few vegetables in pots on the patio or plant a pretty herb garden in containers or a landscaping bed.
- Plant a small raised-bed garden and grow some of that mesclun that's so pricey at the supermarket.
- The next time a photinia shrub dies, and it will, replace it with a dwarf fruit tree or a blueberry bush. Think edible when it comes time to plant for privacy or beauty around your house.

You can go green under your kitchen sinks and vanity sinks, too. All those household cleaners can be replaced with a few simple concoctions made from nontoxic, everyday ingredients. When your infant learns to crawl, you can concentrate your baby-proofing efforts on keeping her away from dangers to your walls such as crayons, rather than Formula 409, because you won't have any chemical cleaners in the house.

You can take care of your skin with a few things you stir up at home instead of what you buy at the drugstore. Do packages that promise shea butter, essential oils, and avocado oil seduce you? Instead of buying premade products that contain only hints of these attractive ingredients, make them yourself entirely out of those things, and, as a bonus, you can

leave out the cocktail of unpronounceable and potentially harmful chemicals.

You can make your own pantry basics, including mustard and mayo, jams, pickles, vanilla extract, and Tabasco sauce. Then you'll know exactly what's in the condiments you're eating and you can adjust the flavors to suit your family's preferences and nutritional requirements. (As an added bonus, you may feel a tad bit superior to those who eat store-bought pantry staples.)

Finally, if you want to stick your toe just over the edge, consider a few laying hens or a couple of miniature goats as productive pets.

Yes, this may raise a few eyebrows, but it's getting more and more mainstream all the time. After all, keeping wolf descendants and tiny tigers probably seemed extreme at one point in human history, but it caught on eventually (and your cat or dog thanks your ancestors).

YOU CAN STILL HOST A BARBECUE

Aside from the fact that my children sometimes use sidewalk chalk to draw rainbows all over the siding, the front of my house doesn't look any different from any other normal house.

The idea of sustainability and simple living in the suburbs (and even in urban areas) can evoke images of rooftop meadows and cornfields in front yards, but it doesn't have to be that way. You can keep things neat, simple, and completely camouflaged.

You can have the neighborhood association president over and open up the patio for grilling and chewing the fat without worrying about the Code Enforcement Officer knocking on your door the next day.

In fact, edible gardening can be downright gorgeous. I have a friend with a stunning heirloom red okra plant next to the lantana at her mailbox. It's beautiful and blends in perfectly, adding texture, color, and form while looking right at home (plus it makes a delicious addition to gumbo!).

Herbs beg to be shown off. Rosemary grows to shrub size in many climates. The soft, green-gray leaves of sage are pettable, pretty, and so much tastier than its ornamental cousin salvia. Why not plant the edible instead? Lavender can't be beat for ornamental value and it adds a perfume-like pizzazz to many dishes as well as fragrant crafts. Salad greens can look spectacular in pots and tidy beds. Strawberries are adorable spilling over onto walkways. The list goes on and on. We'll show you how to do it and how to make it both pretty and delicious.

Ah, but what about those chickens you keep talking about? Poop everywhere! The crowing! And the goats, they'll decimate your yard, right?

It takes careful planning and the right accommodations to make this work, just like with any household pets. But, chicken houses are some of the cutest structures I've ever seen. They can rival the snazziest playhouses and garden sheds for those who want to make the effort or the investment, and even the simplest and most basic versions can be trim and elegant. They can be kept hygienically, and because you need only *hens* for eggs, and *not* roosters, there'll be no crowing at the crack of dawn.

If you ever decide to go as far as goats, they need good fences, like wily dogs. Unlike dogs, however, they won't drive the neighbors berserk with their barking, and they won't chase the mailman. They don't dig out, can't bite, and they don't produce anything that sticks to the bottom of a shoe.

So whether you plant one pot of strawberries or choose to go all out with the works, it's doable with planning and an eye toward consideration for your neighbors and your own family members. From small steps to larger undertakings, we'll show you step by step how you can do it and still remain on good terms with your community.

Low Cost, Low Commitment

DEANNA I saw a bumper sticker yesterday that read *Please spay and neuter your pets*. It had cat and dog paw prints on it. Let me tell you, you're never going to see a bumper sticker advising you to sterilize goats and chickens. Why is that? It's because baby goats and chicks are cash money to anyone who knows what they can do. If you get a puppy and change your mind, it's the pound or a rescue and tons of guilt. If you try baby chicks and goats and change your mind, put them up on Craigslist for twenty bucks and they'll be gone before lunch. The same is true for rabbits, bees, or any other typical farm-type baby animal. If you don't go for eye-candy pedigree versions, all you'll be out is the gas it took to get them to your house and maybe a bag of food.

Gardening is low commitment, too. *It's stirred up dirt fertilized with trash*. As long as you don't build raised beds from gold or get lassoed in by the expensive, bagged, organic dirt, it costs almost nothing. And if you hate it, just ignore it for a few months and it turns back into a well-fertilized lawn. No sweat. At worst, you'll be out some elbow grease.

Composting, unless you bought one of those unnecessary fancy contraptions, costs nothing. It's just a glorified pile of trash. If you decide to quit, it will flatten out as it decomposes (a trait that depresses us avid composters) and disappears in no time.

In short, simple living is simple. It shouldn't involve expensive equipment, special tools, or fancy contraptions. This is how pioneers lived when they had no stores, so it shouldn't cost much of anything. If you abandon it, it just turns back into what it was—just as the land did when pioneers moved somewhere else. There's no negative impact.

It's not like taking up car rebuilding. Hobbies that are based on manufactured items take up useful space. Simple living makes space useful.

You can, of course go broke stuffing your cabinets with gadgets if you like. Yogurt makers, bread makers, dehydrators, soymilk makers, herb kits, shitake logs, seeders, spreaders, greenhouses, I bought all these things in the beginning. Now, I use almost none of them. You need no gadgets to go simple. Don't get suckered in.

But don't you need some things? Yes, eventually. Eventually the chicks and goats get too big for the dog kennel and may need a real fence and real houses. The same is true for kitchen gadgets. I've said to myself about twenty times now, "This carrot peeler just isn't making skinny zucchini noodles like I want. I wish there was something else out there." So I put a ten-dollar julienne slicer gadget on my Amazon wish list.

The time to buy is after you've settled into your simple life and know your challenges and your commitment level, not in the beginning when you're feeling it all out. Get an idea of what you like and what you struggle with, then make purchases that will enhance your experiences or help you solve a problem. After twenty tries, you may decide that the slow-cooker method of yogurt making just doesn't give you the results you want. If that's the case, then go buy a yogurt maker.

Simple living is a lifestyle change, but it's an inexpensive one. Try it. If you hate it, quit! No risk. Most cases, you've only wasted calories and a little effort.

2

I GREW IT MYSELF! OR, BUT YOU DON'T UNDERSTAND, I KILL EVERYTHING

Gardening is central to back-to-basics living. There's nothing like growing something in your yard and eating it at dinner (even if you grow only one basil plant in a spot where another plant died last year). Entire books exist on gardening, and it can seem a daunting hobby, but never fear. We're too lazy for an all-consuming hobby. Gardening truly is a trial-and-error process.

Daisy and I find that each gardener has both strengths and catastrophic weaknesses. I can grow the mess out of squash, sweet potatoes, basil, strawberries, and asparagus. Daisy could feed a third-world country with her lettuce, greens, and tomato crops. My friend Missy has the gift of green beans, peas, and okra. And we all live within twenty minutes of each other, so climate isn't the answer.

Just get me near a tomato plant and it fails. And Daisy, well, she can't grow squash. She's tried foil, organics, companion planting, and once even wrapped the entire bed in white tulle, but no luck with squash (except that time she set out to grow red potatoes in a trash can and ended up with butternut squash in there instead. That's still a mystery.) And, none of us can grow carrots! We know only one gal in our area who can get decent carrots. We don't know how she does it. I say she's made a pact with the devil and waters them with babies' tears.

So, don't worry about killing things. We've all done it. And we'll all do it again this year. Just remember that there will always be some plant you can't do anything with and others that you can grow better than anyone you know. That's why God invented trading.

This chapter will teach you what you need to know to grow some food in a container or a raised bed. If you *really* get into the details of it, then we'll give you a list of those wonderful exhaustive gardening books that make us tired.

Let's Start With Dirt, You Can't Kill That

COMPOST: TO BUY OR TO MAKE?

DAISY If you're going to garden, you need to have compost. You have two choices for obtaining compost: You can buy it or you can make it.

Compost is sold at nurseries, home-improvement stores and discount stores. When you buy compost, it's typically harvested from a single source, which could be cows or chickens or mushrooms. This single source limits the amount of nutrients in the compost.

Homemade compost comes from numerous sources—coffee grounds, yard waste, peels

If at First You Don't Succeed

Deanna

The first vegetable-plant murder that occurred in my yard was an accident. Daisy was digging my very first garden. I was eight months pregnant with my first child. So out of the kindness of her heart, Daisy agreed to do the work for me. She lugged bags of compost. She dug in the soil amendments. She was the one sweating. I'd shopped. I'd ordered a fancy set of tomato and pepper plants from a magazine. One of each flavor. And then it happened.

"I think I snapped its neck," Daisy said as she examined a tomato seedling she'd just transplanted. That was the first of many plants that died that year. Daisy was responsible for only one. I killed the rest with my typical feast-or-famine attention span. Drown them one day, drought them for a fortnight. I never fed them, and I was lazy about staking. Out of twenty-four tomatoes, bell peppers, hot peppers, lettuces, and I can't remember what else, only the hot peppers survived to produce fruit.

You likely have high hopes for your first garden, and that's a good thing. Maybe you'll have great success with everything you plant. If not, don't give up on the idea of gardening. Try to identify what went wrong and work to fix those mistakes next year, or try different plants next season. Keep trying until you find something you can grow with success.

What Goes in the Compost Pile?

While you can put a lot of waste in a compost pile, there are a few limitations. A quick rule of thumb is no meat or dairy and no waste from carnivorous animals. This type of waste will introduce harmful bacteria to the pile and kill off all the good bacteria that turn the waste into usable soil. Here's a list of good and bad things for your pile.

GOOD	BAD
yard waste (minus dog poo)	any kind of meat
fruits and veggies	any kind of dairy
paper, newspaper	veggies cooked with meat or dairy
plain cardboard	cat, dog, and human feces
coffee filters and grounds	magazines/glossy print pages
tea bags	
chicken, goat, cow, horse manure	

and ends from every vegetable you've eaten in the last year, chunks of plants you grew last year—so it will have a billion different nutrients. For that reason, homemade compost is much richer and more effective than store-bought. However, you can mimic the richness of homemade compost by mixing different kinds of store-bought composts.

How to Improve Store-Bought Compost

1. Buy *six* different kinds of compost in any varieties you can find—mushroom, chicken, cotton burr, cow, etc. You need only one bag of each variety.
2. For small jobs, mix a shovel full of each type of compost in a bucket.
3. For larger jobs, pour the entire contents of each bag on one end of a tarp and roll the compost to the other side of the tarp by lifting the heavy end. This rolling will mix all of the composts together.

How to Make Compost

Homemade compost is really just a glorified pile of trash. There's a science behind it involving moisture, temperature, and ratios, but you don't need to understand the science to have a successful compose pile that produces piles of rich soil.

1. In your yard, pick a spot for your compost that's not too far away from the back door or you'll never hike out there to dump your stuff.
2. Decide if you want a container or just a pile. (We'll show you how to make containers in the next section.)
3. Into your pile dump all your yard leaves, vegetable ends, grass and shrub clippings, and basically anything that was once a plant. You can also add paper, plain cardboard, black-and-white newspaper, manure from grazing animals (herbivores), tea bags, and coffee grounds. Your only limitations are no meat, dairy, or products from the back ends of cats, dogs, and people.

That's it, just three easy steps. You can collect your kitchen waste in a bucket and dump it once a day or dump it after every meal. Nature will take care of the rest.

Daisy, the Curb Robber

Daisy

On my walk this morning, I crossed the road to check out some prime yard-waste bags down the street. Finely mown grass and shredded leaves packed hard into super-sized clear plastic bags. I wanted them. I felt a longing mixed with a whiff of fear that I wouldn't find the time to get over there with my station wagon and claim them before the garbage trucks came to take them away.

Sure, I felt a little weird, pulling up and stuffing other people's garbage tightly into the back of my vehicle until no more would fit. I pictured the lady of the house sitting at her kitchen table, coffee mug paused halfway to her lips, mouth agape, as she watched me make off with her lawn clippings, but it was worth it.

Here are some things that make a particularly good haul:

- clear bags so you know what's in them
- bags of grass from neighbors who you know don't have dogs (poo grass is yuck and introduces harmful bacteria to your compost)
- bags of small leaves or leaves that have been shredded by a mulching mower
- bags of pine needles, which make wonderful free mulch for garden paths
- discarded windows to put over raised beds for a mini greenhouse
- shrub and tree clippings (if you have goats this will keep them busy for the day)
- cast-off containers that would make good planters
- newspapers and big pieces of cardboard for weed blankets and composting
- plastic jugs for handy frost protection

Be on the lookout. Curb robbing is addictive. Note: I learned the hard way that it pays to carry an extra empty bag and a small broom or rake with you on your forays in case a bag breaks halfway to the car and you need to clean up a mess. Wear gloves and work clothes.

If you want to speed things up:

- *"Turn" it periodically.* Stir the compost periodically to aerate it and increase airflow. Depending on your container, stirring could involve a shovel, a handle, or rolling your container across the yard. The rule of thumb I've heard is if you've turned it fifteen times (no more than once per day), it's done.
- *Start with smaller pieces.* Small stuff breaks down faster than big stuff. The more you chop or smash your ingredients, the faster your compost breaks down.

COMPOST CONTAINERS: PRACTICAL OR BEAUTIFUL, BUY OR BUILD?

DEANNA After a few years of experience, I've become a try-before-you-buy kind of gal. Not so much that I want to try the actual product before I buy it, but that I want to try the process before I go get a gadget.

How can you know what you want your gadget to do unless you're already engaged in the activity the gadget is designed for?

You might love to shovel your pile or you might hate it. Maybe you're a leave-it-in-the-ground-and-never-touch-it type. Maybe you're the type who starts three different containers so you never have to sift it. Maybe you're like Daisy and you throw all your vegetable trash directly in your newest garden bed to get it ready for next year. You won't know your style until you try.

So *don't* go out and buy some expensive composting contraption. Compost for a year or so, and *then* go get a gadget. What do you do until then? Try one of these options:

1. *Fencing-wire compost bin.* Use zip ties to secure a roll of chicken wire or horse fencing into a large circle. Place your compost inside.

2. *Kickable trash bin.* Drill several small holes all around a plastic trash can that has a lockable lid. Fill it and kick (or push) it periodically to turn the contents.

3. *Underground bin.* Drill several small holes all around a plastic bin that has a tight lid. Bury the can almost to the lid. Fill it with compostable materials. The underground bin is a good option for meat, bones, and dairy that can't be added to an above-the-ground compost pile.

Mr. Pile and Me

There was a time in my life when composting was my sanity. It may sound strange to make friends with a pile of well-rotted plant matter, but it was there when I needed it. When all the kids were under the age of three and I needed a five-minute hobby with some peace and quiet, Mr. Pile was out there just cooking away, waiting for me to come turn him.

Deanna

I had a simple chicken-wire/zip-tied cylinder full of kitchen cuttings, newspaper, mowed leaves, and grass cuttings. Nothing special, but I doted on him. I'd bring him some bean pods from the feed store or grounds from the local coffee shop. Sometimes, I'd go out on trash day and scour the neighborhood for interesting discarded plants and vines to add.

Our clandestine interludes were nothing if not steamy. That first shovel plunge let loose a heat wave that warmed my heart. Ah ... cooking compost.

After many an afternoon rendezvous, our time was over and I spread his remains among the raised beds. But, he was not to be forgotten easily. He left me a gift. Undigested acorn squash seeds produced a volunteer patch in his place that has never been equaled in my garden. Au revoir, Monsieur Pile. And thank you.

GETTING FANCY WITH YOUR COMPOST

DAISY We're all about the basics here, but just so you know, composting can get as fancy as you like. We live in a world where people carve portraits into pencil lead and stack their firewood in the shape of houses, so of course composting has not escaped humanity's desire to complicate the most basic things.

While composting really is as simple as we've described, sometimes things don't go as you expected or you want to speed up the whole process, or you're just one of those people who like to go the extra mile—c'mon, you know who you are, you just made a mental note to Google *firewood houses*.

Here are six ways to take your composting to the next level:

1. *Pay attention to ratios.* Compostable materials fall into two categories: browns and greens.

Browns are carbon-rich material. They tend to be dry, dead, and often wood-based. Dead leaves, straw, newspaper, and cardboard are all browns.

Greens are nitrogen-rich material. They tend to be wet, alive, and often green in color. Food scraps and fresh grass clippings are examples of greens.

The optimal ratio of browns to greens is five to one. That's five wheelbarrows of dead leaves (brown) to one wheelbarrow of fresh grass clippings (green), for example, or five flakes of hay to one nice bucket of vegetable and fruit scraps. Five armfuls of wood chips to one armful of manure. Okay, so you're not going to grab an armful of manure. Even I, for all my love of manure, don't clutch it to my breast. But you get the point.

2. *Pay attention to moisture.* This is where I often go wrong. My compost pile isn't lidded or covered in any way whatsoever, so moisture escapes from it. I often think the rain is sufficient, but most of the time, the leaves act as a kind of roof, protecting the inner recesses of the pile.

Take your hose out there and souse it well if it gets dry beneath the top layer (you'll notice the dryness when you turn the pile).

You may want to place the hose in the pile, beneath the top layer so the water soaks through the pile and doesn't roll off the top. I also like emptying the dirty chicken drinking water over the pile when I freshen their water. Yes, chickens will poop in their own water, as well as kick dirt into it. They let it all hang out.

3. *Use a compost thermometer.* Man has done it again. He invented the compost thermometer and called it good. If you get one of these, you are officially a composting nutter. I love you. Just be aware, you've lost your veto rights to the next crazy gadget your significant other wants to buy.

A good composting temperature is between 135°F–160°F (57°C–71°C). The temperature of the pile increases based on the type of bacteria in it and the activity level of those bacteria. Outside temperature actually plays little role.

The bacteria will heat up if you keep the brown and green levels balanced and keep the pile moist.

4. *Use a compost sifter.* I made a wooden frame around a square of hardware cloth and attached broomstick handles to either side so I can set it over a wheelbarrow and sift back and forth until the fine, fully composted soil falls out underneath, leaving the larger, not-quite-ready bits still in the sifter. It's not necessary, but it's a useful toy to have around.

Alternatively, just use a section of hardware cloth with no frame. Deanna uses an old plastic baby gate. Any port in a storm, as they say.

5. *Use the lawn mower to shred leaves into smaller pieces.* This speeds up the decomposition process. I also shred old chicken bedding straw with the mower to use as a top mulch around my plants.

6. *Create multiple piles.* Having multiple piles is a great way to accomplish the aeration necessary to keep the pile active. After one pile is full, create a new one by shoveling that pile into the space set aside for your second pile. Then, over time, refill the space just vacated by your first pile with more greens and browns.

Get fancy, if you like, but don't sweat it. Your pile of trash will turn to gardening gold, even without these extraordinary measures.

Level One: Container Gardening

DAISY You're looking at your typical suburban yard wondering how on earth to introduce edible gardening into the mix. The foundation planting is already established, the lawn looks so . . . permanent. You're concerned that if you dig something up and change your mind later, there will be an ugly gaping hole somewhere.

Or maybe not everyone in the household is convinced your itch to have a few vegetables isn't going to end in disaster.

How do you stick your toe in the water without worrying about taking a bath?

One solution is container gardening. This option is also good for apartment dwellers, renters without digging rights, and people with physical issues that prevent them from traditional gardening. It's an excellent way to start small and get a feel for whether or not you want to keep at it.

Container growing isn't particularly complicated, but there are some considerations that will help ensure your success.

SELECT THE RIGHT-SIZED CONTAINER
Choose a container that's the right size for your plant. Large vegetables need larger pots. Check a plant's size at maturity (listed on the seed packet or plant label) for clues as to how large your container needs to be.

Tomato plants or other big growers, like squash or cucumbers, require containers that are at least five gallons in capacity.

Smaller containers and bowls are perfect for growing plants like leaf lettuce, herbs, and mesclun. Remember, though, that the smaller the pot, the more frequently you'll need to water it.

You can plant in any sort of container. It doesn't have to be expensive or specially designed for plants. Buckets, barrels, boxes, recycled jugs, and garage-sale finds are all potential planters. Just ensure that they're nontoxic, i.e., don't plant edibles in a container that you suspect is decorated with lead paint.

A collection of less-than-beautiful pots can be corralled inside larger containers such as window boxes and baskets. Those large, white plastic buckets that economy-sized laundry powder comes in look just fine painted and decorated.

If you repurpose a container as a planter, drill or punch holes in the bottom for drainage. Put a plate underneath to collect run-off if you put the pot on your patio or porch.

USE A GROWING MEDIUM

The reason I say growing (or planting) medium instead of "dirt" is because container plants are usually grown in "soil" that is specially mixed for containers and may or may not contain what we think of as dirt.

We recommend organic growing mixes that contain more complete nutrients for your plants and are slower to wash out of the soil. You can purchase organic potting mixes or mix your own from ingredients available at your local home-improvement store.

To make your own, combine:

- 1 part well-aged homemade compost (or a mix of several different store-bought composts)
- 1 part coir or peat
- 1 part sharp (builder's) sand

To this mix, add a complete organic fertilizer according to the proportions on the label.

Always thoroughly wet your planting medium before planting. Place your planting medium in the container (or a bucket if you want to keep your container clean) and add water. Stir, making sure to eliminate any dry spots, like you're mixing up a batch of muffins.

Simply filling a pot with dry potting mix and watering over the top will ensure the water runs straight out the bottom without being absorbed throughout the soil in the pot.

CHOOSE CONTAINER-FRIENDLY PLANTS

While any vegetable will grow in a pot, some types are more suited to container gardening than others. Here are some criteria to keep in mind to help you pick the right plants:

1. *Yield.* Pick plants that will make it worth your while to grow. One container of black-eyed-pea plants might give you just one bowl of peas and one green-bean bush isn't likely to grow enough beans in the entire season for

Recommended Edibles for Containers

These edibles are your best bets when it comes to containers. In addition to these, practically any herb will thrive in a pot.

- Beets
- Carrots
- Dwarf cucumbers
- Dwarf peas
- Dwarf tomatoes
- Eggplants
- Leafy greens, including mesclun and misticanza
- Lettuces
- Kale
- Onions
- Peppers, both hot and sweet
- Radishes
- Strawberries
- Swiss chard

more than a couple of servings. That's a lot of space, time, and effort for a very small yield.

However, one tomato plant will give you a huge yield, so it's worth growing. A single hot-pepper plant is also good bet, as it can produce a year's supply of hot sauce.

2. *When possible choose "bush" varieties.* Bush varieties of plants have determinate growth, which means at a certain point they stop putting out new shoots (new growth) and concentrate on ripening what they have, making them smaller, more compact plants, perfect for containers. This is especially true for cucumbers, beans, and tomatoes.

3. *Choose plants that like close quarters.* In general, when planting in containers, you can space plants closer than recommended on the seed packet or plant label. Use the "between plant" spacing to figure out how close they can go and ignore the "between row" spacing. If you want tomatoes and basil in the same pot, there's no reason to put a two-foot row between them.

PLANTING IN A CONTAINER

When you are ready to plant, be sure your soil is thoroughly damp when you place it in the container.

With container gardening, as with traditional gardening, you can plant from transplants (seedlings or mature plants) or from seed.

To plant from transplants:

1. Fill the pot about halfway with soil.
2. Hold the transplant with one hand while backfilling the pot with soil with the other hand.
3. Continue filling, gently patting in and around the transplant (like patting a baby).

To plant from seed:

1. Fill the pot to an inch from the rim, patting the soil down lightly (like patting a baby).
2. Use a pencil to poke holes in your medium (usually no more than a ½" [13mm] deep; see your seed packet)
3. Place the seeds in the holes and sprinkle them with another handful or two of wet soil and give it another gentle pat.

PUT YOUR CONTAINERS IN SUNNY SPOTS
For some, such as apartment dwellers who have only patios or balconies or one outdoor area to call their own, their locations are limited. The essential thing to remember is that vegetables require at least *six hours* of sunlight *every day.* This amount of light is usually found on southern and eastern exposures.

To find the exposure:

1. Put your back to the building or wall. Point directly in front of you.
2. Using a compass or a landmark, name the cardinal direction you are facing. That is your exposure.

- Eastern exposures get morning and afternoon sun.
- Southern exposures get lots of sun.
- Western exposures get soft evening sun.
- Northern exposures don't get a lot of sun.

Vertical Gardening Tips

Deanna

1. Some plants like to climb. Cucumbers, spaghetti squash, peas, pole beans—they'll climb up whatever you give them. If you give them nothing, some (peas) will just tie themselves up in knots.

- I avoid pole beans entirely. They get tough before I know it anyway. I plant bush varieties.
- I let spaghetti squash and pumpkins scramble wherever they like. I just direct them outside my box and into the yard.
- For cucumbers, I ram two 6' (2m) stakes through my weed blanket and stretch 1' or 2' (30cm–60cm) of 4' (1.2m) chicken wire across them, securing with zip ties.

2. Some plants don't climb, but need support. Tomatoes and bell peppers need support, but they're not going to help you by holding on or doing the climbing themselves. I prefer cages for these plants. They go with my lazy nature. But for a more economical option, drive in a stake (we recommend a piece of wood or bamboo, or those pointy green metal things in the garden section of the home-improvement store). Use gardening tape or shreds of pantyhose or fabric to tie the plant to the stake. Twist ties and zip ties will damage the tender stems. Just remember that with a stake, you will have to go out and physically tie the plant. Cages take up more space but are largely maintenance free because they offer support on all sides.

3. Some plants don't need to go up, but can be forced up if you have limited space. These include squash and zucchini. I've done this before, and it's work winding the little plant around a support every day or so. I don't recommend it, unless you're really motivated. If you're interested in giving this a try, *Square Foot Gardening* by Mel Bartholomew recommends training plants with a structure made from electrical conduit and garden netting. It's brilliant, unbreakable.

Other considerations are shade from trees and buildings. If you've never done so, spend one of your days off paying attention to where the sun hits your surroundings. Take note of the sunniest spots, and plot to locate your containers in those spots if possible.

If you live in a cooler climate, placing your containers against south-facing walls (southern exposure) will keep your plants warmer by radiating the absorbed heat from the structure. This works particularly well if the wall is made of brick, stone, stucco, or other masonry.

WATERING YOUR CONTAINER PLANTS

The planting medium (soil) in containers dries out faster than the ground in a traditional garden, which means containers need more-frequent watering, and often daily watering.

Vegetables grow better when the soil is never allowed to dry out completely between waterings. The soil stays moist, but not water-logged.

Examining the soil is the best way to determine if the plant needs more water. Remember to pay close attention, especially during the hottest weather.

For watering jobs, I highly recommend my favorite garden tool, the watering wand. It turns the flow of water into a gentle, rain-shower-like spray (especially important for seedlings) and puts the water at a lower level, right where you need it. The gentle spray is crucial to allow the water to soak in thoroughly so the plants can develop deep, strong root systems.

(Once you really get into it, you may want to consider a drip irrigation system to water your pots automatically, but this isn't something you must have.)

FEEDING YOUR CONTAINER PLANTS

Because container plants need to be watered more frequently, they will also need to be fed more frequently, as the nutrients in the soil are leached out in the water.

Choose a balanced, organic fertilizer and feed from your local nursery or home-improvement store and follow its recommendations for use in containers.

ADDITIONAL CONTAINER-GARDEN TIPS

- As your plants grow, provide support for tall and climbing plants (like tomatoes and peas) with trellises, cages, or stakes. Going up instead of spreading out is one way to optimize limited-space gardens.
- Top the surface with mulch to help retain moisture and rebuff weeds. You can use shredded leaves, straw, or bark or decorative items such as pebbles, stones, marbles, or cork as mulch.
- Don't forget beauty. Planting flowers, especially edible flowers, such as nasturtiums, violas, borage, calendula, and marigolds, adds to the function and attractiveness of your vegetable containers. Herbs and vegetables mixed is a natural combination.
- Each year, dump your used container mix into your compost for renewal. When you replant the next year, start over with a fresh batch.

Level Two: Garden in a Box

There are many books on raised-bed gardening. We've read lots of them. No matter what the hook, the process is basically the same. With raised beds, there's no magic ingredient, no little detail that will make or break the whole shebang, so just go with our simple formula for your first year and get fancy with the details.

And remember, these beds aren't permanent. If you hate them, you can always move

them or get rid of them. The grass will grow back before the next season, so give it a try!

BASICS TO KNOW BEFORE YOU DECIDE WHAT TO GROW

DEANNA There are many beginner plant lists out there, and while they can be good places to start, it's important to customize your selections for your needs. Rely heavily on the advice of local, experienced gardeners. They will be your best resource. Check with your local cooperative extension office to find master gardeners in your area.

As you select plants, keep the following in mind:

Your Climate

Ask the person in the garden section what your USDA Hardiness Zone is, or look it up online. The department of agriculture established these zones based on average temperatures. Most seed packets and plant tags specify the zones the plants will thrive in.

Check the plant tag or seed packet to make sure your zone is on the list for that plant. Only buy plants or seeds that thrive in your zone. Yes, you will find plants that don't thrive in your zone in your local store. Don't assume that because it's there it works for your climate.

Before you buy, ensure the plant likes your area's climate. Some plants, such as tomatoes, thrive in hot sun. Others, like lettuce, wilt at the first hint of hot weather. Some, like melons, need a long growing season to come to maturity.

Planting dates are often provided for your zone. If they are, obey them. If it's June, but you're determined to plant broccoli, you will be disappointed.

Build and Set Up a Simple Raised Bed

You will need:

- 4 2×8 boards, each 4' (1.2m) long
- 12 deck screws or nails
- electric drill or hammer
- 1 small roll of weed blanket (any kind)
- tarp
- 5 cubic feet of good potting soil (the cheap stuff is often way too heavy and sandy)
- 5 bags of different composts
- water source

1. On your driveway, screw (or nail) together your boards in a square. Don't worry about how crooked the screws are or how maimed the heads of the nails end up. Just make the boards stay together in a square-type shape long enough for you to get it to the backyard.
2. In a sunny location, lay down your square. Cut a piece of weed blanket large enough to cover the bottom of your square (or layer it if necessary). Use a compass to figure out where north is because you'll be planting your large and tall plants on that side.
3. Mix all your dirt and compost on a tarp.
4. Fill the box with your dirt mixture and water it until it's damp all the way through. Stir it with a shovel to get all the dry spots.

If planting dates aren't provided for your zone, go to www.burpee.com and click on a similar plant, under growing instructions at the bottom. Type in your zip code and Burpee will tell you everything you need to know.

Space

As with container gardening, you can ignore the "between row" space requirements. Only the "between plant" spacing is necessary. If your plant calls for 6" (15cm) spacing, you can fit up to sixty-four plants in an 8' × 8' (20m × 20m) raised bed.

Unless you build a *lot* of beds, it's unlikely you will have much luck with certain crops, such as sweet corn. You won't have any trouble getting corn to sprout and grow, but it needs to be planted in a large block for proper

pollination to occur. With a necessary spacing of one foot between each plant, corn takes up some serious room. It also grows up to eight feet tall, so it will likely shade too much of your precious space to be worthwhile.

Melons are another space hog, although with sturdy trellising, they can be done.

Yield

As with container gardening, some crops are more worth growing than others in raised beds.

I love to grow a succession of sowings of mixed salad greens from which I can harvest the larger outside leaves, leaving the inner leaves to grow, and so get an almost continual supply for my family's unquenchable lust for salad.

Other high-yield plants are cucumbers, eggplants, peppers, annual herbs, and, of course, tomatoes, all of which keep producing over a period of time. Additionally, these veggies can be pricey to purchase at the market, especially the organic versions. Growing my own means I can luxuriate in unlimited organic mesclun every day of the week if I want to. And I do want to!

I tend to avoid "one-off" plants that take a long time to maturity, hog bed space, and are harvested all at once, such as heads of cabbage, cauliflower, and broccoli. This isn't to say you shouldn't grow these things. Just be aware that because the capacity of raised beds is limited, you need to concentrate on maximizing it both in terms of space and your wallet.

Pests

Almost every beginner plant list includes some type of squash, but squash is off my easy-to-grow organic list because my area has problems with squash pests of all kinds. The plants take off well and grow big, but bugs keep them from maturing to harvest.

Ask local gardeners what the local bullies are and stay away from the bullies' favorite victims unless you're willing to resort to non-organic methods.

This goes for furred and feathered nuisances as well. Suburbanites can have problems with rabbits, squirrels, birds, and even deer. Choose plants that aren't on the top of their favorites list if you find you are likely to have a battle royal on your hands. Find more pest advice at the end of this chapter.

Personality

Some plants are more forgiving of neglect than others. If you are unlikely to want to spend time tending to the needs of a "garden diva," choose less high-maintenance plants.

Tastes

Peas may grow great in your area, but if everybody in your family hates peas, there's little

reason to waste space on them in your garden. Show your tentative list to your family members and get some input before you plant a whole bed of beets to discover you're the only one who loves them.

EASY RAISED-BED MAINTENANCE

DAISY Make your garden easy on purpose. One of the main reasons I enjoy my garden as much as I do is because I've tailored it around my laziness. Over the years, I've noticed what I will and won't do to maintain it, and I made changes based on my tendencies.

If something dies or a particular bed keeps getting away from me, it usually isn't hard for me to figure out what went wrong. Everyone is different, so listen to your own reluctance to do this or that and think about what needs to change to eliminate the difficulty.

Here are some of my issues. I think they're pretty universal:

I hate hose wrangling. If I have to do a lot of unscrewing and winding and lugging of hoses, I soon dread watering, and my garden thirsts to death. I bought a good hose long enough to reach my plants and I leave the thing out in the garden all the time. All I have to do is turn on the spigot and go.

I don't like having to hunt my garden down. I love stepping out the kitchen door and being a few short steps away from everything. I want it right near the house where I can see it from the windows and enjoy it all day long, and easily access its bounty when I'm preparing a meal.

I don't like weed battles. I kind of enjoy normal weeding, especially now that we have chickens and weeding is like picking treats for your pets. *But,* I quickly tire of epic battles with aggressive, underground invaders like Bermuda grass. I've largely conquered Bermuda with wide borders of landscape cloth, cardboard and newspapers, topped with mulch, all around my garden. An early investment in time and effort saves so much weeding angst later on.

I don't like dirty vegetables. I was raised to despise grit (my mother washes and picks over every raisin), and it takes some of the pleasure out of gardening when cleaning lettuce and greens becomes a huge chore. Having raised beds gives me salad so clean I hardly have to wash it at all. It is pure pleasure.

Store-bought dirt is pretty pitiful. When you're first starting out, especially with raised beds, buying dirt is almost unavoidable. If I could stand the wait, though, I would start my gardening first with a massive composting effort and lasagna beds (layers of newspaper and greens and browns) rather than bothering with the expense and uselessness of store dirt. It is virtually lifeless, lacking in the beneficial microbes and worms and nutrients of real soil. Having my own composted garden soil makes all the difference in the success of my plants.

Be honest with yourself about what you will and won't do. The growing season is a long one, and when you enjoy your garden, it will be less of a chore and more of a joy.

Beginner's Lists Picks and Pans

Deanna

Using the principles Daisy outlined in the previous pages, this is my beginner plant list. Of course, plant according to your own climate, pests, personality, and tastes, but these are my top beginner plants according to maintenance requirements, space, and yield:

Beets
Bush green beans
Bush sugar snap peas
Edamame
Green onions
Hot peppers
Leaf lettuce
Okra
Radishes
Sweet potatoes
Swiss chard

These plants are popular and not very difficult, but they do require more attention for frequent watering, trellising, and pest control:

- Bell peppers: good yield with consistent watering
- Cucumbers: great yield with proper trellising, checking for pests
- Greens other than chard: great yield but more prone to pests than chard
- Pole beans: great yield with trellising and attentive harvesting—the beans get tough and stringy if overripe
- Tomatoes: great yield with staking, consistent watering, and checking for pests

These plants are not easy in raised beds:

- Carrots: beds aren't usually deep enough and thinning is difficult
- Corn: not enough room for enough plants to pollinate
- Dry beans: there's not enough room to grow enough for more than one meal
- Grains: a raised bed will only grow a couple of servings
- Peanuts: there's not enough room to let them spread out and flop over to put down nuts
- Potatoes: beds usually aren't deep enough; they are better suited to large deep containers or traditional row gardening
- Squash: Pests! Unless you are willing to use chemical pesticides, this is an art we've never mastered. I grow big bunches, because I use Sevin dust. Daisy is 100 percent organic, which, in our area, equals no squash.

Sample Garden Plan

Deanna

When I first started gardening, I had no idea what to plant, where to plant it, or what grew well with what. So, for you beginners, we're going to skip all that and just give you a recipe. Find more plans in the appendix.

You will need:

- 2 tomato stakes (any kind)
- 1 cherry tomato plant
- 1 regular tomato plant
- 2 pepper plants
- 1 bunch onion sets (at least 32)
- 1 package petite marigold seeds
- 1 package chard
- 1 package basil seeds
- 1 package bush-bean seeds
- 1 package radish seeds

1. Smooth the surface. Using your finger (or what have you), divide the square in half both ways and do it again on each side to get sixteen squares.
2. With your fingers, poke ½" (13mm) holes in your raised bed. Place them according to the chart on this page.
3. Open your marigold seeds. Pinch out four seeds. Put two in the first hole, and two in the second, and cover them. Put two seeds in each hole in your garden corresponding to the names on the chart on this page.
4. Put your plants in the dead center of the corresponding squares on the chart. Dig down to the bottom of your bed and set the tomato plant about an inch from the bottom. Bury it up to the gizzard. I also do this with my peppers, but you don't have to.
5. Go eat dinner.
6. Water it tomorrow, and the next day, and as needed after that.

North Side

two petite marigolds	one cherry tomato	one salad tomato	two petite marigolds
one basil*	one pepper	one pepper	one basil*
nine bush beans	four chard	four chard	sixteen onion sets
nine bush beans	eight radishes / two petite marigolds	eight radishes / two petite marigolds	sixteen onion sets

North Side

two petite marigolds	one cherry tomato	one salad tomato	two petite marigolds
one basil*	one pepper	one pepper	one basil*
nine bush beans	four chard	four chard	sixteen onion sets
nine bush beans	eight radishes / two petite marigolds	eight radishes / two petite marigolds	sixteen onion sets

*People in cool climates may be able to put up to four basil plants per square.

Level Three: Row Gardening

DEANNA Many people have argued that intensive gardening methods, such as container and raised beds, produce far more food per square foot than row gardening. In my experience, that is true. So, if you are really low on space, intensive planting is the way to go. However, if you want the most produce per plant—and you have the space and equipment—row gardening is where it's at.

Plant production is higher because the big plants (like zucchini and butternut squash) can really get their roots deep, spread out, and send off fruiting shoots in all directions. In my row garden, my four cucumber plants have produced enough cukes to feed the neighborhood! The same is true for zucchini.

In my backyard, I use a hybrid of the two methods. I "row garden" all my big plants like zucchini and cucumbers, giving them plenty of room to let it all hang out. And I intensively plant (in containers or raised beds) my smaller plants, like chard, bush beans, and onions that don't care a hoot about having lots of extra room.

THE BIG IFS

We only recommend row gardening under two conditions:

1. *You have enough garden space that raised beds seem impractical to you.* I'm not going into the compost production business anytime soon, so filling my 32' × 32' (10m × 10m) garden with no-dig raised beds is expensive and impractical for me. Daisy has about the same area as mine for her garden, but she is a compost junkie and watering a bunch of raised beds by hand sounds like fun to her. I think "fun" is turning on my sprinkler and walking away.

2. *You have access to a rear-tine tiller.* My husband borrows a rear-tine tiller and tills our entire garden in thirty minutes. You can try it with a front-tine tiller, but it's going to take more time and a lot more effort.

If you don't have access to any tillers, *don't* work up the soil by hand. Double digging is just too much work. Go with raised beds. If, someday, you make a friend with a six-hundred-dollar tiller, then you can rip out the wooden boxes and till it all under. I did.

HOW TO DO IT

Well, this might not be the official way to make a row garden, but this is how I do it.

1. *Kill the grass.* You can be organic. Or, you can haul out the Roundup. Regardless, you want to kill that turf before you try to till it, especially if you have Bermuda grass. Any living pieces will re-root and fill your garden in a matter of weeks.

2. *Decide how to fertilize your soil.* You have a couple options:

- You can have your soil tested through your county extension office.
- You can add compost to your garden area before tilling.
- You can use fertilizers in the hole and foliar sprays if the plants look hungry.

I chose the last option the first year I put in a row garden. After that, I collected leaves and other compostables in the fall and let the goats and chickens run (and poo) all over it throughout the winter.

3. *Till once or twice.* I like to till twice before I plant, once to stir the dirt and then a second time a few weeks later to get the grass I missed the first time.

4. *Plant.* I use two row designs:

- Large plant rows where I put four feet between each plant.
- Intensively planted rows where there are only inches between plants. As I already said, I plant rows of chard, beans, onion, and pepper the way they would be planted in a raised bed. I still put four feet between each row, but knowing that those plants aren't going to take up the full width, I plant multiple rows of them. There's no reason to plant a single thin line of onions or bush beans.

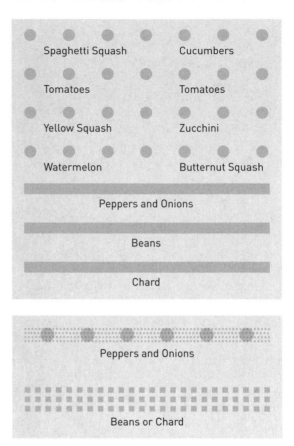

See the example in the charts on this page.

5. *A few weeks after planting, till the rows and columns.* Columns are the space between the plants in a row. I put all my "no-space" rows in the front and my spaced rows in the back. So in the front, only the rows are tilled (because there are no columns) and in the back, both the rows and columns are tilled.

6. *Water weekly, or more often if needed.* Watering for short amounts of time each day will cause your plants to grow shallow roots. It's best to give the garden an inch of water at a time. Run your sprinkler in the garden for a few hours once a week (or more if it's hot and dry). If you're worried about getting the right amount of water, set empty tuna cans around the garden and turn off the sprinkler when an inch of water has collected in them.

HOW TO TRELLIS IN A ROW GARDEN

The beauty of row gardening is that you can plant vegetables that need a lot of room. Veggies that like to spread out often need support, so you will need to add trellises to your garden.

You can make trellises out of just about anything. Pole beans are light, so you can use any kind of material to support them. For heavier plants, such as cucumbers and spaghetti squash, I recommend making your trellises out of cattle panel. Get the one with the *big* holes. I bought 16' (5m) of panel for twenty dollars at a farm supply store. You'll also need a few U-posts and some zip ties to put up the panel.

This year I placed my cucumber trellis smack in the middle of my garden. This was a mistake!

Sneaking Edibles in Among the Ornamentals

Deanna

For gardening in the front yard, herbs and fruit are where it's at. They blend in with your other shrubs and require little care. Additionally, they can be quite lovely. Some vegetables hide well, too, but there's no fooling the neighbors with corn or tomatoes. Here are some suggestions to get you started.

- Strawberries make a beautiful evergreen ground cover for a sunny spot.
- Rosemary can be pruned to look just like a shrub.
- Fruit trees can completely replace your other ornamentals. Dwarf varieties look beautiful and produce fruit sooner than their standard-sized relatives.
- Berry bushes make fine foundation plantings.
- Asparagus* makes a wispy fern-like privacy border with pretty berries in the fall.
- Sweet potatoes** look just like ivy spilling over a wall or as ground cover.
- Parsley* and cilantro* and bush beans* fit easily between the monkey grass.
- Thai and other hot peppers* look like their ornamental cousins.
- Cucumbers look like large ivy scrambling up an iron trellis or spilling over a patio railing.

*Annuals that will not be there in the late fall and winter.
**Perennial plants with foliage that dies back in the winter.

I know, tall plants go in the back, but I had planned to let my cucumbers ramble all over the ground instead of trellising them, so I put them in the "short plant" category. They soon became such a hairy, tangled mess that I had to trellis them!

Unfortunately, now they are shading my hot peppers and watermelon, not a happy arrangement.

FINAL THOUGHTS ON ROW GARDENING
Overall, I've found row gardening to be the least work-intensive gardening method I've tried. I till a few times a year. I water about once a week. I feed the plants and assault the local pests every two or three weeks.

However, the harvest can really get away from you. I've pulled in pounds and pounds of zukes and cukes from four plants each. And my spaghetti squash is so dense that I can't even see the little mystery animal that has made her home in it. (Every time I go back

Nothing Beats Homegrown

Deanna

Daddy grew up on a farm, but he didn't learn much about gardening. He once asked my grandfather, Pop, why Pop never taught him how to grow food. Pop said, "You never asked." (Which was a really strange answer because Daddy was forced to go fishing, rabbit hunting, and squirrel hunting.) But, even with his appalling lack of gardening interest and experience, Daddy always had one lone tomato plant growing in a container on the balcony. "The sorriest tomato you ever grow will taste a thousand times better than anything you can get in the store," he'd say. That's really true, and I've grown a lot of sorry tomatoes in my time. So, even if you have no experience, no space, and only one square-foot patch of sun, follow the instructions in this section and grow yourself something in a pot. It'll be the best thing you ever ate!

there, I hear her scamper off, but I have yet to see a whisker or feather.)

But, as a reminder, only attempt row gardening if you have plenty of full sun space and a friend with an enormous tiller.

Soil Contamination

DAISY Before you execute a plan to grow edibles in your yard, it pays to consider the possibility of soil contamination.

It's likely you have little idea of the history of the land beneath your feet. With a little legwork, though, you can learn a lot about the land's previous life. Most of the time, what you learn will be reassuring.

City records, county-court archives, and even informal conversations with local old-timers can set you on the trail of discovering how your land was used in the past. Common sources of ground contamination to look for include landfills, factories and other commercial industries, gas stations, auto/machine repair shops, and agricultural and other chemical outfits.

If any of these activities took place on your property, soil testing is available. Contact your local branch of your state's Cooperative Extension Service and ask them to direct you

to laboratories that test for soil contamination. For national labs, conduct an internet search for "soil testing."

When you've selected a laboratory, describe the type of contamination that may have occurred (based on your research). Testing is done for specific types of toxins, and the more specific you can be, the better. Follow the lab's instructions for collecting your samples.

Once the results are in, you can get information concerning the health effects of particular contaminants from the Environmental Protection Agency website (www.epa.gov). You can compare your results against the Soil Screening Levels established by the EPA to help determine your risk.

If you determine the levels are high enough that they need to be addressed, several methods are available to clean up, or remediate, the soil. They are divided into two main categories: physical and biological. Of the physical remediation techniques, excavation (having the soil removed and replaced with clean soil) is probably the most affordable method, although still not cheap.

Biological methods are less costly than physical remedies but take somewhat longer to achieve results. They include phytoremediation, which uses plants to clean up the soil, and

Gardening Is Full of Surprises

Watching the grass grow is supposed to be the epitome of boredom, but watching your garden grow is full of surprises. I grew a crop of popcorn one year that inexplicably produced miniature ears. Daisy grew a crop of watermelons that made fruits the size of oranges. No one knows how that happened. She once grew a crop of pole beans so high and so heavy that it crashed down in the middle of her yard. And I accidentally grew a bumper crop of sweet potatoes that took over my entire backyard. My kids couldn't even walk through it. One potato was six and a half pounds! (We named it, and my son took it to school for show-and-tell.)

Sometimes the basil goes bonkers and you end up with so much pesto that you're handing it out to the postman. (I've never recovered from that year. Daisy and I made *vats* of pesto, and I was still handing out full-grown plants to the neighbors.) Sometimes the winter squash volunteers in the middle of your compost pile or shoots twenty feet out into the yard. Other times, your kale is coming up turnips, and you didn't even plant any turnips!

Don't get worried, though. Most plants are predictable and grow according to plan, but every good garden has a few surprises in store to keep you on your toes.

---

microbial remediation, which uses microbes to break down toxins. Thirdly, compost remediation (adding large amounts of compost to existing soil) helps dilute the level of contamination to acceptable levels.

Perhaps the simplest solution is to use raised beds over landscape fabric, which prevents vegetation roots from contacting the contaminated soil.

The fruit of a plant (e.g., tomatoes, cucumbers, peppers, squash, tree fruits and nuts, etc.), is most likely to be free of toxins. Root vegetables and leafy plants such as lettuce are more susceptible to uptake of contaminants and heavy metals. Thorough washing of leafy vegetables removes much of the contamination that is the result of soil splash and wind-blown dust. Peeling your root crops can help moderate the amount of lead.

Planting Seasons and Frost Dates

DEANNA "To everything there is a season." That's the difference between a successful garden and a frustrating, pitiful garden. I can tell you right now that almost every gardening disappointment has to do with seasons or squash bugs. The solution to the latter involves a spray. The solution to the former simply requires a calendar. I can't tell you how many friends I've seen fretting over wimpy broccoli plants in August or still waiting in September for the squash to come up.

The easiest way to know what to plant in each season is to go to your local nursery and see what's up front. You'll see rows and rows of plump, young transplants. Don't look at those clearance tables in the back—there's a reason these they're priced to sell: They've passed their prime planting season.

But how do the garden centers know what time of year is the best to plant? It's all about heat and frost and how the plants will react to each. Some plants (tomatoes, cucumbers, and peppers, for example) hate frost of any kind and will keel over dead the second frost touches them. If you put a transplant in the ground and then you have a frost, you'll have to plant all over again.

Other plants (such as broccoli, cabbage, and spinach) are cool-season plants. They don't really mind frost, but they hate the dead of summer. If you plant them too late in the season, they won't have time to mature before the heat hits, and then you'll get no harvest. These plants need full sun and cooler temperatures.

And what if you decide to start a garden over the Fourth of July weekend? Will your tomatoes have time to grow before the fall frost sets in?

Or what if your zucchini gets killed by the borers and you want to try another batch? Will they have time to produce fruit before the winter kills them?

You can find the average frost dates for your area in three ways:

1. Check a website such as victoryseeds. com/frost.
2. Ask a gardener buddy, or find a local master gardener through your county extension office.
3. Ask at the locally owned nursery.

I prefer to ask the nursery and the gardeners because they say cool things like, "The official date is April 15, but you can plant such-and-such on St. Patrick's Day if you throw some straw on it" or "Fall frost is supposed to be October 15, but I haven't seen a frost in October in ten years. Some years I have tomatoes all the way into December."

Once you've determined your two frost dates, check out the fall and spring planting charts in the appendix. Just plug in your dates and the chart will tell you what weeks to plant everything your heart desires. It takes about five minutes and then you never have to think about it again!

Starting Indoors From Seed, or Not

DAISY Most of the time, in most climates, seed-starting indoors isn't an essential part of vegetable gardening. This is truer in moderate and warm climates, of course, but true to some extent in most places where gardening is possible.

From personal experience and from listening to gardeners across the world, especially beginning gardeners, I can say that getting an early start on the season is often fraught with disappointment.

The first experience most budding green thumbs have is when they plant a few seeds in a cup in the windowsill. Early excitement leads to frustration when the happy little seedlings reach a point and then seem to stop growing properly. They get "leggy" and pale and lean unhappily toward the light, appearing nothing like the strong, stout, hunky starts

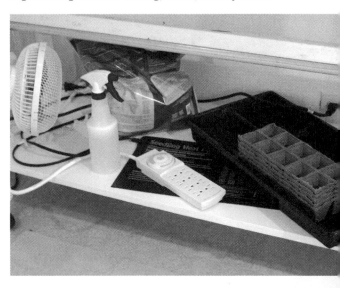

from the nursery. Even worse, they frequently yellow and lose their leaves or fall over dead. So sad, especially when the kids are involved and watch their charges keel over like that.

The next step is usually rigging up a grow light in hopes that it will be the key. This can be a simple lamp or a special setup. Whether you go all out with expensive grow lights or build your own do-it-yourself-style with a shop light, things are starting to get more complicated.

Before you know it, you have a heating mat, a fan, mist bottles, special fertilizers, and a timer for the lighting. It's getting expensive, and worst of all, you're still having only mixed results with your seedlings. And we haven't even talked about hardening off yet. That's a whole 'nother kettle of fish.

I don't mean to be a wet blanket. It's very possible you'll turn out to have success with your indoor starts. Although this sounds very dire, my overall message is good news. Most seeds sowed directly in the garden will catch up to or even surpass their indoor-started counterparts. Give them a little early protection with frost covers or plastic milk jugs that have the bottoms cut out, and you can start even earlier. Also good news for your wallet, the small, inexpensive, multi-packs of vegetable plants in the nursery are your best bets, not the big, expensive, single-plant containers. Once planted in your garden, the smaller ones will soon catch up.

If you do decide to start some plants inside, here are some tips that will help you have success:

- Use an unopened bag of seed-starter soil. (Avoid compost, regular potting soil, real dirt, and fertilizers; they can promote fungal growth.)
- Use clean containers with good drainage. Use new containers or used ones dipped in a mild bleach solution and rinsed thoroughly.
- Obtain seeds from reputable suppliers to increase the likelihood they are disease-free.
- When you sow, instead of making a hole and burying the seeds, place them on the surface of the planting medium and, instead of covering them with soil, cover them lightly with fine sphagnum moss, chick grit, or sterile coarse sand.
- Water from the bottom. This means pouring water in the tray instead of the pots. Allow the pots to soak up the water from the bottom. Stop watering when they stop soaking it all up.
- Provide air circulation, such as a small fan in the room, near, but not directly blowing on the seedlings.
- Thin seedlings to promote good air circulation. Snip them off with scissors. Pulling them out by the roots may damage nearby seedlings.

Give it a try if you must (I know I did), but set a few seeds from the packet aside for sowing directly outside later on. They may come in handy.

Average Seed Storage Time

1 Year: onion, parsley, parsnip, spinach

2 Years: corn, leek, okra, pepper

3 Years: asparagus, beans, broccoli, Chinese cabbage, carrot, celery, kohlrabi, peas

4 Years: beet, brussels sprouts, cabbage, cauliflower, chard, eggplant, kale, pumpkin, radish, squash, tomato, turnip, watermelon

5 Years: collards, cucumber, lettuce, muskmelon

1. Add these numbers to the packaging dates and record this information on the seed package.
2. Store your seeds in the refrigerator in a pickle jar with sachets of dry milk.

Seed Saving and Storing, or Not

DEANNA First, let me say that I don't save and store seeds. Leftover seeds are spread among my neighbors and friends. Any storage I've attempted has resulted in my children scattering the seeds all over the floor. Unless you are the last owner of a two-hundred-year-old heirloom seed, I wouldn't worry about it. When you get your seeds, buy the small package of seed instead of the plant-an-entire-field packet.

Seeds can last three to five years with proper storage. So, just in case you do want to store them, here's how.

You will need:

1 tablespoon dry milk (absorbs damaging moisture)

1 shred of hankie, or other small cloth

1 rubber band

1 clean pickle jar with the lid

1 Felt-tip permanent marker

1. Place the dry milk in the center of the cloth and gather up the sides.
2. Fasten closed with the rubber band.
3. Drop the cloth inside the pickle jar.
4. Gather the seed packets and find the date on the back. (If you only see a sell-buy date, assume that the seeds were collected and packaged one year ago.)
5. Write the expiration date on the front of the packet and drop the seeds in the jar with the milk packet.
6. Place the lid on the jar and refrigerate the jar.

After I started gardening in earnest, my outlook changed. My first summer with a serious garden, I felt as if at least a quintillion of those critters had grabbed forks and were sitting down to a smorgasbord in my backyard.

Where did they come from? How did they know I was growing squash? Aphids, maybe, I could understand—everybody has roses—so they jumped onto my tomatoes from there, but I guarantee I was the only person within a mile growing sweet potatoes and yet here came golden tortoise beetles, who eat little else but sweet potato leaves.

At first I was in a frenzy. Every time I saw an unfamiliar creepy-crawly, I panicked. I was sure it was the beginning of a plague and I might as well get out the flamethrower. I wanted to keep my garden organic, so I pored over organic pest remedies and recipes, searching for solutions. I mixed up concoctions that smelled like death, clogged up sprayers, and may or may not have repelled a bug. I was getting carpal tunnel from all the spritzing, and the challengers kept coming. There were crushed aphids under my fingernails, squash borer guts all over my driveway, and bowls full of beer and turgid slugs.

This was suburbia. I was surrounded by lawns, streets, and houses. I hadn't realized a host of vegetable predators was poised anywhere near enough to pounce with such precision, but they came from hill and dale and were delighting in my garden.

I'm relieved to report that things have settled down a bit now. I no longer experience either the anxiety or the intensive effort of those early years. And it's not because, as I once believed had to happen, I found the perfect spray for every pest.

It's because of what is known officially as *Integrated Pest Management* (and unofficially by me, as Real Life Gardening). Here's the idea:

Common Garden Pest Solutions

DAISY There are almost ten quintillion insects in the world. That's not a made up number, like gazillion. It's a real quantity, all nineteen zeroes of it.

Before I started gardening, the only insects that landed on my radar were mosquitoes, ticks, and, to a lesser extent, flies, plus the occasional yellow jacket. They were nuisances, but I could deal.

SIMPLE PREVENTION

- *Choose disease- and insect-resistant plants.* Most of your heirloom, open-pollinated, or other fancy-word seeds and plants are more vulnerable to disease and bugs than your run-of–the-mill hybrid. True, the former sound sexier, but for your first few years of gardening, be sure to include some tried-and-true hybrids so you have a good harvest.
- *Feed your plants.* Well-fed plants are strong, healthy plants. Humans can't fight off infection without a hearty diet, and neither can plants. Choose a balanced, organic fertilizer and feed from your local nursery or home-improvement store. Follow the directions on the bottle.
- *Wise watering.* Water your plants at the roots. Blasting the leaves spreads fungi and other diseases.

ADVANCED ORGANIC PREVENTION

- Use row covers to keep out bad bugs.
- Plant beneficial-insect-attracting plants like dill, cilantro, and marigolds. Beneficial insects eat the bad insects!
- Use companion planting. Some plants run interference for each other by repelling each other's enemies and attracting each other's friends. See the companion planting chart in the appendix for details.

BUT, IF THEY COME ANYWAY . . .

1. *Calm Down.* The first sign of an insect or disease infestation doesn't necessarily mean you need to drop everything and head to the stinky aisle of the home and garden center. A few caterpillar holes in your mustard greens is not an emergency that calls for the big guns. Take a wait-and-see approach. That might be as bad as it gets. If you are reasonably alert and keeping an eye on the situation, that's the important part.

2. *Stop Before You Stomp.* When you spot an insect in your garden, identify it before you squish it or spray it with something. It's hard to believe at first, but some of those insects are your friends. They're called beneficial insects, and they prey on the bugs that eat your food.

For example, the ichneumon, a small, harmless wasp, lays its eggs inside aphids. When the wasps hatch, they consume the aphids. Num num. In the meantime, though, they look like strange, white, bloated bugs on your tomato leaves. If you don't stop before

- Some bugs are dumb and can't find their way under a piece of gauze, so row covers can help (not with borers, though. They also have teleporters and GPS).
- Spray. Botanical insecticides are commonly available at garden centers and discount stores. Look for ones marked "approved for organic gardens." If you want to do the least amount of damage to beneficial pollinating insects, spray late in the evening when the flowers are closed.
- Don't grow pest attractors. You may also decide, like me, that evasive measures include buying your summer squash at the market because you've exhausted all the organic squash bug, borer, and beetle defenses known to mankind. You will discover your own particular nemesis. Pick your battles wisely.

HOW DEANNA DEALS WITH PESTS

DEANNA About every two weeks, I inspect my garden for pests. If my chard or beans are really taking a beating from the bugs, I spray them with repellent/insecticide (either homemade or an organic kind from a big-box store). They're usually some combination of pepper, lavender, rosemary, or neem oils. I come in smelling beautiful!

Essential oil sprays work fine for all my crops except squash. As we've lamented throughout this chapter, we have horrible squash vine borers in our area. So, I give in and use Sevin dust on the trunk. I've never found anything else, organic or conventional, that will keep my squash alive. Borer moths lay eggs on the vine and the little worms hatch and bore into the center of your squash trunk, killing the *entire* plant. I can stand holes in my leaves, or bug-bitten veggies, but don't kill my whole plant! Anyway, there's no need to dust the universe with Sevin. Just that fat trunk

you stomp, you might interrupt this beneficial parasitic arrangement.

Other insects cause only minimal damage, like the golden tortoise beetles on my sweet potatoes. They might make a few small holes in the leaves, but they won't do significant damage to a crop. You can enjoy their pretty golden carapaces without fear.

By identifying the insect before you go into attack mode, you'll learn how scared you should be (if at all), and what the appropriate controls are for that particular creature.

3. *Take Evasive Measures.* This is a multi-pronged approach.

- For many bugs, hand picking and crushing works fine. This is especially true of squash bugs (not borers, which come with force fields, cloaking devices, and time machines) lying on the ground. No need to kill beneficial insects by sprinkling the flowers, just put the shaker can under those big beautiful leaves and sprinkle down that big, fat stem. And don't worry about getting it all covered. A good sprinkle every other week, after you water, should keep the borers at bay.

Gardening Conclusion

Gardening is really satisfying. Even the smallest homegrown cherry tomato can bring joy to your heart. However, because humans have been gardening and writing about it for thousands of years, there's an overabundance of information out there. Don't short out your circuits trying to read up on everything. We did that and it didn't help one bit. Even our chapter may contain too much information, so here are the basics:

1. Mix up a box of quality soil (see the recipe on page 32).
2. Plant our beginner garden plan (page 42) whenever your garden center is stuffed to the gills with baby tomato and pepper plants.
3. Water at the roots every couple of days with one of those nifty ten-dollar water wands.
4. Feed with a balanced, organic fertilizer according to the directions on the bottle.
5. Buy a bottle of organic bug killer and use as directed if invaders attack.

If you do those five things, you should have a great first gardening experience. Ignore everything else we said until you've mastered these steps. You can do it!

3

DID YOUR BACKYARD JUST BAWK?

Chickens in the suburbs—are we crazy? Well, maybe, but not because of the animals we own. You can keep a quiet, clean flock in your backyard. This chapter will tell you everything you need to know about getting started with this rewarding—and surprisingly relaxing and entertaining—endeavor.

The Perfect Backyard Companion

DEANNA The other day, I was talking to the feedstore owner, who was marveling that he has to order more and more chickens to sell every year. What he found most amazing was the fact that the new buyers were all young couples! It seems that suburban chickens are catching on. But, why? I have several hypotheses:

1. *Eggs:* There has been a lot on the news about chicken mistreatment lately. Plus people are beginning to recognize that eggs from free-range chickens are higher quality than those from caged chickens. Unfortunately, a dozen free-range eggs cost more than a chicken!

2. *Trash consumption:* As mentioned in chapter one, a single chicken can consume hundreds of pounds of leftovers, and what we suburbanites would consider inedible foods (such as peels, rinds, and stems). This translates into almost-free eggs for us (when chickens eat your scraps, there's less feed to buy), a less stinky trash bin, and a smaller contribution to the landfill.

3. *Organic pest control and fertilizer:* Chickens eat bugs. They are not vegetarians except under very restrictive conditions (such as those found in commercial chicken farms where the chickens *never* see the outside world.) Left to their own devices, chickens will eat every bug in your yard. No spiders, beetles, or worms will survive. Once the surface bugs are gone, chickens will scratch down and find all the bugs hiding under the soil. And chickens leave behind free fertilizer for your lawn.

Unlike dog poo, chicken poo doesn't need to be buried. In fact, chicken poo is a fine addition to your compost pile. It's considered an "activator," which means it will help jump-start the microbes working to decompose the waste in the compost pile.

4. *Self-sufficiency:* The recent economic scare showed people how helpless they'd be if there were a complete economic crash. Keeping a few chickens and a small garden gives you skills you need to feed yourself and the security that goes with knowing you aren't completely dependent on the grocery store.

5. *Entertaining, low maintenance pets:* There's nothing as relaxing as watching the chickens peck around the yard. At my house, we find watching our animals as entertaining as watching television. We have twenty-four-hour live access to our chicken and goat "channels," and they are always putting on shows.

Plus caring for chickens is not like caring for a dog or cat. There's no veterinarian visits, no illnesses to treat, no letting them in and out of the house, no walking, no special preparations for summer or winter. They put themselves to bed at night, and often don't even want to come in out of the rain. (In my experience, "mad as a wet hen" only refers to dunking a chicken in a bucket. Rain is fine; it brings out the worms.)

6. *Educational:* The farther we are from our food sources, the more out of touch we are with our world. Raising a chicken to maturity and maintaining it as it makes your breakfast is educational. I can't tell you how much my children understand about nature just from keeping chickens and goats.

There's a significant difference between keeping productive animals and keeping companion animals. You view productive animals differently and are more inquisitive about the role they play in your life and all of the details that go into that role.

Common Chicken Myths

DAISY It used to be that everybody had a few cluckers around. Take a look at old photographs. When I started keeping chickens, I began to notice them in places I never had before—vintage black-and-white pictures. Many old photos include chickens in the background. No one in the photos is paying a bit of attention to them. The human subjects are posing by a horse and wagon, sitting on a porch, or standing out by the general store. Scattered about, minding their own business, are a few hens or the occasional cockerel, embedded into the fabric of daily life, even city life.

That's not the case anymore. Our casual co-existence with domestic fowl is gone, and having chickens around seems weird. People have questions about chickens now, and wonder about things people used to learn simply by observing their surroundings. It's understandable that we need basic information. Great-grandma would have a giggle at our ignorance, but that's okay. We know how to e-mail and she didn't.

Here's a little chicken primer for the twenty-first century:

MYTH NO. 1: CHICKENS BELONG ONLY ON FARMS.

Not so. Chickens have coexisted in populated areas for millennia. It's only in recent times that chickens have been banned to farms and factories. It's perfectly normal to have a small flock to provide a family with its own egg supply, even if you have a only small yard to keep them in.

MYTH NO. 2: IN ORDER FOR THE HENS TO LAY EGGS, YOU HAVE TO HAVE A ROOSTER.

Nope. Egg production (ovulation) is independent of the presence of a rooster. You only need a rooster for fertilization so the eggs can become chicks.

MYTH NO. 3: CHICKENS ARE FILTHY AND SMELLY.

While chickens do poop anywhere they feel like it, unless you have free-range birds, their manure is going to be restricted to their coop and their run. The poop in the coop is cleaned out periodically to do great things for your compost pile (and later the garden). A well-maintained coop is low or no-odor and beats the pants off a kitty-litter box.

MYTH NO. 4: CHICKENS WILL WAKE THE NEIGHBORHOOD.

Roosters are the big noisemakers. They are the crowers, and most suburban and urban flocks omit the rooster. A hen does set up a cackle to announce the arrival of her latest egg, to

Municipal Codes and Homeowners' Association Rules

Daisy

If you live within the city limits, you are subject to the city's laws, called municipal codes. To find out the law in your particular city or town, a good resource is www.municode.com. Many cities' laws are available on this website's free Municipal Code Library. Often these laws are also found on your own town's website.

Another approach is to telephone your city and ask to speak to the official responsible for animal control. Be warned, however, that sometimes an official may be a law unto himself, ignoring the rules on the books and preferring to go by "tradition" or his own interpretation of the laws.

I recommend knowing what your codes are before you broach the subject with your city. Being informed will make the conversation a lot more two-sided. It's not necessary to give them directions to your chicken coop when you phone to ask for information. Make a polite inquiry after you have done your homework.

Homeowners' association rules are similar, but layer on top of your municipal codes to provide an additional set of regulations that apply only to a specific neighborhood within a city. They may prohibit owning chickens even when your city says it's okay. If your home is located in a development with a homeowners' association, check with the association to get a list of their requirements. If they prohibit chickens and you feel strongly about it, you may consider a push to have the rules amended.

complain that another chicken is occupying her favorite nesting spot, or when she's startled, but their little "bawk-bawk" pales in comparison to a barking dog, the whine of a leaf-blower, or a teenager with a new drum set. It's a short-lived cackle, and because hens roost quietly from dusk to dawn, they won't disturb anyone's sleep.

MYTH NO. 5: CHICKENS CARRY BIRD FLU AND OTHER DISEASES.
Bird flu has never been found in domestic flocks in the United States. In fact, experts consider an increase in at-home egg production to be an answer to the threat of diseases such as avian influenza, which are aggravated by overcrowded poultry factory conditions.

When it comes to other diseases, such as salmonella (uncommon in home flocks, by the way), protect yourself simply by washing your hands well after handling chickens and cleaning the coop.

Suburban Chicken Issues

DEANNA We keep small, rooster-free flocks so we don't have many of the traditional chicken issues, such as noise and stench. (Roosters are noisy; hens are pretty quiet. A large number of chickens produces a large amount of poo. A few chickens will not produce enough poo to raise a big stink.)

However, we have our own special issues. There are three main challenges to keeping chickens in the suburbs:
1. Predators
2. Poop
3. People next door

PREDATORS
Wild predators: At my house, we don't raise our flock for meat, but everyone knows chickens are delicious. Skunks, raccoons, and hawks

know that, too. And because suburbia is often recently razed forest, the wild animals are rarely far away.

Predators are prevented in two ways: good fencing and guard animals.

1. Good fencing: Daisy's neighborhood is prone to hawks and raccoons. So her chicken coop and roaming area are covered and very strong. Predators can't go under it, can't fly into it, and can't go through it.

2. Guard animals: My mini-goats live with my chickens. Mini-goats are big enough that a raccoon or skunk isn't likely to mess with them. In all my years of keeping chickens, the only predator attack I ever experienced happened when the goats went to a spend-the-night party with their boyfriend . . . for a month. The leaves were off the willow, which usually obscures my animal yard, and the dog-sized critters (my goats) were nowhere to be found. It took the predator about two weeks to figure out that things were safe for it to move in.

Domestic predators: Regardless of how many times your neighbors tell you that their free-roaming dog will never hurt your chickens,

What Does "Free Range" Mean?

Free range is one of those terms that gets tossed around and nobody really knows what it means. I'm no exception. In its truest sense, it means that you have acres of property, no fence, and the chickens roam around in a herd wherever they like. But, almost nobody has that situation, and if they do, they probably have fewer chickens every day because of foxes.

Deanna

Pastured is the buzzword to look for. Ignore free range. Pastured means that penned or not, a decent percentage of the chicken's diet comes from foraging on grass and bugs. Chickens in a very small pen can be pastured, as long as the pen is moved every few days. Chickens in a humongous pen can be "not pastured," "un-pastured," or whatever you call it—if there's nothing to forage.

Technically, my chickens are pastured about half the year. They are free to roam grassy areas some of the year and are confined during others. That all depends on the state of my garden and my children's ability to keep the gates closed. The other half of the year, the grass in their pen is picked clean, the bugs are all dead, the kids don't play outside and set them free so often, and they live on feed and kitchen scraps.

unless that dog is a dang fool, he eventually will figure out how to get to your flock. It could be a matter of days, weeks, or years. In our experience, unless a dog is specifically bred to guard the chickens, you're on borrowed time.

Though they're bred to be companions, dogs are still carnivorous animals designed to hunt. It's instinct for them to go after easy-to-catch meals such as chickens . . . or at least to guard their territory from those unknown winged-beasties.

And though we suburban chicken owners can gracefully handle a hawk or raccoon invasion, if Rover next door is the problem, all hell breaks loose in the neighborhood. So make sure you have *good* fences.

When one of my pullets stupidly squeezed herself into the wolf breed's yard next door, I knew it wasn't the dog's fault that she never came back.

And if he ever breaks through to our side, I'll know it's time to build a stronger fence, not start a war with my neighbor.

POO

The problem with chicken poo in the suburbs is not volume, like on a traditional farm, but *location*. Chickens are indiscriminant poopers. They poop in their water, in their food, in their nests, everywhere. Which is not so much a problem when you have only seven chickens and you keep them in a well-secured pen (as Daisy does). But when they are free to roam and poop on the porch, the steps, the grill cover—that's a problem.

My chickens were "free range" within the confines of my backyard. And it didn't take them long to figure out that the lady with their food came out the back door. No matter where I actually fed them in the backyard, they huddled by the back door, crapping all over the patio, waiting for me to come out with food. My husband *hates* poop on his porch. So now, the chickens have their own yard—an area fenced off with chicken wire where they can poo without irritating anyone.

Just remember, anywhere a chicken can walk is a toilet for the chicken. If you don't want poo on your deck or patio, find a way to keep your chickens off of it.

PEOPLE NEXT DOOR

Many municipal codes allow for keeping chickens. Progressive communities are installing community coops right now to help with waste management. But, in many communities, chickens are a gray area. They are allowed, unless they're a nuisance. The animal control official can override your chicken rights if he's tired of hearing complaints, and one complaint will usually do it.

Because houses are so close together in the burbs, friendly neighbors are a requirement for backyard chickens. If you're next to a grumpy busybody, chickens may not be an option for you, but don't worry, if you get chickens and then run into problems, you can post them for sale (or for free) on the internet and they'll be gone that afternoon. Just don't buy a fancy, expensive breed and don't buy expensive,

Advice From Suburban Chicken Owners

On our website, littlehouseinthesuburbs.com, and in our inner circle of friends who own chickens, we hear a lot of discussion about what it's really like to have a backyard flock. We thought it would be helpful to share some of the chicken chatter to let you hear what's on the minds of those who've kept chickens in the suburbs and lived to tell the tale. Their stories, in their own words, are sprinkled throughout the pages of this chapter. Here's one from Lara:

"Overall, the experience of owning chickens has been fun, enlightening, crazy, hair-raising (hawks, snakes, owls, oh my!), and meditative. Once a week, I ask myself, What the heck are four chickens doing in my backyard?"

permanent housing until you're sure you will have the chickens for a long time.

Getting Your Chicks

DEANNA Baby chicks generally cost about the same as a gallon of milk at the grocery—maybe a dollar more. But how do you get your chickens? Well, there are several ways:

MAIL ORDER OR INTERNET

This is what Daisy did. Some sites (like mypetchicken.com) let you order small batches of baby chicks (about eight in a batch). If you go with a bigger nursery (such as McMurrayhatchery.com), they often come only in batches of twenty-five! So, you'd need to plan to split them with some friends.

The benefit (or drawback if you hate making decisions) to mail order is you have a nearly unlimited number of breeds from which to choose.

Baby chicks are mailed at one day old. There's a magic little window where they don't need food and water and can make the trip.

What Does "Straight Run" Mean?

Deanna

Straight run is a term used for chickens that haven't been separated by sex. In many cases, farmers will want to order only hens, only roosters, or a mixed batch of both sexes. This mix is called a straight run.

Straight-run batches are good for meat birds (who cares if they lay eggs or not, right?), breeding specialty birds, and people who want to perpetuate their flock on their own. But for the purposes of most suburban backyards, straight runs are a bad idea. Roosters, like most male farm animals, are loud, aggressive, armed, and come with a libido that cannot be satisfied by a tiny flock of gals.

But how can hatcheries tell the difference? With most breeds, I simply don't know. Mojo? Voodoo? Crystal balls? But, in the case of my favorite breeds, I know they tell by color. At hatching, the boys are one color and the girls are another.

In my area, the farm folks really use craigslist.org. This is where I found my chicks. A family down in Mississippi had ordered twenty-five of the exact breed I wanted from McMurray. I got my chicks for four dollars a piece and I was able to buy only four.

FEED STORE

If you have a farm co-op or feed-and-seed store in your area, these folks will order chicks one to two times per year. You can get your chicks just before Easter.

And if you make friends with the farm co-op or feedstore folks, or if you pay ahead, they will often order the breed you want, but you may be limited to a choice between just a few breeds. Or you can wait and see what the folks order.

Just remember that feed stores order for both egg and *meat* breeds. Meat breeds will not necessarily be good layers. Ask what breeds they are ordering and what the breeds are known for (laying or meat).

HATCH YOUR OWN

You can always get fertilized eggs from a farmer if you like. This is the least expensive way to get chicks, but the one fraught with the most disappointment.

Remember the axiom "Never count your chickens before they hatch?" This is especially true of home-hatched chickens. Unless you have an incubator and warmer, your turn out will be low. And the duds will be S-T-I-N-K-Y. (Did you read *Charlotte's Web*?)

Plus you can't guarantee they're going to be hens. After they turn into roosters, they're loud and dangerous to catch, so unless you feel skilled at sexing chicks (or your pal at the feed store is), I wouldn't recommend any "straight run" chick hatching or shopping.

> *"We started keeping chickens six years ago. The things that most surprised me were: how easy they were to care for, how funny they can be, how each can have her own personality, and most of all how relaxing they can be. I love sitting and watching them scratch and cluck around their pen. It's better than a fish tank."*
>
> —AUDRA, BLOG READER

WHITE HOUDAN BANTAM

SILKIES

Choosing a Breed

DAISY Like goats, cows, cats, and dogs, chickens are among the domestic animals humans have genetically tinkered with over the centuries. The result is an incredible range of characteristics, including blue chickens and chickens with fluffy feet and fancy topknots.

When I finally made the commitment to getting my own hens, I was very nervous. I had such a yearning for them, but it felt like a big deal—a huge potential mistake. And, because it was my idea, any fallout would be on my head.

Selecting the right breed seemed to be a key component to success. I stalked chicken websites until my eyes were glazed over and my shoulder was cramped from moving the computer mouse. I read a lot of contradictory information: *Breed A is friendly. Breed A is cranky. Breed B is loud. Breed B is quiet*. It was enough to make you crazy.

It doesn't have to be that way, though. In the end, I was pleased with my choices. I suspect I would have been happy with any of a number of breeds and my obsession with finding the perfect one was unnecessary. In addition to the breed characteristics, each hen has her own personality, and when your birds are well taken care of, they will likely be healthy and contented regardless of breed.

Here are some characteristics to consider when deciding which breed is for you:

- Egg-laying capacity
- Ability to withstand very hot temperatures
- Ability to withstand very cold temperatures
- Egg color (white, brown, extra dark brown, blue/green)
- Temperament (docile, shy, feisty, friendly)
- Noise level (but they're all hens, so this is not such a big determiner)
- Appearance

PLYMOUTH BARRED ROCK

BLACK AUSTRALORP

- Size
- Heirloom status

Start your decision-making process by clearly identifying your reasons for wanting chickens in the first place. Are you looking primarily to fill up those egg cartons? Do you need birds that can weather life in the Arizona desert or the Canadian Rockies? Do you want fancy feathers or is temperament most important to you? Maybe you want to help perpetuate heirloom breeds.

Where you acquire your flock will determine how much choice you have in terms of breed selection. If you plan to get your chickens from your local feedstore, you'll generally be limited to a number of common breeds. Ask the proprietor which breeds he plans to stock in the spring and do your research on those.

If you intend to have your brood shipped to you from a hatchery, your choices open up to just about any breed imaginable.

With your requirements in mind, do some research and develop a list. The internet is

a vast compendium of information on breed characteristics. Your library or bookstore will also have books exclusively on the subject of raising chickens, and these books will include breed information. See the chicken resources page in the appendix for ideas of where to start. Do some homework, but don't sweat it.

MINIMALIST EGG LAYERS

I have no use for poofy chickens. I think they're pretty, but I want birds that produce large eggs almost every day and don't peck my kids when hugged. Fancy-pants breeds usually lose out on one or more of those counts. So, if you're like me, these breeds are your best bets:

Red or Black Sex-Linked: All the chicken farmers I know (I live in the Southeast) say that the red or black sex-linked chickens are your best consistent layers. Mine are healthy, friendly, and lay fat eggs every day the first year. They're hearty, cheap, and easy to get rid of if you don't want your chicks anymore. I will never order another breed again.

RED SEX-LINKED

BUFF ORPINGTONS

RHODE ISLAND RED

Buff Orpingtons and Black Australorps (Often called Orps and Lorps for short): Daisy has both and loves them. I have Buffs, but they aren't laying yet. Though not expensive and certainly prettier, Orps and Lorps may not be as hard-core layers as your sex-linked breeds, but they still will lay more days of the week than not. Orps are friendly, and if you want fluffy yellow chicks with entertainment value, Orps are easy to train into "lap chickens."

Rhode Island Reds and Barred Rock: These old-fashioned favorites are attractive and seem as consistent as Orps and Lorpes for laying. I've never had Barred Rock, but I've heard good things. My Reds are good layers and hearty, but they lay *small* eggs compared to red sex-linked, which are almost identical in color (slightly lighter than Rhode Island Reds.) If you like to buy medium-sized eggs at the store, Reds are the chicken for you.

Heirloom or Heritage Breeds

Deanna

As with puppies, there are associations that have strictly defined terms relating to breeds. Some breeds are new. Some breeds are old. Some are pure. Some are mixes. But, when it comes to chickens, heirloom or heritage status usually refers to a breed of chicken from prior to the mid-twentieth century. They will have a low to moderate growth rate, are naturally mated, and genetically prepared to live long, outdoor lives. Conversely, factory-farm chickens are short-lived, not suited to outdoor living, and grow to that double-wide market weight in less than eight weeks.

Heirloom chicken breeds are often in danger of extinction, have historical significance, and thrive in a pasture-based environment. They grow to market weight in no less than sixteen weeks. They are also lots prettier.

Basic Care and Feeding

STAGE ONE: SIX WEEKS AND UNDER

DEANNA Baby chicks are mailed at one day old. There's a magic little window where they don't need food and water and can make the trip. Once they arrive at your house, you will need:

- a cardboard box
- newspaper to line the box
- a lamp for heat
- flat-bottomed containers or feeders for food and water
- chick starter (food)
- water

Things to remember:

- The chicks can't stay outside or overnight without a lamp until the nights are 70°F (21°C) or higher.
- Food and water should be left in the cardboard box around the clock for free choice eating and drinking.
- They can and will poop on or in anything you put in the box, including poultry feeders and waterers. If you use feeders

and waterers, the amount of poop that gets in their food and water will be less than if you use a bowl.

- Chicks choke easily. If you choose to give them scraps or other animal feed, they will be fine as long as the pieces are small and similar in size to chicken starter. Dried corn and cracked corn are much too big for baby chicks. If you must use dried corn, buzz it in your coffee grinder and sift it before feeding. Remember, there's no such thing as a smart chicken. They will totally eat something they can't swallow.

STAGE TWO: SIX TO TWENTY WEEKS

Eventually, the chicks will get big enough to jump out of the box. When they reach this stage, everything continues similarly, except you will need to cover the box with a screen, some hardware cloth, or just get a deeper box. You can discontinue chick starter and move to a pullet-grower feed, but we've never done that. We usually still have too much chick starter lying about.

After the chicks can get out of a shallow, open-topped box, Daisy and I prefer to keep them in dog kennels as opposed to chicken-rearing contraptions. Use little kennels for little chicks and bigger, wire kennels for pullets.

I also like to let my baby chicks out to play with my kids. I have a "super gate" that I bought years ago to protect my Christmas trees from curious little ornament smashers, and the gate makes a hexagonal pen. I stick it out in the backyard with the kennel inside and let the chicks and my kids play all day in good weather. After the nights stay warmer than 70°F (21°C), instead of bringing them in the garage, I just lock the chicks in the kennel at night.

STAGE THREE: TWENTY WEEKS

At about twenty weeks of age, your chicks will be almost full size, but won't be laying yet. At this stage, they require:
- food
- water
- a dark corner to hide in
- protection from predators

Any method or contraption you use to accomplish these things is fine. Chickens are very tolerant creatures.

At this point, I usually have at least a makeshift coop for the chickens to stay in at

night. My first coop was a doghouse with a tunnel of chicken wire over my super gate. I've also used the same method (minus the gate) with one side of the chicken-wire tunnel nailed to the doghouse and the other staked to the ground. This setup worked just fine. I let the chickens roam in the day, and lifted the corner of the tunnel at night to let them in the doghouse.

The coop they move to at twenty weeks can be the coop they stay in for the rest of their lives.

Food options for adult chickens include:
- Lay crumble or lay pellet—designed specifically for laying chickens. The pellet is usually cheaper and they waste less (this is available from your local feedstore, or you can look on the internet.)
- A combination of *sweet feed* (regular livestock ration with added molasses) *and kitchen scraps* (including egg shells). This is what my chickens live on. We

1. lay crumb   3. sweet feed
2. lay pellets   4. scratch

feed them everything but chicken, not because they won't eat it, but, as I mentioned before, because it grosses me out.

- "Scratch," which is a blend of cracked corn and whole grains you can purchase from a feedstore, but only if they have abundant scraps and a *large* area to forage for bugs.

STAGE FOUR: MATURE ADULT HENS

Your hens will be fully mature around four to eighteen weeks and will lay their first eggs at twenty to twenty-four weeks. After they start to lay, you will need a couple of other things.

- *Grit* . . . also called dirt. If you have a factory-ish situation where the chickens are locked up all the time, then you will need to buy grit from a feedstore for the chickens' gizzards. (The rocks in the grit stick in the gizzards and help the chickens break down their food). If you have free-range chickens, regular dirt from your yard is fine.

- *Calcium*, only worry about this if the eggs get soft shells. I've never found it necessary, especially for a small flock with access to eggshell-containing scraps.

- *Wormer feed.* Purchase this at your feedstore or online. The conventional method is to give your chickens a half a pound a few times a year, though many people now consider indiscriminate worming unnecessary.

Chicken Mortality

DEANNA Chickens are not particularly intelligent animals, and their lack of intelligence often causes their demise, literally.

Chickens often die. This is a fact of chicken ownership. Unless you're Daisy. Her chickens live in the "padded cell" of chicken homes. It's contained, covered, and inescapable. Mine, however, have some freedom. And that freedom leaves them open to making some of their own decisions, which often prove to be fatal.

By all means, take proper care of your chickens, but don't get too emotionally attached to them. They will find ways to bring about their own demise. Here are some examples from my own flock.

CASE NO. 1: THE HEADLESS CHICKEN
I keep my goats in the same pen as my chickens. The goats scare away potential chicken

> *"I was surprised about how easy chickens are to keep—much easier than the cats, the dog, and the boyfriend!*
>
> *Aside from their weekly coop clean and maintenance (which takes about twenty minutes), I spend less than five minutes a day on chicken chores. That's not to say that the only time I spend with them is chore time. They're incredibly entertaining with fantastic personalities. Within a fortnight of bringing them home, I got to use the phrase 'please stop pecking at my bum crack' and got an indignant buh-wark! in return.*
>
> —LOUISA, BLOG READER

predators, such as raccoons. One time my goats were out of town for a month for breeding. The raccoons decided it was time to make their move. Raccoons ran around the chicken fence making weird noises until the chickens couldn't stand it anymore and popped their heads out for a peek. Chomp. Headless chicken.

Now, I don't handle dead things—they give me serious anxiety. So when my five-year-old daughter came in crying because Monty "has a big boo-boo" on his neck, I refused to go take a look. But, children instinctively know that dead things should be buried. So, she begged and I still refused to budge. Then she said, "But what if I put a towel over her? Then will you come?" At that moment, I knew I was a bad parent. My kid was stronger than I was. But, I still couldn't handle the thought of looking at the dead chicken. Finally I said, "If you cover her with a towel, I guess I'll go."

I timidly tiptoed around the corner of the house (shamefully clutching my daughter's hand for support) as if poor Monty was going to jump out and get me. After a few minutes next to the covered corpse, I meekly slid the towel back. "Where's the head?" I asked. This is the point when my daughter had the nervous breakdown.

"Head!" she yelled. "Where's the head! The chicken doesn't have a head? Aaaaaaahhhh!"

Whoops.

CASE NO. 2: CHICK VERSUS DOG
One of my Buff Orpington pullets liked to squeeze through our privacy fence into the common area. Actually, all three liked doing that. But one day, one stupid chicken squeezed into the next-door-neighbor's yard, where a dog that closely resembles a wolf lives. That was the end of that chick.

Teleporting Chickens

Deanna

Chicken manure is like gold to gardeners. But, chickens aren't discriminating about where they deposit that gold. My husband cannot abide back-porch plops, so my chickens are contained, mostly. They have 1,800 feet (550 meters) of my 5,000-square-foot (1525-square-meter) backyard. I've clipped their wings and put them inside a 5-foot (1.5 meter) fence, but unless I keep them locked up tightly in the henhouse, they get out. Apparently, they have the ability to teleport. And I swear, the second they break out, they make a beeline for my back porch.

I've plugged every hole. I've blocked every opening with bricks. I've even lined the base of the fence with cinder blocks. The little devils are geniuses of escape, but the fact is, chickens are so dumb. I must have been missing something.

I sat out in my yard the other day, studying the chickens in their pen like a detective studying his clues. What was I missing? Where is the hole? Nothing. Then I heard my husband say out the bath-room window, "There's a goat staring at me." That window is 8-feet (2.5 meters) off the ground! How was Sylvie up that high?

The bottom half of my house has a brick exterior and the top half has regular siding. Where the brick and siding meet, there's a brick ledge that is the width of one brick. I discovered my goat stand-ing on that ledge. How did she even get up there? I wondered. And then I realized if she could get up there, the blasted chickens could too!

I marched back out to the animal pen to connect the dots. There was a pile of cinder blocks next to the air conditioner. From the ground, the animals could get to the blocks. From the blocks they could get to the ledge. From the ledge . . . where could they get to? Then I saw it. They walked the ledge all the way down to the 1-foot (½ meter) of fence sticking up over the ledge. The goats couldn't leap from that narrow ledge, but a chicken could. One hop to the top of the fence, one ungraceful, 5-foot (1.5 meter) plop to freedom. Finally I got 'em!

CASE NO. 3: THE HANGED CHICKEN
No more than twenty-four hours after the chicken-versus-dog incident, I looked out my curtains toward the chicken yard and saw one of my Rhode Island Reds hanging on the fence.

She had decided to jump from one section of my yard to the other and somehow caught her head in the 1" (2.5cm) space between the boards in the privacy fence.

My anxiety over handling dead things returned, and I called a friend to remove the carcass. But it was the middle of a work day and my friend was gainfully employed and couldn't rush right over.

I kept my children out of the yard all day and my husband returned home before my friend was able to come over. He took one look out the window and died laughing! He said, "Oooo, hatin' it! Looks like the mob hung her out there as a warning to the other chickens."

My husband graciously removed the chicken from the fence and concealed her in a black plastic bag. As he headed for the garbage can I said, "Are you seriously walking through my kitchen with a dead chicken?" He replied, "Would you rather I dance?" And he boogied the rest of the way out the door.

CASE NO. 4: CHOKING HAZARDS

I'd had a few guinea hens die from choking. They'd eaten something too big for them to swallow, even though they had plenty of reasonably sized feed at their disposal. I explained this experience to the owner of my local feedstore, and he told me it's not uncommon for chickens to choke to death. He told me if a chicken starts to chock on feed, you have to rub the chicken's neck to move the feed up and out of the neck or down into the stomach.

"I expected to enjoy watching them, but I didn't expect to catch my kids just sitting outside the coop watching them—or my husband, who will go out to the garage and when he doesn't return, I'll peek out and see him laughing at them."
—STEPHANIE, BLOG READER

One day I saw one of my Buff pullets strain her neck past the ample amount of bite-sized food in front of her and eat an enormous corn kernel. She started to stagger. She pumped her neck up and down. She tripped.

I scooped her up and started rubbing her neck trying to get the kernel up or down or anything!

She closed her eyes. I could tell she was fading. I threw her in a bucket from my kids' sandbox, grabbed my keys, and dashed out the door. I raced into the feedstore and dumped her out on the counter to discover she was fine!

It was that typical case where you take your car in for some weird noise and when you get to the dealership the noise is gone.

The store owner looked her over and declared that she'd passed whatever it was. He fed her some chick starter, told me she was underweight, and sent me home with egg on my face.

Types of Coops

DAISY Coops and/or runs are usually the biggest part of the start-up expense when you budget for chicken ownership.

Housing your chickens can be done with a relatively small outlay, especially if you or a friend are handy with a hammer and saw. It can also be as fancy and expensive as you want it to be. For some people, a big part of the charm of having chickens is housing them in a handsome and efficient structure. Small coops can be just as charming as big, elaborate ones.

I lucked out on my coop. I already had a roomy, well-built building that, over the years, had various uses including a playhouse and a

Run: An area where chickens can scratch, peck, and play.

storage shed. It has two large windows and a secure door, with a screened door to boot. The shelves along the inside are perfect for roosting. All I had to do to modify this arrangement was construct a run on one of the sides that contained a window, put a chicken walk from the window down to the run, and fill the coop with straw and nest boxes. Voilà.

This situation is fairly rare, though, and most people in the suburbs won't have a ready-made "coop" already on the property. When it comes to constructing a coop, there are three basic types:

- Chicken tractor or ark
- Stationary coop
- Shed coop

THE CHICKEN TRACTOR OR ARK
A chicken tractor is so called because it is built to be moved from one spot to another and most often has wheels or runners to facilitate

Wing Clipping

Deanna

If your chickens are in a pen with sides shorter than 5' (1.5m) and no roof, you will need to clip their flight feathers. Not that they will fly anywhere, but they can hop a 4.5' (1.35m) fence in a second.

Feather clipping is really no big deal. It's not "pinioning," which takes the whole wing tip off. You're just trimming some feathers. It's like cutting bangs on a squirmy kid. And if you've been handling your chickens since they were young, it's even easier.

You will need:

- sharp scissors
- a friend to help until you get good at it

1. Hold the chicken, however you can, and fan out one wing. For first-timers, it may be best to have the friend hold the chicken while you fan out the wing.

2. The ten long feathers at the end are your troublemakers. Cut off a few inches or so. The chicken will jump from the vibration it feels on the feathers as they are cut, but cutting the feathers doesn't cause the chicken pain. Think back to a child's reaction to the first snip of her bangs; the chicken's reaction is not much different.

   There are theories about whether it's necessary to clip only one wing or to clip both, but I recommend trial and error. My chicks are scrappy scramblers and one wing is still enough for them to struggle over the fence, so I clip both.

3. Have your friend help you turn the chicken around and clip the other wing, following the instructions in steps 1 and 2.

4. Set the chicken free and check yourself and your friend for poop.

5. High five your friend to celebrate a job well done.

the nesting box from the outside so the keeper can easily remove the eggs. The chickens move in and out of the coop into an attached run.

THE SHED COOP

Like mine, this coop is more of a full-sized building. It's large enough for people to walk inside and have full access to the nest boxes, roosts, and all chicken areas. It also has access to an attached run area. It can be specifically built to house chickens or you can convert an outbuilding or a lean-to into a coop.

When deciding which type of coop is for you, evaluate your needs, your budget, and your vision of how you plan to interact with your birds.

Size of Coops

DEANNA So how much area do you need? The rule of thumb for backyards is 4 square feet (½ square meter) in the coop and 10 square feet (1 square meter) in the run for each chicken for scratching, foraging, and exercise. Factories only allow one square foot (930 square centimeters) per chicken and no outside run at all. This is cruel.

Now, you aren't married to these numbers. It all depends on your set up.

PERMANENT STRUCTURE AND PERMANENT RUN

Daisy's eight chickens have a large coop (8' × 8' × 8' [2.5m × 2.5m × 2.5m]) with access to a large run (20' × 15' × 8' [6m × 4.5m × 2.5m]). They don't leave that area and she doesn't move the pen around. It's a permanent structure.

This is a situation where you need to be careful about square footage. Even if the floor space in the henhouse wasn't sufficient, she has shelves and roosts going up the walls that increase the milling-around area.

easy, wheel-barrow-type movement. It doesn't have an engine and doesn't till the ground. It's a nice arrangement for you and for the chickens because it is relatively small and inexpensive to build or buy. It gives the chickens access to fresh grazing ground as it is moved from place to place. It features a covered roosting/nesting area at one end and an open-to-ground section where the chickens spend the day pecking and scratching and feeding.

THE STATIONARY COOP

This is an immovable coop. It has a pop door that can be locked at night for extra security against predators. It often has a place to access

Each chicken needs four square feet in the coop and ten square feet in the run.

MOVABLE STRUCTURE AND NO RUN

My friend Laurie keeps her chickens in a tractor that is moved around her yard every few days.

If you choose this option and move it every few days or so, you don't need a run because the chickens will have plenty of space to scratch and fresh weeds and bugs to eat each time you move the tractor.

Give the gals a little extra on the coop space requirements—at least 6 square feet (½ square meter) per hen, and you should be fine.

PERMANENT OPEN STRUCTURE AND FENCED YARD

I have a bi-level tractor that has the roosting area above a chicken-wire run at the base. Technically, I could keep the four chickens I started with in the coop, especially if I moved it periodically, but we don't have near the

predator problems I originally suspected. The chickens are more of a danger to themselves than predators are to them in my area.

So, now, with eight chickens, four roost on top and four walk in the run door and roost in the upper level of the coop. I never shut them in and they have full run of at least an 800-square-foot (74-square-meter) pen with the goats. (I think having the larger animals with them has discouraged ambitious predators from venturing into my yard.) And on days

"When my eldest was a colicky infant, the only thing we found that calmed her was spending a couple hours in the barnyard watching the chickens in the late afternoon."
—SANDY, BLOG READER

Tips for Nesting Boxes

- The standard size for a nesting box is about 12" (77cm) square.
- A couple of inches of nesting material like straw, wood shavings, or hay serve as a soft landing surface for the eggs and is instinctively a part of the nesting experience for hens. The material also helps keep the eggs clean.
- Provide one box for every two to four hens.
- Most boxes have a small lip along the bottom front to keep the eggs and nesting material from being shoved out.
- The most-favored locations for nest boxes are somewhat dark and away from activity.
- Some people put a fake egg or a golf ball or something similar in the boxes so hens recognize the boxes as places to lay. If you get a fake egg, leave the price sticker on it (or mark it) so you aren't always reaching for it when gathering eggs!

when the children don't close the gate, they have double that space.

Because I never lock my chickens up, my coop size is almost irrelevant. I could have ten more chickens without changing coop size, and if there wasn't enough room to roost on or in the house, they'd roost in the tree or on the window to the goat house, what have you.

PERMANENT STRUCTURE/FREE RANGE
Another friend of mine has chickens roaming all over her ten acres, but has too many predators to let the chickens roost where they will, so she locks them all in the coop at night. All they need is room enough to cram in and sleep and a dark spot to lay their eggs.

NO COOP/NO PEN
Another lady I know has a big flock, no coop, and they roost in the trees. She finds eggs all over! But, she also has Alsatian guard dogs and lots of tree cover, so predators aren't a concern.

So, you first need to assess your situation before you build a coop. What is the predator situation like in your area? Do you have raccoons and hawks? Daisy has hawks dive-bombing her coop. That's why hers has a hardware-cloth

"When I was younger, I raised many types of birds from parrots to finches. Hens are, by far, the easiest to care for and most rewarding, hands down. Mine meet me at the back door and follow me around like I'm a rock star and they're my entourage while I walk or do chores.

They are their own community, but they include me, and this has even given me many insights into human affairs. My husband laughs when he sees me walking down the hill to the house, dog in the lead, chickens running to keep up alongside, and three cats pulling up the rear. Without chickens I would not be as happy as I am."
—ROSE, BLOG READER

roof! And she finds coons in her driveway frequently enough that she knows that if she had my set-up, she'd have no chickens.

Nesting Boxes

DAISY I obsessed a bit over everything chicken, including nesting boxes, as I was preparing a home for my flock. I guess you could say I was nesting myself.

Again, I discovered that I needn't have worried about it. Have you ever stressed out over finding the perfect toy for a child and lo and behold all he ended up playing with was the box the toy came in? Nesting boxes are sort of like that. You can buy or build the cutest nesting boxes only to find your hens prefer to nest on top of it or in the corner of the coop on the floor.

You can try to coax them into the box by saying, "But look! Look at the cute box I made you!" But be prepared for them to ignore it and continue to nest on the floor.

That said, chickens will usually warm up to nesting boxes, and the boxes serve a good purpose. They are handy areas where your hens can feel safe during the vulnerable time while laying their eggs, and they safeguard those eggs until you arrive to collect them. You have three options when selecting a nesting box:

1. *Purchase a prefabricated box:* They're available by mail order or at farming supply stores.
2. *DIY:* Plans and guidelines abound if you want to build a box yourself or have a carpenter construct one for you.
3. *Improvise:* An improvised nesting box can be made from a bucket turned on its side (so the chicken can nest inside it), plastic or wooden boxes, or, for temporary use, even sturdy cardboard boxes.

You really can't go wrong when selecting a nesting box. It just depends on your preferences, budget, and ingenuity.

Cleaning and Keeping Eggs

DAISY Most of the time, in a well-kept henhouse, pristine eggs sit in the straw waiting to be collected. But sometimes they have a little something-something caked or smeared on them and the subject of cleaning comes up.

In discussions about cleaning eggs, you'll hear the word "bloom." In short, a bloom is a coating, courtesy of the hen herself, deposited on the outer surface of the shell, that helps protect the contents of the egg from contamination. It is a protein, a mucous secretion of the hen's cackleberry chute, to get scientific. "Cuticle" is another name for a bloom.

Bloom is necessary because eggshell is permeable, with about eighty thousand microscopic pores on the surface of one egg. Bloom blocks bacteria and other harmful objects from entering the egg, and also keep the egg fresh longer.

Among their many other issues, factory eggs have been washed to make them more attractive to the public, and this removes the bloom. A coating of mineral oil is substituted to prolong eggs' shelf lives. Like most man-made interferences, this substitution is unequal to nature's solution.

Now our own homegrown hens' eggs get dirty sometimes and may need to be washed, which leaves us with a sort of Catch-22: leave the bloom and the surface contaminants can't penetrate the egg, but they are still there on the outside, looking gross, getting into the egg when you crack it open, getting on your hands when you handle it, and looking really not cool at all sitting on your counter or in the fridge. Heaven forbid one should present a poopy egg to a friend, family member, or customer!

But, see, the bloom is there, protecting the inside of the egg, you explain and point and nod authoritatively, but no, the horror is still frozen on their faces, and understandably so.

What to do?

The general consensus is that washing dirty eggs is indeed fine. It's best to do it just before using the eggs to take advantage of the natural protection of the bloom for as long as you can, but a washed egg is a lovely egg as well, and much more presentable to the general public. So here are both methods:

NON-QUEASY, BLOOM-LOVER'S EGG STORAGE
1. Collect eggs every day or so.
2. Place them in the fridge in their natural state until you're ready to use them.

> Bloom or Cuticle: A naturally occurring protein secretion surrounding the exterior of an egg.

How Often Do Chickens Lay Eggs?

Deanna

The first year, a good laying chicken will lay four or five days a week—about one egg a day. (My Red Sex-Linked laid seven days a week the first year!)

The following fall/early winter, your chickens will go through a three-month molt and will lay no eggs during that time.

The hens will also be more sensitive to weather. Older chickens have less tolerance for heat and will stop laying in intense heat to help control their body temperature. They also stop laying when the days get short. To combat this, you can hang a light in the coop, but neither Daisy nor I are up for that.

Assuming, like us, you do very little to monkey with the natural laying tendencies, egg season is traditionally Valentine's Day to Halloween. The first year, my chickens laid right through my mild mid-south winters. But the second and third years, they followed the traditional schedule.

None of my chickens have reached this stage yet, but I hear that at some point, years down the road, they stop laying entirely, like chicken menopause. This is somewhat of a mystery, as most chickens in our country don't die of natural causes. I will be pretty darn excited about my chicken-keeping skills if I ever have one that lives long enough to stop laying. I think I might even make her a tiny crown or paste a commendation on her roost.

3. Cover them with foil if you have squeamish people in your household. "Ack! A feather in the fridge!"

4. Rinse the eggs well before cracking them.

If you got really lazy about egg collection, which can happen because fresh unwashed eggs suffer few ill effects of laying around unrefrigerated for days, you may have concerns about freshness. If there is doubt, place the suspect egg in a glass of water. If it lies on its side on the bottom, it's fresh. If it touches the bottom but one end begins to tilt upward, it's still good, but perhaps better suited for baking. If it floats, it's past its prime.

EGG BEAUTIFICATION FOR THE
GENERAL PUBLIC

1. Prevention is best. Collect eggs soon after they are laid if possible. Maintain clean bedding and make the bedding deep. Straw makes excellent bedding. Keep roosting areas up and away from the nesting sites.

2. If you must wash the eggs, use water that is 20°F (-6.7°C) warmer than the temperature of the egg itself. This will prevent the shell from developing thermal cracks, which would shorten the life of the egg.

3. A vinegar solution or a mild soap followed by a dry towel is fine. You're not really trying to get an absolutely aseptic shell. Just remove the exterior contaminants that gross people out and might fly into their food when they crack the egg.

4. Once the eggs are washed, refrigerate them immediately for best results. These eggs are no longer protected from invading bacteria and cannot be casually left on the counter for days like unwashed eggs.

Fresh Egg FAQs

DAISY Deanna and I have been surprised by people's reactions to our home-grown eggs. It's out of the ordinary enough that some can't imagine that something that comes from a suburban yard could qualify as perfectly normal and edible. Here are some of the questions we and other suburban chicken keepers have gotten, and our responses.

CAN YOU EAT THE EGGS YOUR CHICKENS LAY?

Yes, of course! They are just like the eggs you buy in the store, except we think they're better.

HOW OFTEN DO YOU COLLECT THE EGGS?

We recommend you collect eggs once or twice a day. This has nothing to do with the eggs going bad, however. Because of the protective coating, an egg can stay out in the heat for days.

Egg collection has more to do with egg production. And, it depends on how many chickens you have laying. But, if any of them see eight eggs sitting in the box, they're likely to switch from egg-producing to egg-sitting.

ARE YOU AFRAID YOU'RE GOING TO CRACK A BABY CHICK INTO YOUR SKILLET?

You can't have chicks without roosters, and we don't have roosters. If there's no male in your flock, it's guaranteed that all of the eggs your hens lay will be unfertilized.

For those with a rooster, if eggs are collected regularly, there won't be enough time for any potential embryos to develop.

AREN'T THE EGGS DIRTY?

Not usually, and if they are, we wash them before cracking them.

WHAT DO THE EGGS TASTE LIKE?

They taste like store-bought eggs, except ours have a flavor-edge because they're fresher and from unstressed chickens that get plenty of exercise, fresh air, and a diverse, well-balanced diet.

In short, they taste eggier, meaning they have a fuller flavor. If you have much experience with homegrown or local, organic produce, you will know what this means. Homegrown tomatoes don't taste *different*, they're just more *flavorful*.

I SAW YOUR CHICKENS EATING BUGS AND PECKING IN THE DIRT. IS THAT GOING TO GET INTO THE EGGS?

Well, sort of, but in the best way. Chickens are omnivorous, and the benefits they get from insect protein and minerals helps keep them healthy and their eggs nutritious and tasty. The grit, sand, and small rocks in the soil goes into the chickens' gizzards and helps them grind up their food so it can be digested. The dirt either remains in the gizzard or passes through the digestive tract and exits the bird through its waste, not its reproductive tract.

The insects are digested in the chickens' gizzards and stomachs, and are absorbed as energy. There's no direct connection between the digestive tract and the reproductive tract, so nothing the chickens eat will appear in or contaminate the eggs they produce.

THAT EGG LOOKS FUNNY. IS IT OKAY?

Sometimes eggs come out a little different. They may have an unusual shape or be covered with little grainy bumps or be covered in a sort of grainy crust.

The unusual shape can result from the shell having received a crack prior to being laid (called a body check). The hen's body deposited more calcium over the crack to fix it and that's what causes the misshapen appearance.

The grainy bumps are calcium deposits. These conditions don't affect the quality of the egg.

Factory chickens—those that produce store-bought eggs—produce these same sort of eggs, but you don't see them in the store because they are culled only because consumers are more comfortable with uniformity, not because the eggs are defective.

A FEATHER AND SOME STRAW STUCK TO THE EGG WHEN I PICKED IT UP FROM THE NEST. WHAT DO I DO?
Just brush it off. The egg is damp when it hits the straw, and as it dries, sometimes the bedding or a stray feather gets dried on to it. It won't harm the egg.

Conclusion

Keeping chickens, like everything else weird we do, seems like a much bigger deal than it really is. Chickens are easy productive pets. They aren't as snuggly as a puppy, but they certainly earn their keep! They'll kill your bugs, eat your weeds, and make your breakfast.

But, we know making the leap to get your first little flock can be stressful. Daisy worried over it for months! So just in case you're overwhelmed, here's a quick summary of the basics:

1. The easiest place to get chicks is the farm supply store. The second easiest source is the internet.
2. Baby chicks need baby-chick food, water, a box, and a light to keep warm.
3. In addition to food, water, and warmth, big chicks need safe places to roam, lay eggs, and sleep.
4. Chickens poop a lot and will poop wherever they are allowed to roam.
5. Don't get roosters.

4

MINI GOATS: INTERESTING, UM, . . . DOG YOU GOT THERE

When you imagine a goat, you may picture a large, bearded billy goat chomping on a tin can—far more suited for a barnyard than your backyard. Standard goats can grow to more than two hundred pounds, and they definitely aren't for the average suburban spread. Miniature goats are the result of intentionally breeding a standard goat with a dwarf, or pygmy, goat. They usually top out at around sixty pounds, and they are perfect for small suburban backyards. Because I own goats and Daisy doesn't, the "I" in this chapter will always refer to me, Deanna.

Mini-Goats Make Great Pets

DEANNA Many people say that they get a mini-goat for two main reasons: grass cutting and milk. While these are both very good reasons, they are hardly exhaustive. I got goats for neither of these reasons. Oh, I had dreams of homemade cheese, but that was secondary.

The real reasons I got goats were allergies and child-damage potential. I wanted a pet that wouldn't make me sneeze and couldn't hurt my kids. So, after a suitable mourning period for our seventeen-year-old dearly departed canine, I replaced him with a pair of mini-goats instead of another dog. Here's why:

- *No top teeth.* Goats cannot bite.
- *No claws.* Goats cannot scratch.
- *No horns.* A farm veterinarian can easily de-horn a goat and it will only cost about fifteen dollars.
- *Not big.* A fifty-pound goat isn't going to be able to do any real damage to a human child, even if the goat wanted to. Most medium-sized dogs are around fifty pounds. Labradors can weigh far more than that.
- *Nontoxic poo.* Dog and cat poo is nasty and must be dealt with in some fashion or the yard starts to smell like a sewer. Goat poo is little pellets that disappear into the grass and have no scent.
- *Not stinky.* Speaking of no scent, goats don't smell. Wait, lemme resay that. *Girl* goats don't smell. Have you heard that phrase "smells like a goat?" That's *billy* (male) goats. They stink to high heaven on a good day. Female goats, though, have no scent at all. You can pet their fur and then put your hand straight to your nose. Nothing. Try that with a Labrador.

- *Hardy.* Goats are not prissy. As long as they have a way to get out of the wind and the cold, you don't need to do anything special to house them, even in foul weather. No need to bring them in for the night.
- *Good sleepers.* Goats sleep at night. No hunting, howling at the moon, or barking at the neighbor's porch light.
- *No digging.* (See the no claws part.)
- *No running away.* My goats see me as the shepherd. They come when I call and aren't comfortable being on the other side of a fence from me. If I go in the gate, they follow.
- *Quiet.* Goats do make noise, but the loudest noise they can make is still several decibels quieter than the softest dog bark. I've never heard anyone complain about the noise my goats make; in fact, mostly I get compliments on how quiet they are.
- *Entertainment.* I don't know why, but we can watch goats graze for ages. We call it the Goat Channel.
- *Yardwork.* First, they eat all the leaves off every shrub, so if you want to preserve your bushes, keep the goats away. If there are no shrubs, they start with the fallen leaves. Then they edge around the fence. Then they eat all of the weeds. Then they start in on the grass. Grazing isn't necessary for goats. You can feed them hay and they'll leave your lawn alone. If you want their lives to be especially happy, give them fallen branches and vines from the neighborhood to munch on.

Oh, and they make milk too, but after all that, it seems like a bonus.

Municipal Codes and Homeowners' Association Rules

If you live within the city limits, you are subject to the city's laws, called municipal codes. To find out the law in your particular city or town, a good resource is www.municode.com. Many cities' laws are available on this website's free Municipal Code Library. Often these laws are also found on your own town's website.

Here's the first rule about getting mini-goats: Don't ask permission. Just go read your codes and make your best decision. There is a commonly held myth that you need tons of space for a goat, but that's only something city people think. Miniature goats are small stock, in the same class with rabbits, chickens, bees, and mini-pigs. Most people, even your animal-control officer, may not understand that distinction. So, asking him is often asking for trouble.

Ignore codes about big animals. See what your town codes say about mini-pigs and fowl. Most codes don't specifically mention mini-goats, but if they have rules against mini-pigs (or all swine in general) and chickens (or all domestic fowl), you can bet you can't have a goat either.

But, regardless, it's all about neighbors. I know of a family in a town where you cannot have goats, but their neighbors never questioned that rare, "Swiss-breed of dog" they were walking. My town tried to forbid my goats, but my neighbors all signed a petition to let me keep them.

Homeowners' association rules layer on top of your municipal codes to provide an additional set of regulations that apply only to a specific neighborhood within a city. They may prohibit owning mini-goats even when your city says it's okay. If your home is located in a development with a homeowners' association, check with the association to get a list of their requirements. If they prohibit mini-goats and you feel strongly about keeping mini-goats, you may consider a push to have the rules amended.

Issues With Goats in the Suburbs

Assuming your municipality allows mini-goats, the only problems you can really have are poo, fences, and neighbors. Fortunately, each problem is manageable.

POO

With goats, the poo issue is much smaller than it is with chickens. Like chickens, goats poo where they stand. So, if your husband is picky about the porch, he won't like all those little pellets rolling everywhere. However, unlike chicken poo, there's no smell and the pellets sweep away. You cannot sweep bird poo. It's gloppy. Not so with goats. Their poo is like rabbit pellets. And you'll only notice it in your yard if the goats chew the grass down super low. If you want to keep your patio or an area of your yard poo-free, simply put up a barrier, such as a fence or gate, to keep the goats out.

FENCES

- You must have one. Goats on a chain are miserable and have a tendency to accidentally hang themselves.
- It must be a strong fence. Goats like to scratch themselves by walking back and forth along the fence. Our suburban privacy fences are *perfect* for goat keeping (I've heard farmers say that if they could afford that style of fencing all around their property, they'd have it), but chain-link fencing is also fine. The fence should

Advice From Suburban Goat Owners

On our website littlehouseinthesuburbs.com, and in our inner circle of goat-owning friends, we hear a lot of discussion about what it's really like to have mini-goats in the city. Quotes from actual suburban goat owners are spread throughout the chapter. Here's one:

"I was worried about our neighbors. What if the goats got out? What if they destroyed a plant on the fence line that was a prized heirloom passed down for thirty generations? Our neighbors behind have told us on many occasions that they love watching our goats and will pet them if they're by the back fence. They loved seeing the new babies in the spring, too. Our neighbors on one side are apparently deathly afraid of goats. The one time the goats got out, they went straight to those neighbors' yard, and they very kindly called someone to take the goats back to our yard and close the gate. Our other neighbors don't seem to mind. One has even asked if he could borrow our goats to clear some brush in the spring. When we have goat babies, we make sure to invite all the neighbor children over to see them. Parents are amazed at how well behaved even the big goats are with children."

—Lindsay, blog reader

be 4'–5' (1.25m–1.5m) tall. I have one 4' (1.25m) fence and one 5' (1.5m) fence. Neither of my goats can "jump" the fence flat-footed, but Lily can get over the 4' (1.25m) fence if she banks off the side of the house like a free-runner.

- Goats will consider everything within the fence-line as food. So don't include your prize roses or baby trees in the enclosed area. Goats know if it's green, it's good for them, and they will eat it. No kidding.

NEIGHBORS

This is the big concern with goats in the suburbs. Like most things in the burbs, you can usually do what you want unless someone complains.

Goats can be heard all over the neighborhood. Not because they're loud, but because their sound is out of place. It's not a normal suburban sound. We tune out lawn mowers and dogs and traffic noises, but a goat bleating gets the attention of every passerby.

For the first few months I had goats, people kept asking me if there was a child crying in my backyard. (Some breeds are quieter than others. LaManchas are reputed to be the quietest. Nubians and Boers, not so much.)

However, unless your neighbors are just plain grumpy, there's nothing much to aggravate them about goats. Goats' noises aren't intrusive, they don't smell, and they can't bite the neighbor's child. So, you're in trouble only if you live next to a Mr. Wilson type.

OBERHASLI

NIGERIAN DWARF

Obtaining Goats

So where do you get goats? There's no goat store. I suggest craigslist.com. That's where I found mine. Well, one I got from Craigslist, but the other I got through a friend of someone I called on Craigslist. (Once you're "in" with a goat owner in your area, you'll find that they all know each other.)

If you don't want to use the internet, I suggest you contact your local feedstore and get the name and number of someone who has goats. Baby goats are usually ready to sell by the spring, and if the people you contact aren't willing to sell, they will probably know someone who is.

Breeds

The first rule of selecting a goat is don't buy pedigree unless you're going to breed for profit (and this book doesn't contain any information on that). There's no reason for a pedigree goat. It's like paying for a show dog when you just want a friend to take on walks. A good mixed-breed goat costs between twenty and fifty dollars. Pedigree goats can be in the hundreds or more.

As with any type of animal, different breeds of goats are known for specific qualities. When you select a mixed-breed goat, you can combine traits from the two different breeds into one goat.

When it comes to selecting the right breed for you, you first need to decide the reason you want the goat. Is it for cuteness, milk volume, cheesemaking, companionship? It's all up to you.

SIZE
Any suburban goat should contain at least part pygmy or Nigerian dwarf. Both breeds are small and produce milk that is high in butterfat. Pygmies, however, are the stockier of the two, because they're meat goats. Dwarfs are noted for their gentle personalities. Pygmies are great pets, but they are considered louder than dwarfs.

SAANEN

ALPINE

MILK PRODUCTION

Dairy goats are breeds that overproduce milk—that is, they produce more milk than their kids need to survive. Dairy breeds include Alpine, LaMancha, Nubian, Oberhasli, Saanen, and Toggenberg.

Any of these could be crossed with a pygmy or dwarf to create a miniature goat that would produce more milk than a straight dwarf or pygmy goat.

For milk, the LaMancha breed is where it's at. Mini-LaManchas are known to produce a great deal of milk. As I've heard, most other minis are "like milking a mouse." But, if you're just getting milk for your family, you may not care about huge volume. A few cups a day might be plenty. It would be for my family.

CHEESEMAKING

Cheesemaking is all about the milk fat. Volume of milk doesn't necessarily mean lots of cheese.

Nigerian dwarfs and Pygmies are both great choices for cheesemaking, as they have higher butterfat. You get less milk per goat, but more cheese per gallon of milk. Any of your minis will have pretty high milk fat because they're crossed with a dwarf or pygmy, but if you want to maximize butterfat, stick with a purer version of these mini-breeds.

Don't buy a goat just because it has four legs and bleats like a goat. Talk to the owner, make sure the goat is friendly, has human interaction a few times a day, and preferably hasn't come from a sale/auction barn. Sale barns are where farmers go to get rid of their problems, and even if a particular goat didn't have a problem when it got there, it very likely picked something up while there. Buy one that has good milking lines on both sides (if you're milking).
—LINDSAY, BLOG READER

Pick the Right Personality

When you pick your goat, pay attention to the breed's personality traits. One of my goats, Lily, is part Nubian, which may be why she's so stubborn and independent. She's forever thinking she can butt her way into my kitchen. And when I pull down a branch for her, she can never wait for me to get it low enough, she's got to climb up my side. Ouch! She's the one that butts the chickens. She's the one that muscles her way into the feed box. She's trouble. And for most of the winter, I think about how nice it would be to not have goats, especially that one.

Then summer comes. I take her out in the tall green grass . . . and I forget all the trouble she caused. A goat with a mouthful of dandelions makes it all melt away. I never watch a dog eat, but watching those goats, especially that naughty, mouthy one, chomp giant bouquets of clover makes the world seem bright and good.

Then the neighborhood children come to feed them. They run their hands down branches, stripping a boutonniere of leaves for them. Lily responds to the light little pic-pic-pic sound of leaves being plucked like it's a clanging dinner bell. Sylvie, the well-behaved, quiet goat, is much too shy to let the neighbor children feed her. But Lily takes mouthful after mouthful from green-stained fingers.

I just sit in the shade and smile. Drivers slow down and wave, neighbors stop by to talk. It's like the clock suddenly turned back seventy years and I think, "I'll always have goats, especially that one."

MEAT

These breeds are bulkier because they were created for meat production: Boer, Spanish brush, kiko, and myotonic (fainting).

FIBER

These breeds are renown for their hair, which is used to make fabric: cashmere, angora, and pygora (A pygmy-angora cross can be used for both fiber and milk).

PERSONALITY

As with dog breeds, goat breeds are noted for specific temperaments and noise levels. Keep personality in mind when selecting the right breed for you and your backyard.

- Oberhasli, Saanen, and LaMancha are considered quite docile.
- Alpine, Nubian, and Toggenberg are considered willful and independent.
- LaMancha and Oberhasli are considered to be extremely quiet breeds.
- Nubians are considered especially vocal (read: loud).

MINI-NUBIAN

MINI-TOGGENBERG

COMPANIONSHIP

Dwarfs and LaManchas, Oberhasli, and Saanen are the sweetest dairy goats. So the mini-LaMancha wins this category (two gentle breeds will pretty much guarantee a gentle cross). Keep in mind the pygmies and Nubians are considered to be *loud* goats. No goat is as loud as a dog, but if you want the sweetest, quietest mini-goats, you'll want a dwarf LaManchas.

> *I'd have to say what has surprised me the most about our pygmy is her personality. I always assumed that goats would be just like any other "barnyard" animal, and that's not even close to the truth. Her attitude is much more like that of a dog. She'll follow us around off leash, sleep on our doorstep, run to get in our cars, and play in her hay. Her intelligence and personality surprise us daily.*
> —EMILY, BLOG READER

Alpine, Nubian, and Toggenberg are considered the most willful and independent of the dairy goats. Lily's dad is a pedigree Nubian, and boy is Lily obnoxious—independent and loud—but, as my bottle baby, she's also the most affectionate.

CUTENESS

I can't lie—I bought my goats for cuteness. I wanted something adorable to stick a pink camouflage collar on and play with in the backyard. So Lily is a dwarf-Boer mix and Sylvie is just a pure white brush goat. Nothing special about them, except that I thought they were precious when I saw them. I wanted pretty goats that would make good pets and possibly produce milk.

For the rest of the characteristics, LaManchas seem to me to be the best choice, but I didn't choose LaManchas for my own pets. They have little or no ears, and I don't find them quite as cute as other breeds. (I know, it's totally shallow and subjective.) Bottom line—buy a goat that you adore. It makes it that much more fun.

Bottle-Feeding Baby Goats

When I first got Lily, she needed a bottle. The only problem was she wouldn't come near me. And once I got ahold of her, I had to pry her mouth open and shove the bottle in. She was really wiggly!

I thought that after the first time, she'd figure it out. But she didn't. For two days, I chased that goat at feeding time. I was so beat up and cut and bruised, I looked like a roller-derby queen. When I bought Lily, the owner had just walked up to her and picked her up. She scrambled a little, but I guess the presence of the rest of the herd had given her a sense of security, so she didn't run. She wasn't so calm in my backyard. Wow, she was fast. Imagine trying to tackle a miniature deer.

"Goat people" told me that I just needed to sit out there with her for a few days and let her get used to me. I sat out for hours. Nothing. I was afraid she was going to starve before she got used to me. And then we encountered a second problem. The minute she got hungry, she started yelling! People walking their dogs wanted to know if that "screaming child" was okay.

Finally, someone said the most important words in my baby-goat-feeding career—*drag chain*. That made all the difference. My scrapes and bruises soon healed, and not long after that, Lily figured out I wasn't trying to kill her. And as soon as she figured out the whole feeding thing, she stuck to me like glue. Thank heavens for drag chains.

Baby Goats—for Suckers Like Me

Baby goats are more trouble than bigger kid goats you can buy. But they're so *cute!* You will need a few things to take care of them that you wouldn't need for big goats.

FORMULA AND BABY BOTTLE
Goat formula can be found at the feedstore. Follow the directions on the bucket! Overfeeding on formula is serious. It can give the goat diarrhea, which can lead to death. If your goats want more to drink, just double the water next round.

Any baby bottle will work fine, just cut the tip so the formula flows freely when the bottle is turned upside down.

DRAG CHAIN
For the first week or two, your goat will not come to you any more than a wild deer would. She will run from you every time you try to bottle-feed her. Put a dog collar on her and attach a five-foot (1.5m) leash with the loop cut so the goat can't get it tangled and hurt herself.

If you can get within five feet of the goat, you can step on the chain and reel her in.

WARMTH
If you get your baby goats in the cold season, you can be a sucker like me and keep them in a wire dog-kennel in the kitchen at night. Once you can't stand cleaning up goat mess each morning, move the kennel to the porch, fill it with straw, close the kennel door, and cover it with a tarp and blanket. Some people also add a heat lamp for extra protection. Or, you can make them some adorable wool goat sweaters!

EAR PLUGS
A baby goat that is without its herd for the first time is going to be upset, which means it's going to be *loud*. The only way to stop that is

Adult Goat Basic Care and Feeding

I will always buy goats that still require bottle feeding, because this feeding process creates a bond between me and the goat, and the goat will think that I'm its mother. But for a hassle-free goat experience, get goats that have already been weaned from bottles and de-horned. Mature goats need very little in the way of care and feeding. They need:

- a friend
- water
- grass or hay
- livestock feed
- minerals
- shelter from rain and wind
- hoof trimming (occasionally)
- dose of wormer (occasionally)

to carry her around all of the time. The second you set her down, she will probably go back to yelling. After she figures out you are the one with the bottle, and settles in a bit, you should be back to quiet happy little goats.

PATIENCE

Chasing goats, hitting goats, yelling at goats—not the way to become friends.

If your goats are older (as in weaned), the best way to make friends is to hang out near them while being quiet. Oh, and a little sweet feed in your hand or near your feet never hurt. You watch them, they'll watch you.

The more they are used to seeing you around, especially if you are the food person, the more they'll start making friends. They will come up for pets and pull on your sleeves if you're stingy about showing your affection.

But, like deer (which are a close cousin to goats), they're skittish. So quiet, calm, and patient is the way to go. Let them get used to you.

FRIENDS

Goats are herd animals. A single goat is a pissed-off goat. You don't want that. Buy her a girlfriend.

When I had only Lily, I borrowed a spend-the-night friend until I could find another mini. The temporary friend, Rosie, was a full-sized goat, but just a baby. After I found Sylvie, I took Rosie home.

WATER

Like almost all animals, goats need 24/7 access to water. I've used a five-gallon bucket to hold the goats' water, but the best water container is a rubber, flat-bottomed bowl that can be purchased at the feed store. The goats can't tip over this type of container, and because it's rubber, it won't break in the cold. Plus, when water freezes in it, you can flip it and stomp the back to pop out the ice.

HAY OR GRASS

Goats will eat the yard, or the branches your neighbors throw over the fence, or your shrubs. But after they've run out of green stuff (like in the winter), they will need 24/7 access to hay.

When they don't have any other options, goats will eat hay, and, in the winter, it's their main source of sustenance. There's no need to buy expensive hay. Mixed-grass hay is fine.

The biggest hassle with hay is keeping it dry. If you throw a bale in the backyard, it will mold in the center after the first rain. I keep mine in a wire dog-kennel with the kennel's bottom tray on top, held down with a brick, to shelter it from rain.

LIVESTOCK FEED

You don't have to get a specific brand, just make sure the packaging mentions goats. It's mostly just a supplement to the hay and something to make the goats feel that life is good.

MINERALS

Minerals come in a block or a bag from the feedstore. It's like a salt lick you would give to a rabbit. Select blocks designed specifically for goats. Minerals for sheep will not include copper, so avoid those.

SHELTER

The general recommendation is to give goats a three-sided shelter that faces south. I use an old Little Tikes playhouse. I put in half a bale of straw and voilà, goat house. In the winter, I wrap it with a big tarp to keep out the wind. Done!

You can use anything as long as it will keep out the rain and the wind. Dog-igloos work fine, as do old dog houses. I've even seen goats use a wood pallet under a lean-to. I tried for ages to get them to sleep in the nice little house I made, but they preferred that darn old pallet under the lean-to. Silly animals.

FENCES

As mentioned before, your typical suburban pine privacy fences are great goat fences. But what if you don't want your entire yard to be a goat bathroom? Then you'll need to put in another fence. You can build a short privacy fence, but even dwarf goats will be able to bank off the side of the house and get over at the ends. The only fence I've found that will keep them in, other than a full-height (6'

[1.75m]) privacy fence, is horse panel, found at your local farm supply store. "Goat panel" is too short, plus it won't hold in chickens. I wonder if it's meant to be electrified, which won't work for suburbanites with small children. Horse panel is taller and has smaller openings. I pounded U-posts into the ground and attached my fence with zip ties. But, that is a temporary measure.

If I had full-sized goats or wanted my ties to last more than a year, I would need to twist the fence to the posts with wire.

Two mini-goats need a 20' × 20' (6m × 6m) pen to be happy. The grass in that area will mostly disappear, probably just from foot traffic. If the goats are in a larger area, about 40' × 40' (12m × 12m), the foot traffic and grazing shouldn't wear out the grass.

WORMER
Like every other animal, goats get worm and bacterial infections; however, lucky for you, a ten-dollar tube of wormer lasts years. For my goats, I use Ivermectin (for horses) every three

How Not to Put Up a Goat Fence

1. Borrow a friend-of-a-friend-of-a-friend's manual transmission, diesel, sixteen-foot flatbed truck with a lift and drive sixteen miles per hour to the farm-supply store, never killing the engine (thank you, Jesus) yet lightly grinding the gears twice.
2. Arrive at the store and realize that you can't possibly park this monstrosity, so take up six parking spaces so you don't have to make a turn.
3. Find it impossible to remove the key. Struggle for a few minutes, then flag down a couple of good ole boys in the parking lot who look like they would know how to de-key a diesel truck the size of your house. Key successfully removed. Lessons given on key removal.
4. Enter the store and ask for a goat panel.
5. Laugh out loud when they show it to you, because a lame goat on Benadryl could jump it backwards. Four feet? Must be meant to be electrified. Can't do that with small children around.
6. Buy two 16' (5m) long, 5' (1.5m) high horse panels.
7. Bring the mammoth truck around to the back of the store. Again, fail to remove key. Get the elderly salesman to give lessons.
8. Help the elderly salesman get the panels over the lift that neither of you know how to use, into the bed of the truck, and drive home at seventeen miles per hour. (Never been in a car that needed fourth gear before thirty miles per hour.)
9. Have a mild nervous breakdown while trying to turn left out of the lot, calling on all the saints that can be remembered whilst adrenaline is pumping. "Saints Therese, Teresa, Lewis, John of the Cross, Philomena, Sacred Heart of Jesus, Mama Mary, Elizabeth, any relatives that can hear me, people who are holy that I don't even know . . . all y'all pray I get back without wrecking, please!"
10. Drop panels at the house and return the mammoth truck. Thank the whole host of heaven for their much-appreciated assistance.
11. Again, fail to remove key. Struggle for a few minutes. Pray some more. Finally get key out.
12. Return key to owner who can't believe you didn't call stranded on the side of the road. (In my case, the phrase "superwoman" was used. Yes!)
13. Go home and bang in U-posts in a relatively straight line, attach panel with zip ties, and install a gate kit from a hardware store. Voilà!

to six months. A pea-sized amount in their food does the job.

TRIMMING HOOVES

When my goats still lived on the back porch, before my hubby put the kibosh on all the pooping, I almost never needed to trim hooves. The concrete wore the hooves down naturally. After I moved the goats to a pen in the back, the grassy ground was too soft to wear down the hooves, so I needed to trim them more often. I have used scissors, but that involves a lot of swearing. A rasp is a cheap woodworking tool that does the job quickly and painlessly, much like filing your fingernails.

Goat Illnesses

If you start reading up on the net, you can get overwhelmed with all of the bagillion possible goat illnesses. My theory is that these people have a lot invested in their herds and are doing most of the doctoring themselves. So let me break it down for you. Backyard goats get two illnesses:

1. diarrhea (also called scours)
2. bloat

You know if a goat has scours because its back end will be dirty and it will look like it feels (miserable). Remember how you looked the last time you had the cha-chas? They look the same. If a goat looks pitiful, peek around back. Scours comes from eating something that didn't agree or from bacteria the goat picked up off the ground.

Bloat usually comes from breaking into the grain store and over eating. Goats aren't really made for grain, and too much will make their tummies inflate and rupture! Sounds awful, but both are easily treated.

- For a baby goat with scours, feed it less formula.
- For an older goat with scours, give it some of the wormer.
- For bloat or suspected bloat, use a dropper full of baby gas drops (simethicone).

Breeding

If you don't intend to milk your goats and you don't want to sell goat kids, you can skip this section, as you don't need to breed your goats. You can breed once a year, but it's not necessary.

If you continue to milk your goat on a regular basis, you can breed every couple of years to keep the milk production high. This is called "freshening," but it's not necessary.

If you intend to breed, don't buy a buck to live on your property! Bucks are stinky and obnoxious. Here are your options:

- Make friends with someone who has a buck and trade the kids for the stud fee.
- Pay a stud fee and sell the kids yourself.
- Buy a buck with a friend (who has lots of property and can, therefore, easily keep the buck) and share the cost of maintaining him.

TIMING

Don't try to detect heat. I'm not even going to tell you the signs. It will make you crazy staring at your goats' behinds. So, here are three options that will let you get the boys and girls together at the right time.

- Have a buck stay with you for a month.
- Have your girls go stay with the buck for a month.
- Use a "buck cloth" (see the sidebar on page 100).

Breeding facts:

- Does generally breed in the fall.
- They go into heat once a month.
- Gestation is about 150 days.

I was surprised by how soothing it was to sit in a cold barn on an early spring morning, lean my head against a warm goat flank and listen to the rhythmic sound of milk going into the bucket while I milked. I was also surprised by how endearing baby goats are.

—OAT BUCKET FARM, BLOG READER

How to Walk Your Goat

Walking your goat has two perks:

1. It files their hooves for you.
2. You'll be famous.

If you ever want to draw attention to yourself, take your mini-goats for a walk. I've had people pull off of the main drag into my neighborhood, just to find out what this crazy lady had on the leashes.

Walking a goat is hilarious fun. It's very low stress, compared to dog-walking. Just be sure to take a shower and brush your hair before you go. People will be noticing you.

Here are some tips for a successful walk:

- Goats must be leashed because they'll shoot off to heaven-knows-where if they get scared, which happens a lot.
- Goats are generally followers, not leaders. You may spend a great deal of the walk with your arms behind you as they trail along.
- Goats don't generally pull you toward something. You have to pull them away from something, like your neighbor's weeds or mailbox shrubbery.
- Goats are most easily walked in the road, not on the sidewalk for two reasons: (1) there's no need to pooper-scoop their pellets (which is nearly impossible without a mini-dustpan) and (2) they are easier to keep moving (staying on that little cement strip between grassy areas is like keeping a dog moving if there are steaks all over the ground.)
- Goats don't walk in a straight line. They aren't on a mission, like dogs. They browse and meander behind and around you. You will get tangled. I suggest retractable leashes or leashing them together, if possible.
- Goats will let you talk to the neighbors all you want, especially if those neighbors have grass, but they'll happily stand in the street, too.
- Stay away from busy streets as much as possible (goats are frightened by cars and may dart, pulling hard on your arms), as well as dog walkers (goats are even more afraid of dogs than cars).
- While you're out walking, be sure to watch the goats for signs of thirst.

Using a Buck Cloth

A buck cloth is a rag that has been rubbed on the scent glands of a boy goat in "rut." Rut is the season when boy goats think they're hot and sexy and their bodies produce incredible amounts of stinkiness. The gals love it.

To use a buck cloth:
1. Keep it in a sealed, air-tight container. It smells awful.
2. Show it to your gals each day. Most days they'll show little interest.
3. When they wag their tails and sniff like they can't get enough, it's time.
4. Run them straight over to the buck's house.
5. The whole event will take just a few minutes.

KIDDING TIME

Dogs and cats give birth to their litters without our intervention all of the time. Goats can pull that off too. Someday, you might wake up and find two extra goats in the yard. But, for most of us goat owners, you'll have a hand in the blessed event.

Goats typically give birth to two babies at a time. The gestational period for goats is typically between 145 and 155 days (about five months). Write down when your goats were bred so you know when to expect labor.

Before you breed your goats, find a vet or someone very experienced with birthing goats to be your support during the birthing. Ask this person for advice about what to have on hand during the birthing. It will be helpful to assemble these items into a kit so you have them ready at a moment's notice. As the due date approaches, inform your expert and line him or her up as an emergency contact should you need help.

Do your research so you know what to expect. See the appendix for a listing of helpful kidding books and websites.

Bucks are stinky! *We happened to find one through a friend, but if you search Craigslist, you can find ads for farms that will offer a stud service. Or post a seeking ad yourself! I recommend bringing the buck to your property if possible. He's stinky, but your goats will be healthier for it. A single buck isn't likely to bring diseases and problems to your place. But sending your healthy goat to a farm with thirty other goats exposes them to a host of potential problems. We've done both, and preferred bringing the buck here. As long as he has a girl or two to keep him company, he won't try to escape.*

—LINDSAY, BLOG READER

Milking

In the beginning, I thought that milking a goat would be icky. I thought goat udders would feel like private parts, like I was invading someone's underpants. It in no way feels that way. You might as well be tugging on an ear.

Note that the photos in this section feature a full-sized Nubian goat. A mini-goat will be smaller, obviously.

To milk a goat, you will need:

- A pail or collection container that is easy to clean. Seamless stainless steel is traditional, but not absolutely necessary.
- Udder wash—either from the feedstore or homemade.
- A milk stand, to raise up the goat and hold her head in place, and a stool.
- Two funnels and a coffee filter for straining out foreign matter.
- 1 or 2 quart glass jars for storing the milk.

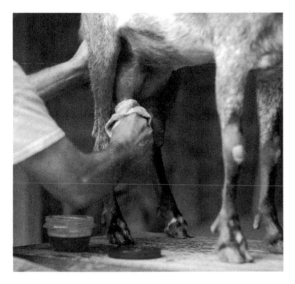 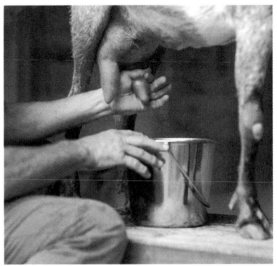

1. To start, wash your hands well. Then wash the goat's udder well with soap specifically made for udders. You can find this type of soap at a feedstore. There are homemade recipes available on the internet; just use caution as you try new products. Washing helps protect your goat from infections.

   Dry the udder with clean paper towels and never dip a dirty towel in the wash solution (single-use items reduce the chance of contamination and infection).

2. Grasp the top of the teat just above the area that feels like a small balloon. Seal off the milk with your first finger and thumb, trapping it in the teat.

3. Close your other fingers in series to flush the milk out of the teat into the pail. Let go and repeat until you get no more milk.

   Never pull on the teat. Simply move your fingers gently to massage out the milk. Then massage the udder to see if you can get more. The hindmilk is the richest in butterfat.

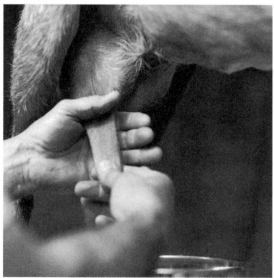

4. To strip the very last of the milk, grasp the teat just above the area that feels like a small balloon again and run your hand down the length of the teat. Don't stretch the udder.

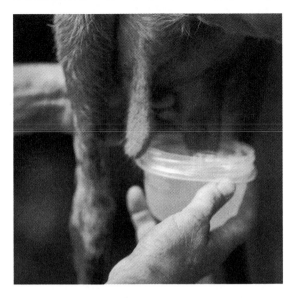

5. When you finish milking, dip the teats in a fresh mixture of udder wash. Consider using small paper cups to dip the teats because single-use items reduce the spread of disease and infection.
6. Place the coffee filter between two funnels and strain the milk into a clean glass jar. Tighten the lid, mark it with the date, and place it in the refrigerator.
7. Then clean your equipment by hand using a dairy disinfectant, or wash your equipment in the dishwasher.

Goat's milk will keep a few days if it's not pasteurized.

Milking Advice From Goat Owners

"Do not pull on the teats or squeeze too high up. They don't like it. Keep things as clean as possible. Your hands will eventually stop hurting. If the doe is pitching a fit, don't stop. Milk onto the ground if you have to, but do not let her get it into her head that stomping, kicking, and jumping will get her out of being milked. Make sure you milk her all the way out." —Oat Bucket Farm

"If they're lactating/milking, add an extra half a pound of feed per kid per day in addition to their regular ration for a full-sized goat." —Maven

"We milked twice a day this past season, and we won't be doing that again. Yes, you get more milk, but it's a lot of work. If you let the kids nurse during the day, and separate them at night (to milk in the morning), you have the option of getting away for an evening because you have automatic "milkers" (the kids). We were tied to our house for seven months, and let me tell you, that is no fun.

Goat's milk is wonderful. Absolutely wonderful. And we made goat's-milk ice cream this summer that was incredible. Don't let anyone tell you that goat's-milk tastes "goaty." Some breeds do taste different, but most taste better than cow's milk (no yucky aftertaste) if it's processed properly. We process ours by putting it in the freezer for two hours right after milking. It removes all the gases that can make the milk taste "off." Most people can't taste the difference, other than that it's whole milk, and they comment that it has a sweet aftertaste." —Lindsay

"Keep your lactating girls separated from the bucks. Otherwise every time they mate, the milk will taste awful that day." —Tanya

5

SECRET BEEKEEPERS

I propose you consider inviting tens of thousands of stinging insects to come live with you. Wait, *what*? Beekeeping is the latest thing—and by latest I mean since the twenty-fifth century BCE, if not earlier. Yes, it's been around forever, but only recently has it popped back onto the radar of the average modern city-dweller. Because I keep bees and Deanna doesn't, the "I" in this chapter refers to me, Daisy.

Benefits of Bees

Beekeeping has been experiencing a revival in cities and suburbs in recent years, and for good reason. It's a fascinating hobby that provides multiple benefits to both individuals and society.

For the individual, keeping bees prompts a consciousness shift, a microfocus. Instead of seeing "bugs," you start to notice different species. *Is that one of my bees?* you wonder.

You start to see plants in a different way. The dandelions in your lawn that once plagued you are transformed into golden sources of nectar and pollen, and maybe they can stay.

The hum and stench of the ChemLawn truck next door was never nice, and now you start thinking about community activism to promote organic lawn-care in your town.

The honey in the supermarket becomes a pale shadow of the amber elixir from your own hives.

For society, bees are the unsung underpinnings of agriculture. Over one hundred edible crops, the cotton industry, and the feed crops for the dairy and beef-cattle industries all depend on bees for their viability.

And of course, there's honey itself. It's been used in traditional medicine for millennia, and modern medicine has started to discover it as well, using honey and other bee products like royal jelly, propolis, and bee pollen for their antiseptic, antibacterial, anti-inflammatory, and nutritional benefits. And, of course, it's delicious.

So why doesn't everyone have a hive in his or her backyard? Of all the homesteading arts, beekeeping seems the most complicated and expensive, the scariest, and the most mysterious.

There is a learning curve, and there are start-up costs. But, the learning process is fascinating, and costs can be trimmed.

Scary, well, bees can and do sting, but that's what bee suits are for, and honeybees are generally docile and avoid stinging except as a last resort.

As for the mystery, that's part of the lure of keeping bees—discovering their secrets.

Beekeeping may not be for everyone or for every backyard, but for those who've got the beekeeping fever, it's hard to shake, and can be a very rewarding aspect of your little bit of homesteading independence.

Advice From Suburban Beekeepers

We asked the readers of our website, littlehouseinthesuburbs.com, about their beekeeping experiences. Their stories, in their own words, are sprinkled throughout the pages of this chapter. Here's one from Anny:

"I don't even eat honey, I wanted the bees because I find bees interesting, they are amazing insects . . . I bought my bees two years ago through someone I found online. Now I'm addicted. I want more hives! . . . I live in a major city. I have a pretty small backyard, and I keep my top bar hive in a far corner of my yard facing the six-foot (1.75m) high privacy fence. The bees never bother me, or anyone in the area. My biggest challenge I faced was neighbors fearing the bees, or not knowing very much about them. Most of the neighbors don't even know I have the bees and always ask what that "box" in my yard is. When I tell them it's a beehive, they freak out and tell me about how they once got stung by a bee and it was probably one of my bees. I also have people call me and ask me to remove the bees they have in their yard, and I'll go there to discover a wasp nest, blah!"

The Secrets of City Beekeepers

My dad kept a few beehives, as did his father. My brother, who also keeps bees, has Granddaddy's old hive smoker. Odds are my grandfather learned to keep bees from his parents, and the tradition probably spans a few generations in my family tree.

With this history in mind, and with childhood memories of chewing the honeycomb like gum and the *best* honey ever, I dreamed of becoming a backyard beekeeper, too. Problem was, I lived in the suburbs. Can't keep bees there, right? It's a farm thing, a country thing.

Then I began to hear snippets of news to the contrary. A doctor in the big town of which my small town is a suburb began giving my husband the occasional jar from his own city hives. I heard whispers of people keeping bees on rooftops in New York City.

Maybe it wasn't so out of the question for me, after all.

I went to my first local beekeepers' association meeting as a curious guest, just to get a feel for it. And who did I see sitting there but my next-door neighbor. I call this chapter "Secret Beekeepers" in part because of this. For more than twenty years, my neighbor and I had lived within yards of each other and were always on friendly terms and I never knew he had bees in his backyard.

This says several things to me. For one thing, it says beekeepers are good at keeping secrets. We're that way because we know the powerful emotional response some people have at the thought of a hive full of bees.

The second thing it says to me is that bees can make very well-behaved neighbors. It's likely I would never have known my neighbor kept bees if I hadn't caught him at that meeting. I never observed an unusual number of

"We got bees because I love honey and the good kind is very expensive. I got lucky and found a grant through our extension service that pretty much paid for our first hives—equipment and bees. (Every state has its own extension service programs, but quite a few have these beekeeping grants. They're very much worth looking into.)

When working with bees, I love the way you absolutely have to be present in the moment. If you don't focus on that hive, you're going to get stung. If you do focus, you can mess around with the lives of thousands of stinging insects and barely bother them.

People seem to be very interested in our bees, but I've noticed that beekeeping is more difficult for the layman to grasp than chicken-keeping."

—ANNA, BLOG READER

bees around, never got a sting, and never saw a swarm.

Lastly, it says to me that it's a shame we sometimes feel compelled to keep our bees a secret. My neighbor is now my mentor in the beekeeping world. If beekeepers weren't so concerned with having to give up their bees because of the fears of a few people, they would be much more effective at spreading around this valuable hobby. Beekeepers know this, and it can be hard keeping our bees a secret. We enjoy teaching people about bees, talking about bees, and sharing our honey. But on the off chance of causing offense, we often choose to keep quiet.

Perhaps as more and more urbanites choose to venture into this interesting hobby, attitudes will begin to change for the better, and beekeepers can emerge from the shadows.

Issues With Bees in the Burbs

Beekeeping, for all its resurgence, is still a bit under the radar today in most American cities. When I spoke with my local code-enforcement official, he said in his seven years on the job, mine was the first question he'd had on the subject of bees. This either means that no one has bees in my suburb (and I know that's not the case) or that the beekeepers are doing a pretty good job keeping a low profile.

Here are a few basic recommendations for city beekeepers who want to keep things cool with the neighbors. (As my neighbor proved to me, this is entirely possible.)

Place your hives in a private, out-of-the-way location. A good way to do this is to keep your bees within a privacy-fenced area, typically 6' (1.75m) in height. Out of sight is out of mind. This also drives the bees' flight path upward and away from the human-height zone.

Provide bees with a water source. Keeping water near the hive will prevent your bees from making a habit of quenching their thirst in the neighbors' pool or dog dishes. A simple birdbath or even shallow bin containing water will do. Place stones or floating sticks in the water for the bees to light safely upon while sipping.

HOA Regulations and Municipal Codes About Beekeeping

A city's laws are called municipal codes. They tell you what you can and cannot do in your town. On top of municipal codes, if you live in a neighborhood within that city with a homeowners' association (HOA), you are also subject to the homeowners' association's rules.

To clarify, there are two main types of homeowners' associations. The one to which I refer here is the type with governing rights over your residential subdivision. If you belong to one of these, you know it. Membership is a mandatory condition of buying a house in a development governed by this type of HOA. This type of neighborhood association sets standards for home maintenance and appearance and is governed by a board of directors. The other type of homeowners' association is a voluntary group, which has a mostly social and civic purpose. It doesn't have rules in addition to your town's code.

Most rules currently on the books of both cities and HOAs that pertain to beekeeping are general rules concerning operating a business within a residential area and rules concerning being a nuisance. If you are maintaining beehives for personal use and give the by-product as gifts, you are not violating any zoning ordinances concerning operating a business in a residential area. If you are following responsible beekeeping practices, your bees are unlikely to present a nuisance to your neighbors.

Some cities and HOAs do have rules that pertain specifically to beekeeping. Check your town's website or municode.com for a list of these rules, or phone your town's code-inspector's office for information. Your local beekeepers' association may also be able to advise you.

Sing the praises of the bee. If you choose to discuss your hobby with your neighbors, remind them that bees are not only docile unless disturbed, they also tend to drive away aggressive stinging insects such as yellow jackets. They also help aid pollination of the local flora (including perhaps their favorite backyard vegetables). The occasional gift of a jar of honey never goes amiss.

BEEKEEPING AROUND CHILDREN

I've had many questions about keeping curious (and even mischievous) children from mixing it up with the bees. If you abide by the first principle above and have your bees within a fenced space, it's unlikely you'll have to deal with roving children.

In the case of your own kids, older children can be taught a healthy respect for the hive. Teach them to stay a safe distance from the hive entrance and not to antagonize the bees by striking or disturbing the hive in any way. Kit them out in bee suits along with you as you work your bees and let them learn by helping and observing you.

For younger children unable to understand and stay a safe distance away, an additional barrier such as a smaller, locking fenced area within your larger yard is good. This is also an option for someone without a fenced perimeter who wants to have a special space just for the bees.

Pets seldom create an issue with hives. If your dog does happen to cause a disturbance with the hive, he'll quickly learn his lesson and it should only be a one-time event.

Knowledge drives away fear. Be prepared to advocate for neighborhood bees by knowing their characteristics and how beehives fit into the landscape of suburbia.

CITY NECTAR

It isn't difficult to imagine the sources of nectar and pollen for country honeybees. We envision meadows and fence rows of nodding blooms, blossoming cropland, and fragrant orchards. In towns and cities, though, it takes a little more imagination to think of that environment as conducive to bee foraging.

Actually, though, city bees have some advantages over their country cousins. For one, the biodiversity in urban and suburban areas often rivals that of farmland, where monoculture is the norm. Beekeepers in the city have identified thousands of different flower sources in one draw of honey. Many keepers believe urban honey to be more flavorful as a result.

Also, city sources of pollen and nectar tend to have lower amounts of pesticides and herbicides than agricultural cropland.

City beekeepers report fewer problems with colony collapse disorder, a good indicator of the strength of urban bee colonies.

Because bees have a range of two to six miles from the hive, it can be difficult to determine the exact sources of their honey, but as bees collect nectar from trees, hedges, and every sort of flowering plant, a fresh look at urban areas reveals an abundance of potential bee food.

And it's a reciprocal arrangement. Even though they will probably never realize it, gardeners who have beekeeping neighbors likely enjoy higher productivity because of the pollination help provided by the little foragers visiting their plants.

Mysteries of Modern Beekeeping

After I realized I could keep bees in the suburbs, I faced my next hurdle—a complete lack of knowledge about beekeeping. Even though my family had a few hives while I was growing up, my interest in bees at the time was limited to eating the honey. What went on in those mysterious white boxes at the edge of the woods was beyond me.

So I tried to read up on bees. I consider myself to be of average intelligence on a good day, but soon I began to feel very ignorant indeed. It wasn't clicking. Maybe I wasn't cut out to do this. Maybe there was a window of opportunity when a person could easily grasp beekeeping, as there is with learning a foreign language, and I'd missed it.

I went to beekeepers' association meetings hoping that it would start to come together. It didn't. I attended a day-long new-beekeeper training event because I knew that would help. I'm embarrassed to say it didn't, really.

I knew some things have to be learned by doing, and perhaps beekeeping was one of them. I looked through the supply catalogs distributed at the beekeeper training and tried to pick out the hives and equipment I would need.

Whoa. Entrance reducers? Telescoping covers? Queen excluders? Tell me I wasn't going to need a $550 honey extractor. If I wasn't already in over my head before, I would have been at that point. I faced sticker shock and extreme confusion. I thought I was never going to figure this out, it seemed so complicated.

I wasn't making any progress. I still read, but I found myself going over the same thing over and over and not feeling any more confident.

Then, in my internet research, I started hearing about natural beekeeping. Of course with my inclination toward "natural" stuff, my ears perked up. I heard phrases like "less interference," "simpler," and "less expensive." Sounded good to me.

As I explored the "natural" approach, I realized that the reason beekeeping seems as complicated as engineering a rocket launch is because modern beekeeping has evolved around the beekeeper, not the bees.

The focus of modern commercial beekeeping is on maximum honey production, which is understandable. More honey is a good thing, but it requires a high level of human interference in the process. Manipulated out of the ways they naturally function, bees have become more susceptible to parasites and disease. Rather than stand back and allow honeybees to revert to behaviors that are less conducive to hosting these parasites and diseases, man predictably responded with more interference, most recently in the form of pesticide treatments.

It sort of worked for a while, though at a cost. Then the pests became resistant to those pesticides and we came up with new pesticides to which the pests became resistant, and a cycle was started.

Let's recap. You have bees in a production-oriented, pest-vulnerable, human-designed hive. Lots of pests. Pesticides. Pesticide-resistant pests and pest-stressed bees. More pesticides and more interference. What else can make it hard on the bees? How about less biodiversity in agriculture and more herbicides and pesticides being used on the crops bees need to survive? Then let's move them around a lot on trucks and expose them to foreign diseases as well.

So a lot of what complicates modern beekeeping, even hobby beekeeping, is the man-made solutions to man-made problems in the process.

For the simple hobbyist, like me, what if we got back to basics? What if we encouraged

Langstroth Beehives

The Langstroth beehive has become the standard hive in North America as well as parts abroad. It was developed in the mid-nineteenth century in Pennsylvania by Rev. L.L. Langstroth. This type of hive has many excellent features and represents a great advance in modern beekeeping. The Langstroth hive is highly recognizable with its appearance of stacked boxes, which are commonly painted white.

Because Langstroth hives are so widespread, many beginners may find the Langstroth hive a good one to start with. There are ample resources available for Langstroth hives. The vast majority of beekeeping information available today is related to the Langstroth method, and most of the experienced bee keepers you meet in beekeeper association meetings will use this method.

There are many ways to adapt the use of Langstroth beehives to allow for natural pest- and disease-control methods. You may find using this traditional hive in conjunction with organic controls to be a happy solution to bridging the gap between standard practices and earth-friendly ones.

honeybees to live as closely as possible to how they would in the wild while still managing them and harvesting honey? By eliminating the man-made problems (over-manipulation to maximize honey production), you eliminate the need for complex solutions to these problems. Let bees be bees and they'll take care of themselves while giving you some honey.

Beekeeping the Natural Way

"Whole wheat" is how one of my brothers jokingly referred to the way I decided to begin beekeeping. It was an affectionate (I hope) reference to how I tend to go about things the "crunchy" way, in spite of the fact that I don't consider myself hard-core about natural everything.

The central principles of a more natural style of beekeeping are simple and as follows:

- Let the bees do it their way.
- Don't put anything into the hive you wouldn't let your toddler chew on.
- Don't be a honey hog.

With my whole-wheat approach in hand, I set aside those bewildering modern beekeeping books and catalogs and found a set of plans online for what is called a Horizontal Top Bar Hive (HTBH).

Before you start to go cross-eyed trying to learn all the new terms, let me first say that natural beekeeping can be done in just about any kind of hive, with modifications. This type of HTBH was my choice because it's fairly easy to build and has some features that appealed to me.

HORIZONTAL TOP BAR HIVE

A top bar hive is best described as a long box, usually made of wood. Wooden bars are placed along the top of the box, and bees build comb on the underside of these bars. A removable roof is placed above the bars to protect the hive from the elements. The bees enter the box via holes drilled into either the ends or the sides. Many variations in this type of hive exist.

The Natural Beekeeping Community

Local beekeeping associations are the usual go-to organizations for people wanting to learn about how to keep bees. I adore my local beekeeping association. The people are warm and funny. They have a wealth of knowledge about bee behavior, an understanding of the local flora, climate, and bee history. The old-timers have their own senses of humor and are willing to give a leg up whenever you need it. My personal nickname for them is The Church of the Beekeeper, as meetings are inaugurated with prayer and once a speaker slipped and addressed us as "brethren." I love it.

But I don't ask them for advice on natural beekeeping. They are traditional, Langstroth-hive beekeepers. I recently asked the most progressive among them (in terms of organic pest treatment) if he'd ever heard about top bar hives and he shook his head.

I'm on my own here for the time being. Perhaps this will change soon. I still enjoy the meetings and encourage you to seek out your local beekeepers, but unless yours is in the minority, you will have to look elsewhere for natural beekeeping advice.

There are a few books on the subject and a few online forums and websites that will give you the community you need to provide advice and information until the day you can start your own local natural beekeepers' association.

Here's where I go:
biobees.com
bushfarms.com
thebeespace.net
naturalbeekeeping.info
beesource.com
naturalbeekeepingtrust.org

Resources for top-bar hives and equipment:
goldstarhoneybees.com
thegardenhive.com
beethinking.com
backyardhive.com
honeybeehabitat.com

Books
The Barefoot Beekeeper by P. J. Chandler
Natural Beekeeping by Ross Conrad

Many HTBHs are built on legs. Adding legs to the hive has two benefits:

1. It lifts the hive off the ground, keeping it safe from rot and predators.
2. It's easier for the beekeeper to access the hive.

The important part is that the hive lets the bees build their own comb from scratch, which is the way they like it.

Traditional beekeeping forces bees to build comb on manufactured comb foundation (sheets of wax or plastic used to prompt comb formation) within frames. At harvest, the comb is emptied and replaced in the traditional hive for re-use to save the bees from having to start all over with new comb.

My whole-wheat bees don't do that. They build comb as they would if left to their own devices. They customize the cell size according to nature's dictates, not mine.

In this kind of beekeeping, the honey is harvested comb and all, and the bees build a new comb to store the future honey they will produce.

Allowing the bees to build new combs is the natural way of it and also the more hygienic way, as a fresh new comb is less likely than a re-used, pre-fab comb to host an accumulation of possible environmental toxins.

"Bees work hard. I love to hear them working, not just near the hive, but all around the farm. They work spring, summer, and fall. Even if it's rainy, I know they're toiling away inside the hive, drying the nectar, drawing comb, and keeping their home shipshape. It gives me comfort to know that I can go inside the house after a hard morning's work and eat a lazy lunch, then sit on the porch, and drift off, hearing them working, working, working. Working for me."
—JOE, A BLOG READER

Equipment

My experience with beekeeping is the whole-wheat way, so the information in this chapter is geared toward that method. I won't go into complex explanations of or instructions for traditional beekeeping. There are many great resources available for that. See the appendix for ideas and attend a meeting of your local beekeepers' association.

Here is the basic equipment you'll need for top-bar-hive beekeeping:

- A hive. You can buy one, build your own, or have a handy friend build one for you.
- A bee veil to protect your eyes, ears, nose and mouth.
- A bee suit (optional).
- A hive tool or sturdy knife. A hive tool is a metal bar with a flat end used to pry apart bars that become stuck together by comb and/or propolis (a resinous, glue-like substance bees use to build the interior of their hives).
- A swarm or package of bees.
- A spray bottle of sugar water (equal parts water and sugar). Spray the sugar water when collecting a swarm or when installing a package of bees. It distracts the bees as they drink up the syrup and makes them easier to manage.
- A hive smoker.

Light a hive smoker the same way you would start a tiny campfire, by starting with fast-burning kindling, such as pine needles or shredded paper (each region seems to have a favorite kindling). Pump the bellows of the smoker to stoke the flame with air. Add fuel that is longer-burning such as dry twigs, wood pellets, strips of cotton cloth or burlap. Continue to pump the bellows until the new fuel catches and continue to add fuel until the smoker is about half-full of combustible material. Close the lid and pump the bellows until

the smoker is emitting a good stream of thick white smoke.

After you finish working the hive, completely extinguish the fire in the smoker.

How to Get Bees

You can get bees to your hive in one of two ways. There's also a third outlier option that is rare.

PURCHASE A PACKAGE OF BEES

The first way to get bees is to purchase a "package" of bees from a beekeeping business. This is a literal package (box) of bees, usually sold by the pound (i.e. two-. three-, or four-pound sizes). Some sellers will mail your bees to you via next-day airmail.

This is the most expensive route to getting your bees. Prices vary, but two to three pounds of bees (a decent quantity for a starter hive) will cost from sixty to one hundred dollars plus shipping, which is rather dear for next-day service.

You can also purchase a "nuc," or nucleus hive (a beekeeping term for a small, temporary hive), although they are even more expensive than packaged bees.

If an established beekeeper has enough bees, he or she could give you a nuc to get you started, but conditions have to be right in the beekeeper's hive to make this possible.

FIND A SWARM

A second way to get your bees is to find a swarm. If you have developed a relationship

What Are Killer Bees?

More properly called the Africanized honeybee (AHB), "killer bees" are a strain of bee that was introduced to other parts of the world from Africa beginning with an accidental release of AHBs from a research program in Brazil.

The venom of the Africanized honeybee is no more dangerous than that of the Western or European honeybee (common domesticated honeybees), but the AHBs temperament is more aggressive than that of the Western bee, and AHBs are more likely to attack humans and animals.

The AHBs aggression is the result of the natural selection. The bees most likely to survive conditions in their native land were those who would successfully defend their hive from being robbed by both animals and humans. Hive robbing, rather than beekeeping, was the normal way to obtain honey in the region to which AHBs are native.

The AHB is spreading north into the United States. The knee-jerk reaction of municipalities in which AHBs are starting to move is likely to be to ban beekeeping in urban areas, but this would be counterproductive. Established Western honeybees help prevent the AHB from becoming established in an area. A restriction on these gentler bees would leave an ecological hole that the AHB would willingly fill.

Although the encroachment of the AHB sounds dire, in areas where AHBs have become established, they have usually failed to create the stir once feared. After an adjustment period, they become established and interbreed with the local bees. The AHB hybrids are highly productive and resilient.

This hybrid of the AHB and the Western bee has become the norm in Brazil. If you've eaten Brazilian honey, you are likely to have tasted the produce of these "killer" bees.

with other beekeepers or your local beekeepers' association, let it be known that you want to get a swarm. Many beekeepers' associations have a "swarm list" of keepers the public can call when they have an unwanted mass of apis mellifera (honeybees) hanging around their property. Let the beekeepers know that when they get such a call, you would like to be the lucky recipient of a swarm.

The outlier option, which is rare but not unknown, is for a swarm to move into a ready hive on its own.

Some people have had luck with luring bees to their hive with lemongrass essential oil during the spring swarm season. It's a very long shot, though. You could grow old waiting for this to happen.

Be aware that wasps can take up residence in an empty hive. If wasps moved into your empty hive, you would need to remove the nest and seal the hive. However, you don't need to worry about wasps taking over an established hive. A healthy colony of bees can successfully defend their hive against wasps.

Adding Bees to Your Hive

A package of bees generally includes the quantity of bees you ordered and a separate container within the package that contains the queen and a few workers to attend her. It also contains a can of enough sugar syrup to feed the bees during their transit period.

To install the bees, have the hive ready and open. Don your bee suit and have your smoker and spray bottle of sugar water ready. Spray the bees with sugar water through the wire mesh package.

> "I am a gardener first of all. My reasons for getting bees were: First, the pollination; second, the plight of the honeybee; third, the challenge. I live in a rural county, but my street does have neighbors, and we have close to an acre with woods and swamp to the back. I only have an older couple on one side, they don't work their yard at all. So as far as telling anyone, I only called the county to see if it was legal. I love working with the bees. It is an awesome privilege, sometimes intimidating, but always challenging and rewarding. I have been trying to let the bees do their thing without interfering too much. This was our second season and we got a gallon and a half of delicious honey for our family, but also left a whole box for the bees."
>
> —NANCY, BLOG READER

Open the package lid and remove the can of syrup. The packages are commonly designed so that removing the syrup can reveals the bees. Remove the queen package

The queen is kept separate from the rest of the swarm because she is still new to them and the bees need time to adjust to her and recognize her scent. Until the bees recognize and accept the queen, they consider her an intruder and they will kill her if they have access to her.

The queen package will have a hole in it that is plugged with a piece of "bee candy" (just a piece of hard sugar candy). The bee candy is a sort of timed-release feature. The worker bees will slowly eat away at it and by the time they work through the plug, they will used to the new queen and accept her. Instructions with your bee package will usually tell you how the queen package should be treated.

Suspend the queen package with the bee candy in place between frames within the hive.

Then bang the package of bees on the ground or the hive to concentrate the bees in one clump.

Position the package over the hive with the package opening facing the hive opening and shake or tap the bees into the hive.

Use a hive brush to move the bees out of the way of the hive lid and close the hive. Some bees will cling to the inside of the package. Don't try to get them out. Just set the package on the ground with the opening facing the hive. The stragglers will eventually find their way into the hive through the hive entrance.

Working Safely With Honeybees

Because you are considering beekeeping, you must not be too bothered by the thought of receiving a few stings, but, hopefully, you understand that you should always exercise caution when working with a beehive. This section will give you ideas on how to be safe around your bees.

WORK WHEN THE BEES ARE HAPPY

Happy bees will be much more receptive to your presence than unhappy bees. Honeybees are happiest and most docile in warm, sunny weather. (For your own sake, avoid oppressively hot days, or you'll be miserable in your bee suit.) If at all possible, wait for a good bee day to work on your hives.

Do not work in your hives on stormy days or days that have threats of storms. The bees will be agitated by the weather.

STOP BY WHEN NO ONE'S HOME

The best time of day to work in your hive is in the late morning to the earliest part of the afternoon. The foraging bees will be out, so you'll have fewer bees to contend with, and the home bees will be occupied in the hive. The hive will never be empty, but if you stop by while all the bees are busy, your presence won't be as noticed.

BE CALM AND PATIENT

It may seem like an impossible task, particularly at first, but the calmer you are, the calmer the bees will be. Slow, deliberate movements communicate a sense of safety to the hive, which is what you want. Don't swat. Bees may hover near your face, but if you are protected by a veil, you are safe. Let them hover. They are only guard bees doing their job. Breathe normally, but try not to exhale directly on the bees.

BRING PACIFIERS

If the bees seem agitated, use a smoker or a sugar water spray. The smoke is said to mask the alarm pheromones bees emit when you disturb the hive. The alarm pheromones also prompts a feeding response (the bees think they are going to have to leave so they look for fuel to survive the journey). Spraying sugar water allows them to feed right away. Feeding makes bees less able to sting because a full bee isn't as able to flex its stinger.

Harvesting Honey

Harvesting honey from top-bar hives is fairly straightforward. To harvest from a top-bar hive, the keeper uses a hive tool or a sharp knife to remove an entire comb. Combs are harvested one at a time as needed in the spring. The honey is either used as is (comb honey is delicious), or the comb is mashed with a fork and the honey is allowed to drip out through a mesh filter.

The top-bar setup is generally considered to produce less honey than the traditional Langstroth method, but one top-bar hive can produce enough honey for a single family. If you would like more to share, you'll need to add more hives.

Most top-bar beekeepers harvest honey as needed in the spring when new stores are coming in. This gives the bees the entire summer to rebuild their food supply for winter.

Harvesting in the fall is complicated for a few reasons. You have to estimate how much honey to leave the bees for the winter, and if you guess wrong, you would need to implement supplemental sugar-syrup feeding to get the bees through the winter. It makes common sense to me and to other natural beekeepers that honey, rather than sugar, is a more complete food for the bees. If bees are left to feed only on their honey, as nature intended, the colony will be healthier.

Even if you harvest a modest amount in the spring, your bees still may need supplementary feeding during times when they produce an insufficient honey store. Stress and environmental conditions, such as drought or too much rain can affect honey production. But this is hopefully the exception rather than the rule.

Colony Collapse Disorder

Bees today face many threats, including the much-publicized colony collapse disorder (CCD). CCD is a phenomenon characterized by the sudden abandonment of a colony by its worker bees, effectively decimating the colony. CCD is still the subject of much research and debate, and a definitive explanation of what causes CCD is yet to be found. There are a few current theories. One is that CCD is caused by a combination of environmental stressors (climate change, pesticides, poor nutrition, et al.) that weaken honeybees and make them easy prey for pests and disease. The most recent theory, as of 2010, is that CCD is caused by a co-infection of a virus and a fungus. Researchers and beekeepers continue to search for solutions to this widespread problem that has caused the honeybee populations in some areas of the world to decline by as much as 50 percent.

Health and Safety in the Hive

Honeybee colonies can fall victim to a number of pests, notably the varroa mite, tracheal mites, wax moths, hive beetles (their larvae ruin honey and comb) and even ants, yellow jackets, skunks, and mice. Bears can also be a problem in some areas of the country.

Disease concerns include nosema (a unicellular parasite that causes widespread damage to bee health), foulbrood (a bacterial disease), chalkbrood (a fungal infection), and sacbrood (a virus of bee larvae).

One of the best protections against pests and disease is promoting the development of a healthy hive.

I believe allowing the bees to build their comb from scratch makes the hive better able to fend off assault, particularly in the case of the dreaded varroa mite. The top-bar method (and adaptations of traditional hives that allow the bees to build their own comb from scratch) allows the bees to do just that. When you prevent problems, you don't have to resort to chemical methods to control pests and diseases.

Other methods of controlling varroa mites include dusting the bees with powdered sugar

"Everybody everywhere is interested in beekeeping. At least, I've never met anyone who, when the subject was raised, did not express a lot of interest. Bees and honey are, somehow, just one of those things that fascinate people. People love to watch me harvest honey. And I like to have them watch. They think that anyone who raises bees and harvests liquid gold is pretty clever, and, yeah, I guess we are."

—J.P., BLOG READER

(loosens the mites' grip on the bees), thymol treatments (thymol is a derivative of oil of thyme), and other essential oils.

More comprehensive natural treatments of bee pests and diseases can be found in the Resources for Beekeepers list in the appendix.

The Benefits of Bee Products

As you will see, many of our recipes for good things to eat *and* for skin and home products contain honey or beeswax.

Raw (unpasteurized) honey has a long list of beneficial properties. Raw honey:

- is antibacterial
- is antifungal.
- is an antioxidant.
- has anti-tumor properties.
- is antiviral.
- boosts athletic performance.
- boosts beneficial bacterium in the intestines.
- speeds wound healing (including burns and surgical cuts).
- stabilizes blood sugar.
- strengthens the body's immune response.

Beeswax is close behind in the superiority contest. Beeswax:

- is antibacterial.
- is anti-inflammatory.
- cleans the air when burned in candles by emitting negatively charged ions and attracting and burning positively charged particles.
- is emollient.
- is nonallergenic (unless you have a bee allergy).
- is noncomedogenic.
- is water-repellent.

DIPPED BEESWAX TAPERS

Pure beeswax candles are a delight, both in appearance and fragrance, and also in the way they purify rather than pollute the air as standard paraffin candles do.

Makes three–four pairs of six-inch tapers

Materials:

46 ounce (1.35L) metal can (like a large can of tomato juice)

saucepan

2 pounds beeswax

#3/0 or #4/0 square braid cotton wick (no core)

pencil, piece of doweling, skewer, or chopstick

1. Fill the metal can with pieces of solid beeswax. You will probably need to break or cut the wax into smaller pieces. You can also use beeswax prills or pellets, which are granulated, pourable, forms of wax.

2. Fill the saucepan with a couple of inches (2.5cm-5cm) of water and place the metal can filled with beeswax in the saucepan. Place the saucepan over low heat and allow the wax to melt slowly.

3. While the wax melts, cut your wick to size. For 6' (15cm) tapers, cut the wicking into 24" (61cm) pieces. This will create two tapers at a time.

4. After the wax has melted, prime your wick by dropping it into the wax. Give the wax a stir with a wooden skewer and let the wick sit in the wax for a minute or two to allow the wax to soak in.

5. Extract the wick and stretch it out in a U-shape on a sheet of wax paper. Try to get the ends as straight as you can.

6. Starting in the middle of the wick, wrap the wick around the center of the stick.

7. Holding the stick, dip the wick about 6" into the melted wax in a steady, smooth motion, straight down and then straight up.

Allow the wax to cool briefly and continue to repeat the motion until the taper is the desired circumference. (You may wish to measure the candle holders you are planning to use the candles in to determine the size you need).

As you dip, the level of the wax will go down. Add pieces of wax to the metal can and allow the fresh wax to melt as you go to bring the level of the wax up to the required depth.

8. When your tapers are the desired size, hang them over a dowel, doorknob, etc., to allow them to cool completely.

9. Use a sharp knife to trim off the drip bump at the base of the candles to allow them to fit easily into the candle holders.

Pure beeswax candles are rather pliable, so store them on a flat surface or continue to store them in a hanging position. Beeswax candles may develop a filmy, white "bloom" after a while, which can be removed with a soft polishing cloth if you like.

To use, cut the candles apart and trim the wicks to ¼" (6.5mm).

Conclusion

If you give beekeeping a try, I hope you're smarter than I am and it isn't as confusing to you as it was for me, especially at first. If it does send you reeling a bit, I hope you gain comfort and confidence from my experience. Beekeeping is a path less traveled than some, and like most best-kept secrets, it's full of new concepts, new people, new sights, sounds, and smells. Give it a try and become a small part of the secret life of bees.

I got into bees because we wanted to get away from using sugar. I want to make sure that the honey I eat is as chemical-free as possible. You can't control what the bee gets into when it's out and about, but you can control what goes into the hive. I was shocked at all the chemicals that even local beekeepers want to put with their bees. Moth crystals … really?

I was careful to buy my starter bees from a guy who uses only organic practices with his bees. He also bred them to be very gentle. If you buy bees from someone who uses lots of chemicals, the bees are really not strong enough to survive on their own.

I live in a rural area, but I do have neighbors. I took the time to educate them about bees. The first important lesson to teach is that not everything that flies is a bee. The second was that if it is stinging you just for the heck of it, it is for sure not a honeybee. I invited them over to see how gentle the honeybees were at the hive and the neighbors quickly lost all concerns about the beehives.

I like to grow my own food, so the honeybee is here on the farm to pollinate my crops. The increase in vegetables plus the honey production make the bee a valuable addition to my small farm."
—KIMBERLY, BLOG READER

6

MY PANTRY WAS NEVER SO YUMMY

Food is something that recently grew in the ground or moved on it. It provides vitamins, minerals, proteins, and other nutrients that build and fuel our bodies. Highly processed foods are "derived" from something that grew in the ground or moved on it, usually two years and twenty-five chemical processes ago. These "foods" may be edible (and some may even say tasty), but they aren't nourishing. That's what's amiss with them. They really aren't food.

Take That, Tanker of Corn Syrup!

DEANNA Now we aren't saying you can't have a layer of processed, totally fake BBQ sauce on your bleached-flour, mystery-meat freezer pizza now and again, but we think once you make a few of our homemade staples, you won't miss the high-fructose corn syrup version anytime soon. And, you might even start offering to bring the salad dressings and whatnot to parties, just to avoid the processed version.

And if, like us, you're too lazy to run to the grocery for that one bottle of ketchup you need for the meatloaf tonight, this is the section for you!

Homemade Condiments

DAISY When you make something you once assumed, subconsciously perhaps, was the invariant privilege of a factory to create, it gets your creative juices flowing and gives you more power and flexibility over what you and your family eat. Here, we have recipes for basic condiments and "Cadillac" versions of these condiments. This is not to say you will never buy another jar of pickles, but you may never want to.

We're not pretending it's cheaper and easier to make ketchup at home than it is to toss a squeeze bottle of Hunt's into your shopping cart. We also don't guarantee your six year old (or anyone else for that matter) will automatically transition from store-bought to homemade.

We aren't trying to mimic the commercial flavors, we just want to give you alternatives that we think are even tastier.

Four basic food groups: ketchup, mustard, mayo, and hot sauce.

PLAIN JANE KETCHUP
Yield: approximately 2 ½ cups

- 1 6-ounce can tomato paste
- 2 tablespoons cider vinegar
- 2–3 tablespoons brown sugar
- 1 teaspoon garlic powder
- 1 teaspoon onion powder
- 1 teaspoon salt
- 1 teaspoon molasses
- 1 ¼ cup water
- dash Worcestershire sauce or allspice (optional)

Mix all ingredients together in a small saucepan and simmer over low heat until the mixture reaches your desired consistency, about 30–45 minutes. Let sit for at least an hour for better flavor.

Keep refrigerated.

PLAIN JANE MUSTARD
Yield: approximately ½ cups

- 4 tablespoons dry mustard powder
- 2 tablespoons white-wine vinegar
- 2 teaspoons turmeric
- 2 tablespoons water
- pinch each of garlic powder, paprika, and salt to taste (optional)

Whisk the mustard powder, vinegar, and turmeric in a small bowl, adding the water a ½ tablespoon at a time until you reach the desired consistency. Add optional spices and let the mixture rest 20 minutes. Serve. This mustard keeps several weeks in the refrigerator.

COARSE SPICY MUSTARD

This is Coarse with a capital C. Rustic, huge mustard flavor, with visible whole mustard seeds.

Yield: approximately 1¼ cups

- ½ cup apple-cider vinegar
- ¼ cup white wine

¼ cup mustard seed

¼ cup dry mustard

1 teaspoon salt

½ teaspoon turmeric

¼ teaspoon paprika

1 clove garlic, crushed

½ teaspoon coarsely ground black pepper

1 tablespoon honey

1. Combine the vinegar and wine in a small bowl with the mustard seed, dry mustard, and crushed garlic. Cover and place in the refrigerator for twenty-four hours or overnight.

2. Place the vinegar mixture in a medium bowl. Add the salt, turmeric, paprika, black pepper, and honey and stir to blend. Allow to thicken in the refrigerator for several days. It will reach spreadable consistency after three or four days.

NO-FAIL MAYO

DEANNA Homemade mayo is nothing like store-bought mayo. Nothing! If you've never had fresh mayo, you haven't yet begun to live, my friend.

Yield: approximately ¾ cup

1 egg yolk

1 teaspoon lemon juice

1 pinch salt

½ to ¾ cup light-tasting oil (such as canola), divided

1. Dependable mayo is about two things: warmth and the slow addition of oil. So, fill a medium-sized mixing bowl with really hot tap water, pour in the yolk, and let it sit for a few minutes. This process evenly warms both the yolk and the bowl. (If you are using fresh eggs you collected from your own chickens, see the instructions at the end of the recipe to pasteurize your egg first.)

2. Drain the water, but leave the yolk and set the bowl on a nonskid surface. Whip with a whisk for a second until the yolk is a little bubbly.

3. Add the lemon juice and salt. Mix well.

4. Place ¼ cup of the oil in a small container. Add two teaspoons of oil to the yolk. Whip until you can't see the oil. This takes about ten seconds.

5. Continue adding a couple of teaspoons of oil at a time until you've worked through the entire ¼ cup.

6. Refill the container with another ¼ cup of oil and repeat the process, adding 1 tablespoon at a time.

7. If you want your mayo thicker, add oil by tablespoons until the consistency is how you want it. If you go too far, it will start to ball up and cling to the sides of the bowl. Not good.

8. Use immediately or refrigerate. This mayo will keep a few days or more.

After you have made this recipe twice, you'll be able to add the oil with less care. It still needs to be added slowly, but with experience, you can add the oil in splashes instead of teaspoons and tablespoons.

The following method is how I learned to "pasteurize" eggs, but, I don't think a food scientist would agree that the end results are pasteurized. This method allegedly kills any errant germs. But, frankly, I only did it the first two times. It's a lot of effort. And I decided that if eating raw homemade mayo was the way I was going to go down, than that's just how it was gonna be. I live on the edge. However, if you don't have access to healthy chickens and want to play it safe, this is the best way I've seen to have your mayo and eat it too.

To pasteurize a fresh egg yolk:
1. Set up a double boiler. Begin heating water on medium heat. Put some water in the cup, about 1" (2.5cm). And gently drop in your egg yolk.
2. Heat until the water containing the egg is at least 130°F (55°C). Don't go above 140°F (60°C) or your egg yolk will cook. Try to keep it around that temperature for five minutes.
3. To warm your bowl, dip it in the pan and dry it. Then continue the recipe instructions at step 2.

HOMEMADE TABASCO SAUCE

The first time I made my own Tabasco sauce, I did it the wrong way. I will share my experience to prevent you from doing the same. After I put the ingredients on to simmer for a few minutes, I went outside for a second. Which turned into several minutes. When I walked back in the door after, oh, half an hour, I pepper-gassed myself. I gasped, coughed, and fled, choking. My windpipe was searing. Then I took a big breath and had to go back inside, remove the burning peppers from the stove, and evacuate my family who were, sleeping in on a lazy Saturday morning.

We were coughing, sneezing, and choking by the time we got the windows open and the fans turned on. We stood in the yard, stranded. Even the dog was sneezing. So, with one small caveat, here's the recipe. Do as I say, not as I did.

Yield: approximately 1¼ cup
- ⅓ cup tabasco peppers
- 1 cup vinegar, your choice, white, cider, or wine
- 2 garlic cloves
- 1 teaspoon salt

1. Briefly simmer the peppers in the vinegar and salt, watching carefully, in a well-ventilated area. (Do not go out and start to leaf blow the driveway.)
2. Remove the ingredients from the heat, cover, and cool.

3. Add crushed garlic and puree the mixture in a blender or food processor until smooth. Don't stick your nose right in there and breathe deeply (please, for the love of your mucous membranes). Store in the refrigerator. Keeps indefinitely.

HOMEMADE HORSERADISH

Horseradish is so easy to grow in the garden you have no excuse not to have your own supply. At sandwich time, haul out this simple prepared horseradish and take your turkey club or reuben to a new level.

- fresh horseradish root
- vinegar
- salt

1. Scrub the excess dirt from the root and peel the root using a vegetable peeler.
2. The root can be grated using the fine surface of a box grater, or it can be cubed and processed in a blender with just enough water to get things going. If you use the blender method with water, allow the excess moisture to drain briefly in a sieve.
3. Add 3 tablespoons vinegar per cup of grated horseradish. Add salt to taste.

Salad Dressings

DAISY When my family gathers for a potluck, I'm almost always asked to contribute a salad, with "that good dressing you make." They may not realize it, but I seldom make the exact same dressing twice, but it always rivals typical store-bought versions, plus I can leave out the sugar usually found in commercially prepared dressings for sugar-sensitive relatives. With a really delicious dressing, even salad-haters may become converts.

THAT GOOD DRESSING
Yield: approximately 2¼ cups

- 1 teaspoon pressed or finely minced garlic
- 1 tablespoon honey
- ½ teaspoon freshly cracked black pepper
- 2 tablespoons brown mustard
- 1 tablespoon each fresh, or 1 teaspoon each dried basil, oregano, and rosemary
- 1 teaspoon soy sauce
- ½ cup any good vinegar (red, white or rice wine or apple cider)
- 1½ cup extra virgin olive oil
- ½ to 1 teaspoon salt (adjust to your taste)

Combine all ingredients in blender and whir until emulsified. Alternately, without a blender, combine all ingredients except the olive oil in a medium bowl, then slowly whisk in the olive oil until the ingredients are emulsified. Taste and adjust the salt.

Keep refrigerated up to several weeks (but it probably will be used up quickly).

JUST RIGHT BUTTERMILK RANCH DRESSING

Seriously? Ranch dressing? Well, yes, why not? It's got the real flavor the store-bought version merely hints at.

Yield: approximately 1½ cups

- ½ cup buttermilk
- ½ cup mayonnaise (see homemade recipe in this chapter)
- ½ cup sour cream
- 2 teaspoon lemon or lime juice
- 1 teaspoon pressed or smashed and finely minced fresh garlic (release that flavor!)
- 1 teaspoon dried or 1 tablespoon fresh chopped basil
- 2 teaspoon minced fresh chives
- 2 teaspoon minced fresh parsley
- 2 teaspoon toasted minced dried onion
- ½ teaspoon salt
- ¼ teaspoon freshly cracked black pepper

Blend the buttermilk, mayo, and sour cream. Stir in the lemon juice, garlic, herbs, and onion. Add salt and pepper and adjust both according to taste.

Keep refrigerated up to two weeks.

POPPYSEED DRESSING

This dressing is sweet and tangy with the cool crunch of poppyseed and green onion. Bring out the big guns for the staunchest salad-refusers. They'll have a hard time resisting.

Yield: approximately 1 cup

- ½ cup of your favorite salad oil, such as olive or canola
- ¼ cup honey
- ¼ cup of your favorite vinegar
- 2 teaspoon lemon juice
- 1 teaspoon mustard
- 1 green onion, coarsely chopped
- 1 tablespoon poppyseeds
- salt and pepper to taste

Process the ingredients in a blender or food processor until smooth. Adjust salt and pepper. Keep refrigerated.

Seasoning Blends

Packaged in little cello bags and tied with a ribbon or in small glass jars with bail lids, these make great gifts. Keep these blends on hand in your own kitchen to rub into meat and fish and to toss into pasta sauces, salad dressings, and just about anything that needs a tasty kick. Any or all of these blends can be made salt-free if you prefer.

GREEK BLEND

1 ½ teaspoons dried oregano

1 teaspoon dried mint

1 teaspoon dried thyme

½ teaspoon dried basil

½ teaspoon dried marjoram

½ teaspoon dried minced onion

¼ teaspoon dried minced garlic

1 teaspoon lemon zest

SUNSHINE BLEND

¼ cup dried oregano leaves

2 tablespoons fennel seeds

2 tablespoons crushed lemongrass

2 tablespoons dried lemon zest

¾ teaspoon black pepper

1 tablespoon kosher salt

ITALIAN BLEND BLEND

2 tablespoons dried basil

2 tablespoons dried oregano

2 tablespoons dried rosemary

2 tablespoons dried marjoram

2 tablespoons dried cilantro

2 tablespoons dried thyme

2 tablespoons dried savory

2 tablespoons red pepper flakes

SOUTHWESTERN BLEND

2 tablespoons chili powder

2 teaspoons ground cumin

Dried Herbs From the Yard

1. Gather fresh herbs from the garden, preferably during that ideal time in the morning after the dew has dried but before the heat of the sun has had a chance to wilt the leaves.
2. Spread the leaves out on a clean surface to dry, or tie them into loose bundles and hang to dry. This will take several days. If you're impatient or need them right away, you can nuke them in the microwave. Start out at one minute, check for dryness, and continue at thirty-second increments until the leaves are dry and crisp. Time will depend on the moisture-content and thickness of the herbs.

3. Strip the leaves from the tough stems.
4. Working with one herb at a time, crush the leaves into pieces of desired size and store in air-tight jars in a cool, dark place for maximum freshness.
5. If you prefer ground herbs, you can whir the dried herbs in a clean electric coffee grinder. Pack the grinder as full as you can get it (it grinds better with enough leaves in there to get some traction). Grind until the leaves are reduced to the desired fineness. I find it helps to hold the grinder and sort of shake it a little as it grinds.
6. If there are tough bits of stem remaining, you can sift the herbs through a fine sieve to remove them.

2 tablespoons paprika

1 teaspoon black pepper

1 tablespoon ground coriander

1 teaspoon cayenne pepper

1 tablespoon garlic powder

1 teaspoon crushed red pepper

1 tablespoon salt

1 tablespoon dried oregano

HERBES DE PROVENCE

1 tablespoon savory

1 tablespoon rosemary

1 tablespoon thyme

1 tablespoon oregano

1 tablespoon basil

1 teaspoon fennel seed

1 teaspoon lavender

TUSCAN HERB SALT

Sprinkle this over bread dough brushed with an egg wash before baking, or wherever you want a pinch of salt with a punch of herbal flavor.

¼ cup each fresh basil, mint, sage, rosemary, thyme, and marjoram, leaves only, loosely packed

4 cloves garlic

2 teaspoon fennel seed

¾ cup kosher or sea salt

In a food processor or blender or by hand, finely chop herbs and garlic. If using a food processor or blender, add half of the salt and the fennel seed and pulse briefly. Then add the rest of the salt and mix. If not using a machine, combine the chopped herbs, garlic and fennel seed with the salt in a large bowl and press the herbs and the salt together with the back of a large mixing spoon, bruising the herbs to release their oils into the salt.

Spread the herb salt on a baking sheet in a thin layer and allow to dry for several days. When no moisture remains, store in jars with lids.

How to Make Herbal Oils

1. Place the dried herbs and any other ingredients into the dry, sterilized bottles.
2. Warm the olive oil below a simmer (don't boil it) just until you can see some movement in the pan, but no bubbles. While the oil is still hot, use a funnel to pour it into the bottles over the herbs.
3. When the oil is cool, cap it and let it sit for a minimum of two weeks to allow it to absorb the flavors of the herbs. Pour it through a strainer into new sterilized bottles, removing the steeped herbs. If you like, add a sprig or two of a dried herb or a few peppercorns to the new bottles for visual interest, then re-cap. Begin using your oils.

Herbal Oils

DAISY Herbal oils are a little tricky. The issue is rancidity and food safety. The important things to watch are humidity, heat, and light.

I prefer to use dried ingredients in my herbal oils. Also, make sure your bottles are sterilized and completely dry before adding your completely dried herbs.

To do this, you can put them through the dishwasher if you have a sterilize setting. Otherwise, place the jars in a saucepan in cold water to cover and bring to a boil. Boil for five minutes. Remove the jars with tongs and allow them to drain and dry on clean paper toweling.

Store finished oils in a cool, dark place, but don't forget about them. Use them within a couple of months after making them. Label the jars with the date you made them for extra food safety. It won't be hard once you realize what a flavor jolt they give your salad dressings, pastas, and sauces.

ITALIAN HERBAL OIL

For 1 quart of olive oil, add:

   15 whole peppercorns
   2 tablespoons dried rosemary
   2 teaspoons dried crushed garlic
   1 tablespoon dried oregano

   1 tablespoon dried thyme
   2 whole bay leaves
   2 tablespoon dried basil

PROVENCAL HERBAL OIL

For 1 quart of olive oil add:

   ¼ cup marjoram
   ¼ cup rosemary
   12 whole peppercorns
   1 teaspoon dried lavender
   2 teaspoons dried crushed garlic

LEMON OLIVE OIL

This variation produces a lightly lemon-flavored oil that is to die for. It's perfect over delicately flavored pasta dishes, fish, and chicken. I even love it drizzled over popcorn.

Yield: approximately 2 cups

   2 cups olive oil
   3 lemons
   ½ teaspoon kosher salt

1. Remove the zest from the lemons, avoiding the white pith.
2. Crush the zest with the salt in a large mixing bowl with the back of a heavy spoon, the handle of a hefty knife, or a pestle if you have one. You want to bruise and crush the zest and release the oils, but not completely pulverize them.
3. Begin adding a bit of the olive oil at a time, releasing the flavors of the lemon into the oil,

Canning Equipment

Here's the equipment you'll need to can.

Canner or large pot: A canner is just a very large pot with high sides, a lid, and a metal rack that fits inside the pot. The rack keep the jars slightly elevated from the bottom of the pan and make it easy to lift the jars out of the canner. Canners are commonly enameled, aluminum, or stainless steel. They can be found in the canning departments of most large home-goods stores, at garage sales, or online at stores that specialize in canning equipment.

Set of canning accessories: These are commonly sold as a group, or canning kit, which includes: jars, lids, rings, a jar lifter, a lid lifter, canning funnel, a jar wrench and kitchen tongs (optional). These kits also are found at the home center, in some hardware stores, and online.

Jars are reusable until chipped or cracked. Bands (the part of the lid that looks like a big ring) are also reusable unless rusted or bent. The lid is the flat, circular piece of the lid assembly that has a rubber ring on the underside. Use new lids each time.

Note: If you want to go entirely eco, a special kind of reusable lid is available through a company called Tattler. The process for using them is a little different, but instructions are provided with your purchase.

until all the oil is added. Cover and allow to steep for an hour or two.

4. Strain out the zest. Use a funnel to pour the oil into bottles, cap them, and store the oil in the refrigerator for up to several months.

How to Make Herbal Vinegar

DAISY Herbal vinegar is an easy-to-make condiment that layers in flavor wherever it goes. My favorite use is in salad dressings and as a piquant splash over sauteed vegetables.

To make herbal vinegar you will need:

Sterilized glass bottles or jars with non-metallic lids

A selection of herbs, garlic, citrus peels and/or spices

White, red, or rice wine vinegar or apple cider vinegar, minimum 5 percent acidity

1. Insert your herbs and other inclusions into the jars. Try rosemary, basil, sage, and thyme with peppercorns and garlic. Use your imagination and whatever is fresh in the garden. Be generous. If the finished product is too strong for your tastes, you can always add more vinegar.
2. Add room-temperature vinegar to the top of the jar. Close jar.
3. Store it away from heat and bright light a minimum of three days to a month, depending on the strength you want. Strain out the herbs while pouring into new, sterile containers.

Canning Basics

I've heard so many people say, "I've always wanted to try canning, but it scares me." Between the thought of ruining a big batch of precious strawberries and the fear of creating Improvised Explosive Devices in their pantry, many people shy away from home preserving.

Really, though, it isn't rocket science, and anyone can do it. You just have to have a few simple pieces of equipment (see the sidebar on page 133) and follow a few easy rules.

STERILIZE

Before you can anything, you must sterilize the jars. To sterilize the jars:

1. Wash them in warm soapy water or put them through the dishwasher.
2. Place the washed jars in a large pot (your canner is good for this), fill the pot with enough cold water to cover the jars, and bring the water to a boil.
3. Boil the jars for five minutes, then remove them from the heat.
4. Drain them and allow them to air dry on clean paper towels.

To sterilize lids and rings, place them in a smaller pan, fill it with cold water, and bring to the boil. Remove from the heat and allow the lids and rings to sit in the water until you're ready to screw them on the jars.

Once you have the basic equipment and sterilized jars, the rest is as easy as following the directions for each recipe. When you are a beginning canner, start with recipes that have detailed steps for newbies, like the recipes found in canning guides such as the *Ball Blue Book*. These guidebooks will walk you through the process step by step.

You will know you've succeeded when you hear the triumphant *pop* as your jars form an airtight seal as they cool. Very satisfying.

4. For a little bit of pretty, add another fresh sprig of herb, reclose lid, and store at room temperature for up to one year.

Jams and Marmalades

PLAIN JANE FRESH JAM

DEANNA

Fresh fruit taste, soft set . . . To. Die. For.
Yield: approximately 6 cups

3 cups frozen strawberries, crushed and
    warmed
3 cups sugar
1 cup water
1 box Less or No-Sugar-Needed Sure-Jell

1. Stir together the Sure-Jell and sugar, then add the water. Boil over medium heat, stirring constantly, for about a minute.

2. Add crushed strawberries (squished with a pulsed immersion blender, potato masher, or your fork.) **Note: The warmer your berries, the firmer your set.

3. Stir the ingredients until mixed, remove from heat, and pour in a freezer-safe container. (This makes about 6 cups, so you'll freeze the extra.)

4. Cover and leave out at room temperature for twelve to twenty-four hours to set. Refrigerate one container. Freeze the rest.

PEAR-LEMON PRESERVES

DAISY

Pears and lemons are soulmates, two
halves of one ambrosial whole. To me,
the only way to make pear preserves is with thinly sliced whole lemons, peel and all.

Yield: 3 pints

10 large pears (about 5 pounds), peeled, cored, and chopped
4 cups sugar
3 cups water
2 lemons, very thinly sliced

1. Put the pears in a heavy-bottomed pan and add water to cover. Bring to a boil; cover, reduce the

heat, and simmer for 15 minutes or until the pears are nice and tender. Drain.

2. Combine the sugar and water in a large, heavy pot; bring to a boil, and cook 10 minutes (the mixture will be a thin syrup). Remove from heat, and let cool several minutes.

3. Stir in the pears and lemon slices and bring the mixture to a fast boil. Boil rapidly until the pears are transparent (about 45 minutes), stirring occasionally.

4. Pour the pear mixture into a large, shallow pan; skim off foam with a spoon. Cover loosely and let stand in a cool place overnight. Skim off any foam.

5. Heat the fruit and syrup mixture in a heavy pot. Using a slotted spoon, spoon the hot fruit into hot jars.

6. Bring the syrup to a boil; pour boiling syrup over the fruit, leaving a ¼" (6mm) head space; wipe jar rims with a towel dipped in hot water. Cover with the metal lids and screw on the bands.

7. Process in a boiling-water bath for 20 minutes.
    Note: Five pounds of whole pears became 3 ½ pounds after peeling and coring. Also, if you are suspicious that the syrup is too runny and unlikely to gel, when you boil the syrup for the last time just before pouring it over the fruit, test it by putting a little on a cold plate. If it is not starting to congeal

How Much to Can

After I began canning and realized it wasn't nearly as complicated as I once feared, I faced another pitfall: creating my own personal Museum of Jars.

I would read a recipe that sounded irresistible. Everyone will clamor for my homemade **Daisy** chutney or emerald-green jars of pepper jelly, I would think. I daydreamed of being like Pollyanna, bringing jars of calf's-foot jelly to crotchety, misunderstood shut-ins. So I would make lots—and I mean lots, jar after jar of home-preserved goodness. After the lids popped, before they were barely cool, I would arrange them, stack them, and shift them to catch the afternoon sun to bring out their best golden glow.

As the days and weeks went on, I could see the jars weren't moving very fast. I realized I really didn't know any shut-ins who required pepper jelly to accompany their legs of lamb. And no one seemed to know what to do with mango chutney, either, or the two dozen jars of green-tomato pickles. But they were canned. They were the fruit of careful labor. Ergo: They weren't going to be thrown away.

I run across them from time to time, in the recesses of my pantry. At first, I'm like, what is this? Then I remember: Mango chutney, 1998. Hello, old friend.

at all, continue boiling it until the cold-plate test is good for a bit of a gel. Just watch it—boil too long and you've made hard candy. (You are more likely to have a no-gel situation if you have tried to reduce the sugar like I tend to do.)

BLACKBERRY–BLUEBERRY JAM, LOW SUGAR

DAISY I use tart apples in the jam to augment the pectin, which helps it set up. The apples cook down to sauce and are not noticeable in the finished product. I have tried recipes with no pectin and no sugar and they are fine and one way to do it, but in my experience, they don't set up well. Those recipes are good for syrup, but trying to balance the syrup on the toast reminds me of one of those games that used to come in Cracker Jack boxes where you had to guide a tiny bead through a maze—the syrup flows all over the toast and down your fingers. This recipe has more body.

Yield: 5 pints

4 quarts mixed berries (blackberries, blueberries, raspberries, etc.)

4 tart apples, peeled, cored, and chopped

1 cup honey, more if your berries are particularly
tart

⅔ cup sugar

½ package pectin (Sure-Jell, Certo, or the like,
about 2½ tablespoons)

Clean and sterilized jars, lids, and rings.

1. Put the clean, stemmed berries into a large,
heavy-bottomed saucepan. Pare and chop the
apples. I used Granny Smith, but any tart cooking apple will do.

2. In a separate bowl, mix together the sugar and
pectin and add this to the berries along with the
honey, and cook over medium heat. Bring slowly
to the boil and boil gently for at least thirty
minutes or until it looks like and tastes like jam.
Mine took about 45–60 minutes. Use your best
judgment. Take a bit out on a spoon and put it on
a cold plate. Are the juices watery-looking? Keep
cooking until it reaches the point that when you
put a little dab on a plate it has a more syrupy-
like consistency. Let the dab cool a bit. It should
begin to set up a little. It doesn't have to be
terribly thick or gelatinous (you want to be able
to spread it on your toast without undue effort). If
you have much foam, skim it off with a spoon.

3. At this point, turn off the heat and ladle the
jam into the jars within ½" (1.25cm) of the top,
add the lids and loosely screw down the rings.
Lastly, they go into the canner for a 10 minute process, then they're done. Let them cool.
Tighten the lids up a bit. Over the next hour or
so, the lids will seal with a pop. After they seal,
if you press a finger on the top of the lid, the
lid will be pressed in and will not pop back and
forth. That's a good seal.

CLEMENTINE MARMALADE

The honey is perfect with the citrus flavor of the
oranges.

Yield: 3 to 4 half-pint jars

2 pounds clementines (wash the peels very well)

1 cup honey

1½ cups water

1. Slice the stem end (just the stem, really) from
the clementines and slice the fruits in half.

2. Place them in a bowl, cover them with water,
and leave them overnight to soak.

3. The next day, drain the water and slice and chop
the clementines into small pieces. Place them
in a heavy pot and add water and honey. Cook
over medium heat for about an hour, stirring
frequently until the clementines are beginning to
look cooked through and the peel has begun to
take on a deeper color and a translucent quality.
Test a bit of the syrup on a plate left to chill in
the freezer. Tilt the plate, and if the surface of
the syrup wrinkles a bit, it is ready.

4. Remove the marmalade from the heat and pour it through a canning funnel into prepared sterilized half-pint jars. Wipe the rims and add hot sterilized lids and rings. Tighten the jars gently and process them in a water bath for ten minutes.

MEYER-LEMON-VANILLA MARMALADE

Meyer lemons are considered to be a cross between an orange and a lemon, with a distinct flavor all their own. The vanilla bean is a good complement to the sweet and tangy Meyer lemon and honey flavors.

Yield: 4 half-pints

> 2½ pounds Meyer lemons (wash the peels very well)
> 1½ cups honey
> 2 cups water
> 1 4" (10cm) piece of vanilla bean, split length-wise

1. Cut the lemons in half. Cut out the white pith and seeds from each half. Cover the lemons in water and soak them overnight. The next day, drain and chop the lemons.
2. Place the chopped lemons in a heavy pot and add water. Scrape the vanilla-bean seeds out with a knife and add the bean and seeds and honey to the lemons. Cook uncovered over medium heat for about an hour, stirring frequently until the lemons begin to look cooked through and the peel has begun to take on a deeper color and a translucent quality. Test a bit of the syrup on a plate left to chill in the freezer. Tilt the plate, and if the surface of the syrup wrinkles a bit, it is ready.
3. Remove the marmalade from the heat and pour it through a canning funnel into prepared sterilized half-pint jars. Reserve the vanilla bean and cut it into four pieces and add one piece to each jar. Wipe the rims and add hot sterilized lids and rings. Tighten the jars gently and process them in a water bath for ten minutes.

SAVORY & SWEET ONION JAM

DAISY The idea of an onion jam might take a little getting used to, but after you've tried it, you'll understand what the fuss is all about. This jam is delicious in a panini. Use it in place of tomato on bruschetta, or spread it on to bring out the flavors of an artisan cheese over rustic crackers.

Yield: 3 half-pint jars

> 3 pounds thinly sliced white onions
> 2 tablespoons olive oil
> ½ cup balsamic vinegar
> ¼ cup apple cider vinegar
> ¼ cup red wine
> approximately 6 good sprigs fresh herbs, left whole
> 4 teaspoons kosher salt
> 1 teaspoon coarse black pepper
> ¼ cup honey

1. Heat oil in a large heavy pan, a cast iron dutch oven is ideal. Add onions and cook, stirring frequently, until wilted and just starting to caramelize.
2. Add vinegars, wine, and herbs. Season with salt and pepper. Simmer covered about 20 minutes.
3. Remove lid and add the honey. Cook, uncovered, an additional 15 minutes to reduce the liquid, stirring often, keeping an eye out to prevent scorching. Remove herb sprigs.
4. To preserve, spoon immediately into hot, sterilized jars, cover with lids and process in a hot water bath for 10 minutes, or place in freezer containers to freeze.

Keeps several weeks refrigerated.

Homemade Dairy

HOMEMADE BUTTER

DEANNA *Fortunately, making butter is really easy! All you need is whipping cream and a way to agitate it. I use a mixer.*

Yield: one pint of butter (just under a pound) and one pint of milk

1 quart whipping cream
salt to taste

1. Beat the whipping cream in a bowl until it separates into yellow butter and white milk.
2. Reserve the milk for drinking, baking, soups, shakes, etc.
3. Pour a cup of cold water over the butter and beat it again. Pour the water off.
4. Repeat until the water is mostly clear.
5. Smoosh out the extra water and add salt to taste.
6. Eat it with a spoon! (Sorry, I meant to say, spread it delicately on your mother-in-law's banana bread and take tiny ladylike bites.)

SPREADABLE BUTTER

DAISY *I love butter. I've heard you can leave it out in a crock safely or in a special bell-like contraption that holds it under water, but that isn't going to happen in my house, where resides a refrigeration enthusiast.*

So I really like spreadable butter, but rather than pay more for diluted whipped butter from the store, I make my own. The only drawback is having to clean up the blender with all that yummy butter left clinging to it. Okay. There aren't any drawbacks.

½ cup butter at room temperature
½ cup canola oil or light oil
pinch salt

Process all ingredients in a blender or food processor until smooth. Scrape out into a container pop on a lid, and refrigerate.

SOUR CREAM

DEANNA **Yield: about 2 cups**
4 tablespoons cultured buttermilk
2 cups half-and-half

1. Put the buttermilk in a bowl (introduces protective, delicious, lacto-bacteria found naturally in all unpasteurized milk).
2. Splash in the half-and-half.
3. Cover and leave out 12–48 hours to achieve desired thickness and sourness. For the love of Pete, don't stir it! Refrigerate to stop the lacto-bacteria growth.
   Keeps for over a week.

QUICK CRÈME FRAICHE

DEANNA *Crème fraiche is sour cream's understated, elegant cousin. It's less sour, much creamier, and would never have the word "light" on her container. There is no such thing as reduced-fat crème fraiche. Or if there is such a thing, it's an abomination.*

QUICK HOMEMADE CHEESE

½ gallon whole milk (goat or cow)
¼ cup white vinegar or ¼ cup lemon juice
salt to taste

1. Put the milk in a stainless steel pot and heat over medium until between 190°F (88°C) and 200°F (93°C).
2. Slowly stir in the vinegar or lemon juice. Remove from heat and allow to curdle and cool until it's not too hot to touch.
3. Pour into the cheesecloth-lined bowl. Pull together the four corners of the cloth and twist around a spoon. Hang the dripping cheese for a few hours.
4. Salt to taste and check the consistency. I like a fairly hard cheese, so I hang it in the fridge overnight. That's about the max.
5. Untie (add any garlic or herbs or more salt, if you like), place in an airtight container, and chill. Depending on how long you hung it, you should have about 12 to 16 ounces of cheese.
   Keeps a few days in the refrigerator.

2 cups heavy whipping cream
2 tablespoons whole cultured Bulgarian
   buttermilk

1. Warm the heavy whipping cream to 85°F (30°C) and add the buttermilk.
2. Pour into a nonreactive container, like Tupperware.
3. Cover and leave out on the counter for one day.
4. Chill and serve over berries, banana bread, what have you. Keeps about two weeks refrigerated.

EASIEST CREAM CHEESE

Frankly, there are about 385 million ways to make a basic cream cheese, but this is the one that I think is most accessible.

1. Buy a quart of plain, active-culture, single-ingredient yogurt. Even if it says organic, still check the back. No gelatin allowed.
2. Plop it in a cheesecloth-lined bowl.
3. Gather the edges of the cheesecloth and tie around a spoon or other long object.
4. Suspend for twelve hours, allowing the whey to drain. Check the consistency. The longer the draining time, the firmer the cheese.
   Keeps for a few days in the refrigerator.

YOGURT FROM STORE-BOUGHT MILK

To make yogurt, you have to have yogurt or a store-bought culture. That fact was a big disappointment to me. I like doing something from scratch-o-la. But, then I learned why. It's not because the art of yogurt making is lost. It's because in the United States, we pasteurize our dairy products. The naturally occurring, beneficial bacteria that are born in the raw milk get killed with the baddies. So in this country, unless you have your own goat or cow, no cultured milk products can be made sans store-bought starter.

Go buy some plain yogurt. But read the back and make sure there's no gelatin or other nonsense in it. One of the organic brands has, like, ten ingredients on the back. Don't use that.

Cheesecloth

Cheesecloth is made of very light loosely woven cotton. You can purchase it at supermarkets. It is cheaply made, doesn't last very long, and is hard to reuse. Cheesecloth sold at specialty cooking stores is a bit sturdier and easier to reuse, but still doesn't last through many uses. Clean it between uses by washing it in your washing machine.

"Real" cheesecloth leaves a pretty, traditional finish on the cheese, but anything that drains and can take some squeezing will work. Any loose-weave, thin cloth will work. In a pinch, I use a tea towel as a substitute (truthfully, I do that a lot). You can even use a coffee filter, but the cheese will be wetter because you can't squeeze a paper filter.

1 quart milk (whole, 2%, skim, soy, or reconstituted dry milk)
1 cup dry milk powder
½ cup yogurt

1. Heat the first two ingredients to 180°F (82°C) to kill off any competing bacteria. Pour into a covered container to cool to around 110°F (43°C).
2. Add some of the warm milk to the yogurt and mix before slowly incorporating this mixture into the big bowl of warm milk.
3. Cover. Place in the oven on the lowest possible setting for four to eight hours depending on the tang you like. The goal is to incubate it at around 110°F (43°C). If the oven system sounds un-fun, wrap the container in a towel and set it on a heating pad. Just poke it periodically with a thermometer the first hour or two to make sure you aren't killing the culture.
4. Chill when you like the consistency. (Check the consistency by tilting the container. For the love of Pete, don't stir it. I killed three batches that way. Runny, blech.)
5. Serve. It will keep for a few days in the fridge.

To make strawberry yogurt, stir in a dollop of jam.

VANILLA-CUSTARD ICE CREAM

DAISY **Yield: 1 gallon**

5 cups milk
1¼ cups sugar
¼ cup plus 2 tablespoons all-purpose flour
¼ teaspoon salt
5 eggs, beaten
4 cups half-and-half
1½ tablespoons homemade vanilla extract (see the recipe on page 147)

1. Heat the milk over medium heat. Combine the sugar, flour, and salt in a bowl and add this mixture slowly to the milk. Blend well.
2. Cook over medium heat until thickened, stirring constantly, about 15 minutes.
3. Stir about 1 cup of the hot mixture into the beaten eggs. Let this sit for half a minute, then add it back to the pot. Cook 1 minute; remove from heat, and let cool.
4. Chill 2 hours to overnight.
5. Combine the half-and-half and vanilla in a large bowl, add the chilled custard, stirring with a wire whisk. Pour into the freezer can of a one-gallon hand-turned or electric ice cream freezer. Freeze according to the manufacturer's directions. Let ripen 1½ to 2 hours.

Miscellaneous Treats

DEANNA'S STOVE TOP POPPED CORN

DEANNA I have been popping my own corn in the cast iron kettle for ages. When Mr. Caswell and I had some regular microwave popcorn recently, we were shocked at our reaction . . . BLECH! I thought I was being frugal, cutting down on waste, eliminating questionable oils and preservatives. I didn't intend to ruin us for life on the store-bought stuff! But, that's exactly what happened.

So, here's how you can ruin yourself.

1. Go to your local discount store and buy a bag of kernels in the nut/jerky section. (I didn't even know they sold this stuff anymore, but yes, it's top-shelf in a cardboard box, as if they too have forgotten they sell it.)
2. Put a heavy pot on the stove and put in just enough canola oil (or what have you) to coat the bottom of the pot (about a millimeter).
3. Toss in a few kernels and set it right between medium and medium-high.
4. Cover it and wait about five minutes or until you hear the tester kernels pop.
   While I have your attention, I'll tell you how to make popcorn salt. Get out your table salt and your clean coffee grinder. (If you actually grind coffee in it, wipe it out and then grind some white bread in it to remove the residue.) Buzz that stuff for about five seconds and voilà . . . popcorn salt! After grinding salt in the coffee grinder, thoroughly clean the grinder or the salt will corrode the metal.
5. Okay, the kernels just popped. I heard them, so carefully open the lid and put in enough kernels to cover the bottom of the kettle. Cover and wait about five minutes until you hear lots of pops.
6. That rule about the 1 to 2 seconds between pops in the microwave is true here too, but you have to make sure it really means it. When the pops slow, periodically shake the pan hard to make sure all the kernels get a chance at the bottom. When that no longer produces a flurry of new pops, and the corn is committed to that 1- to 2-second pace, take the pot off the heat . . . with the cover still on to catch any remaining jumpers.
7. Open the lid. Sprinkle in your salt, stir, and serve.
8. And then lament that you will never again be satisfied with that mass-produced micro-junk.
9. If you want to be really spoiled, buzz some sugar in the coffee grinder and sprinkle it on to get that yummy kettle-corn flavor.

CILANTRO PESTO

DAISY If you have a bumper crop of cilantro, the best way I know to use a lot of it at once is to make pesto. And wow, if you are a cilantro fan and have never tasted cilantro pesto, you are in for a treat. I use pecans because I have a lot of those, too, but you can use whatever nut you have in abundance (insert your own joke here).

I use this pesto stirred into pasta, in dollops on pizza, mixed into vinaigrettes, and over fish. Stir some into cream cheese for a cracker spread or just eat it with a spoon. Delicious. It freezes very well, too. There will be some oxidation on the top surface, but this won't hurt anything—just stir it in when you are ready to use it. If it bothers you, pour a thin layer of oil over the top before storing the pesto.

Yield: approximately 2 cups

5 ounces (about 4 cups packed) fresh cilantro, washed and roughly chopped
⅔ cup vegetable oil (olive, canola, etc.)
⅔ cup toasted nuts (pecans, pine nuts, walnuts, etc.), chopped
4 cloves garlic, coarsely chopped
⅔ cup grated Parmesan cheese
salt and pepper to taste

1. Put the cilantro, oil, garlic, and nuts in a blender or food processor. Blend until smooth. This will require turning off the blender a few times to

smoosh things down. Philistines who complain about the noise from the blender interrupting their television show do not get any pesto.

2. Remove to a bowl and stir in the cheese, salt, and pepper. Taste and adjust seasonings.

By the way, gardening note here—I haven't planted cilantro in years. I let some go to seed (coriander!) and it spread around my yard and garden by itself and comes up on its own every year. If you love this herb, just leave it alone and it'll come home, wagging its tail.

HOMEMADE BREAKFAST SAUSAGE

 You probably know you can make your own sausage in a slaughter-it-and-toil-for-a-week kind of way, but you can also stir up a batch of breakfast patties super easy with just a little ground meat and a few common herbs and spices. And then you know what's in it.

Yield: 8 patties

1 pound ground turkey
1½ teaspoon salt
1 teaspoon chopped fresh rosemary
1 to 2 teaspoons chopped fresh sage
1 to 1½ teaspoons red pepper flakes
½ teaspoon ground black pepper
1 clove garlic, minced

1. Combine all ingredients in a large bowl and stir to mix well.
2. Shape sausage into patties, about ¼ cup each.
3. Heat a large skillet and oil it lightly. Fry the sausages over medium heat until they're well browned and much of the fat has rendered out. Serve warm.

HOMEMADE "MAPLE" SYRUP

DEANNA If you're like me, watching your kids *dump* real maple syrup on their pancakes is like watching them flush gold down the toilet. That stuff is so expensive! But, I also can't stand to feed them that maple-flavored-high-fructose-corn-syrup junk from the store. So, I now make my own maple-flavored natural sugar syrup.

  2 cups organic sugar
  ½ tablespoon molasses
  1 cup water
  ½ tablespoon maple flavoring

1. Heat the sugar and water over medium until slightly thickened.*
2. Remove from heat and add the maple flavoring.
3. Cool. Oh, and while it's cooling, dip buttered bread in it . . . just to make sure it came out okay.
  * If you lose track of time and let it boil its brains out, it will make maple candy, or as my kids call it, "the crunchy syrup."

PEANUT-BUTTER PLAY-DOH

DEANNA My kids live on this stuff, but I've realized recently that it's not as well known as I thought. Maybe some people just use it for occasional playtime, but in my house, it's lunch. Just remember: No honey until after age one.

  big blob of peanut butter
  decent squeeze of honey
  coffee grinder full of dry milk
  (It's an exact science, you see.)

1. Put the peanut butter and honey in a bowl.
2. Buzz your dry milk in the grinder.
3. Shake some milk into the bowl and stir it all together.
4. Keep adding milk until you think you can make a stiff putty. Mash it until it's well mixed.
5. Roll into balls and pack in the kids' lunches.

APPLESAUCE FROM PEELS AND CORES

DAISY I have my frugal moments, and this may have been the pinnacle. I made about 4 pints of applesauce out of the peels and cores left over from making canned apple-pie filling. I was very discriminating, however, and meticulous about removing all (and I mean all) of the seeds and worms and other suspicious brown spots. These were premium parings from organically grown apples. So if you try this, take note.

1. Place the parings in a heavy-bottomed pan and cook over medium heat until you have a rich, thick sauce.
2. Use a ladle to spoon the cooked sauce into a colander, then mush it through the colander. Work only a little at a time through. This is messy and time-consuming, but worth it. This would have been a lot easier if I had a ricer.
  The finished product will be a smooth, tasty, pink homemade applesauce. All from what ordinarily would head straight to the compost bin.

HONEY CANDY DROPS

DAISY
  ½ cup honey
  candy thermometer

1. Put the honey in a small saucepan over low heat. Stirring constantly, bring the honey to a boil.
2. Put in the candy thermometer and continue stirring until the honey reaches a temperature of 300°F to 310°F (150°C to 155°C). Honey burns fast, so don't leave it. Reduce the heat to a simmer if necessary (if the honey seems to be heating up too fast, or you get a whiff of scorched honey).
3. Immediately remove from heat.
4. Check for the right consistency by placing a few drops of the cooked honey into a cup of ice water. Let it get cold, then feel the drops. They should feel like hard candy. If the honey is still soft, return it to the heat and cook it a little while

longer, and do the ice water test again. Do this until it's right.

5. After the right consistency is reached, remove the honey from the heat and continue to stir it until it cools enough to drop by teaspoonfuls onto a well-greased solid surface. It still needs to be runny, but a little less runny than when you first took it off the heat. Don't wait too long or it will be impossible to remove from the pan. Work quickly.

6. Allow the drops to cool completely. Don't do what I did and put some in the refrigerator to hurry them up. They got too hard and cracked when I tried to release them from the plate. Room temperature is good. When they are cool, take a dinner knife and pop them loose.

Tips:

• Don't skimp on the greasing, or you will have a permanently cough-drop-coated surface. If you have a flexible, nonstick mat, like a Silpat or something similar, it will help to release the drops from the surface once they are cooled. If you are a candy-maker, you probably have some nonstick molds for this, but for the rest of us, a mold isn't necessary.

• Wrap each piece in plastic wrap. Avoid waxed paper, as the candy sticks to it. The candy pieces will also stick to each other, so don't store them together unwrapped. Store in a cool, dry place.

• Use your imagination to come up with add-ins to make them into cough drops. I've thought of crushed, powdered vitamin C, perhaps, or herbal infusions.

Cordials and Liqueurs

ELDERBERRY CORDIAL

DAISY   I love this, and not just because it was the key prop in *Arsenic and Old Lace*, one of my favorite movies. I love the inky purple color and rich, spicy, berry flavor. Plus elderberries are reputed to have medicinal benefits.

Yield: approximately 1 quart

2 cups elderberries

2 cups brandy

1 cup honey

4 cinnamon sticks

4 tablespoons freshly grated ginger root

1. Put the elderberries in a large bowl and mash them with a potato masher until all the berries are popped.

2. Spoon into a large, nonreactive container (at least 1½ quart capacity) with a lid. Add the brandy, honey, cinnamon sticks, and ginger, and stir to combine. Close the container and allow the mixture to steep for at least six weeks, periodically shaking the container to agitate the contents.

3. After the cordial has steeped, strain out the solids through progressively finer sieves and filters, then pour into sterilized bottles and cap securely. Keeps indefinitely.

LEMON CORDIAL

A nonalcoholic version. Add seltzer or soda water and ice for a fizzy lemonade, drizzle over pound cake, or use this to sweeten and flavor iced tea.

Yield: 1 pint

 2 cups lemon juice

 zest of two lemons

 2½ cups sugar

1. Combine the juice, zest, and sugar in a saucepan and heat to just boiling, stirring to dissolve the sugar. Strain out the zest.
2. Pour into sterilized bottles, cap, and process in a boiling-water bath for 10 minutes. Remove from the water bath, tighten the lids, and store in a cool, dark place. Refrigerate after opening. Keeps several months unopened. Once opened, keeps in the refrigerator for about a week.

COFFEE LIQUEUR

A shot of this over a warm walnut brownie with ice cream is the perfect dessert.

Yield: approximately 6 cups

 3 cups fine-ground coffee

 3 cups boiling water

 1 cup dark brown sugar

 1 cup honey

 3 cups vodka

 1 vanilla bean

1. Steep the coffee in boiling water in a medium pan for one minute.
2. Place a coffee filter in its proper place in your coffee maker's filter reservoir (using a traditional Mr.-Coffee-type maker) and strain the brew through the filter into another saucepan.
3. Add the brown sugar and honey and stir over low heat just until the sugar is dissolved. Remove from heat and allow to cool.
4. Add the vodka and pour into sterilized, prepared bottles. Cut the vanilla bean into the same number of segments as bottles and drop a segment

into each bottle. The liqueur will be improved by aging a few days before use. Keeps refrigerated for several months.

BERRY LIQUEUR

An old-timey, slow-sipping favorite. Delicious over ice cream or in a berry trifle.

Yield: approximately 1½ pints

 2 cups fresh or frozen blueberries, raspberries, blackberries, etc. individual or in combination

 zest of 1 lemon

 5–6 whole cloves

 1½ cups vodka

For later:

 ¾ cup thick simple syrup (combine 1 cup sugar and ½ cup water, bring to a boil, remove from heat, and let cool)

1. In a bowl, mash blueberries with a fork or potato masher, then place them into a quart jar. Add the lemon zest, cloves, and vodka.
2. Seal the jar tightly with its lid and place in a cool, dark place. Allow the vodka to stand for three months, gently shaking the jar every few days.
3. After three months, strain out the blueberries and filter through a fine sieve into another clean jar. Add the simple syrup, stir, cover tightly, and allow to age once again for a minimum of one month.
4. To bottle, filter again, this time through several layers of cheesecloth, into clean bottles. Cap and enjoy.

Homemade Extracts

DAISY It's easy and cheaper to make flavor extracts at home, and I think they taste better than store-bought. These extracts make thoughtful gifts for cooks. Each recipe makes enough to divide into several small gift bottles.

VANILLA EXTRACT

1 whole vanilla bean, sliced lengthwise
1 cup brandy

1. Scrape the seeds of the bean out with a knife. Add both the bean pod and the seeds to the cup of brandy in a clean jar with a tight-fitting lid. Stir to combine.
2. Screw on the lid and allow to stand in a dark place for a minimum of two weeks for the flavors to combine. At this point, you can remove the bean pod and pour the extract into smaller bottles. I like to cut the pod into as many pieces as I have bottles and put a piece into each.

LEMON OR ORANGE EXTRACT

2 lemons or 2 oranges
½ cup vodka

1. Remove the peel of the lemons or oranges (colored part only, no pith) and lightly bruise them by twisting them a bit.
2. Place the peels in a jar with a tight-fitting lid and add the vodka. Screw on the lid and steep for at least two weeks. Strain out the zest and pour the liquid into clean bottles. Store in a cool, dark place.

7

I NEVER SMELLED SO GOOD

Many people ask, *Why make your own skincare products?* There are a number of reasons. You can completely customize each batch, and it's far less expensive to make your own. Plus, homemade products aren't full of all the bad stuff found in commercially manufactured products.

Why Make Your own Skincare Products?

Commercially manufactured soaps and lotions are full of preservatives to make them shelf stable and full of artificial fragrances to make them smell nice. To make your soap effective in all water types and work without mechanical scrubbing, they're full of oil-stripping detergents, which actually dries out your skin. (Ever wondered why you *need* conditioner? You have to put back all those natural oils you just washed down the drain with the dirt.)

Then there's animal testing, chemical allergies, and other concerns. In fact, there's a study going on right now that is exploring the effect that commercial shampoo and lotion have on a pregnant woman's ability to absorb choline. (I only know because I'm in the study!)

The second reason to make your own products is simply because you can and it's cheap! It's so empowering to mix your own lotion or deodorant and *not* have to pay six dollars a bottle at the store. It's frugal and super easy. These are some of the simplest, most useful recipes in the whole book and they cost beans compared to the store versions.

Finally, you can make your own beauty products to spoil yourself. I want my products customized to my specific tastes. I want them to smell a particular way, come in specific sizes and shapes. Plus, I can leave out ingredients I don't like and include weird stuff that only I like. I want to be able to toy with formulas and make something a little more or less moisturizing depending on the season, my mood, or the phase of the moon (kidding about the moon).

So, browse through our recipes and make your own something. You'll love it!

Deodorant

DEANNA In the DIY world of home health and beauty products, deodorant seems to be the most feared replacement. Stinking is *not okay* in our culture, right?

But aluminum crammed in your pores cannot be good for you, and it seems in recent years that store-bought deodorant is becoming less and less effective anyway.

For many, baking soda powdered in the pits works fine. For stink control, I find that it does its job swimmingly, but for my sensitive skin, it's way to itchy. Also, it's messy and has no moisture control. My deodorant uses a natural moisture absorber (cornstarch), a natural deodorizer (baking soda), and a natural moisturizer (coconut oil).

But what if it doesn't work? Here's what I suggest—make this stuff ahead and use it on *Saturday*, or on a sick day, or any day you aren't going to see anyone special, so you'll feel secure and not look like a nut obsessively sniffing your underarms all day. Once you get over the stink phobia, let your body get used to it, and you'll never go back.

This deodorant can be used as a powder. But, after while, it was just too messy for me.

If you want a stick, go to the shortening section of the store and buy some solid-at-room-temperature coconut oil. I use Lou Ann brand.

My natural deodorant hasn't failed me yet, even on skipped-shower days and during step classes, I *swear* (and oddly, this also has a double use as a "dry" shampoo for those days when you're in a pinch or just greasy in the bangs; sprinkle in, brush out).

I'm often asked if it will stain your clothes. The answer is no. You need only a light layer for it to be effective. You should not be able to see it after it's applied. (You're not smearing a cup a Crisco under there.)

Find Your Favorite Scent

The recipes in this chapter list various essential oils in the ingredients. Take these as suggestions. If a recipe calls for an oil that you don't like, substitute in an oil you love. If you don't have any experience with the oil listed, go to the health-food store and give that particular oil a good smell before you buy it. If you don't like it in the bottle, you won't like it in the recipe. If you are highly sensitive to smell, try the recipes without adding any oils. The beauty of homemade is that you can customize the product.

Many essential oils have therapeutic properties. Keep these in mind as you add oils to your homemade beauty products. Following is a list of some essential oils and their properties:

- Tea tree: antimicrobial, antiseptic, antiviral, antibacterial, fungicide, insecticidal, and stimulating
- Rosemary: analgesic, antidepressant, astringent, and stimulating
- Lavender: antiseptic, analgesic, antidepressant, anti-inflammatory, antiviral, antibacterial, decongestant, deodorant, refreshing, relaxing, calming, and sedative
- Peppermint: analgesic, anesthetic, anti-inflammatory, antiseptic, astringent, decongestant, stimulating
- Lemon: antimicrobial, antiseptic, antibacterial, insecticidal, and stimulating.
- Eucalyptus: analgesic, antibacterial, anti-inflammatory, antiseptic, antiviral, astringent, decongestant, deodorant, stimulant, pesticide.

HOMEMADE STICK DEODORANT

Ingredients
    baking soda
    cornstarch
    coconut oil (use a solid-at-room-temperature version)
    essential oil, such as tea tree, rosemary, or lavender (optional)
    empty deodorant container

1. Put 2 tablespoons of baking soda and 6 tablespoons of cornstarch* in a bowl with an optional 10 (or more) drops of an essential oil.
   *If you have tough skin, you can go as high as ¼ cup to ¼ cup on the baking soda and cornstarch. My skin is too sensitive for that. And even someone who can tolerate the higher concentration of baking soda may find that he needs to decrease it in the winter. Too itchy!

2. Stir in 2 or more tablespoons of cornstarch until it's the consistency you like.
3. Smash into an empty deodorant container. The mixture will become a bit sturdier after it sets for a day or so.

I have made this deodorant many times without the tea tree oil and it still works great, but if I happen to have the essential oil around, I always toss some in. Also, for those who are worried about stinkiness, essential oils such as tea tree, rosemary, and lavender prevent bacterial growth, and lack of bacteria means no odor.

To use
When applying this deodorant, use a lighter hand than you would with normal stick deodorant, especially the first couple of days, or it will crumble and the crumbs will fall on your bathroom rug. Used correctly, this stuff is invisible. A small supply will lasts for ages because you apply so little each day.

Deodorant on Ice

I live where it gets paint-peeling hot in the summer, and a large part of fall, sometimes in the spring, too. Still, we try to use open windows and fans as much as possible and keep the thermostat as high as we can stand it.

Daisy

What I'm getting around to is the solid version of our homemade deodorant contains coconut oil, which begins to melt at temperatures above 72°F (22°C). So, when it's hot, I keep it in the fridge. I don't find this gross at all, any more than keeping other non-food items in there, like film (showing my age here), medicine, or batteries. (In *The Seven Year Itch*, Marilyn Monroe's character kept her undies in the icebox.) I think iced deodorant is refreshing (and I think Marilyn would approve).

Toothpaste

DEANNA All homemade-toothpaste recipes use either baking soda or soap as their main cleaning ingredient. I can't stand the taste of either, so I'm still using the commercially produced brands. But, Daisy kind of likes the baking soda taste. There are plenty of homemade toothpaste recipes out there, but she just uses plain baking soda and it seems to work for her.

I inquired once at the dentist office about the effectiveness of baking soda as toothpaste. The answer was that baking soda is just fine, as long as you have fluoridated water. Otherwise, you'd need a fluoride source to protect you from cavities. Secondly, they said that if baking soda had a disadvantage it would be that it might be a little too abrasive. So *don't* add anything to it to make it more abrasive (salt, etc.).

Some of those "natural" toothpastes are no more than baking soda with an artificial sweetener (xylitol or stevia) for taste. So if you wanted to make your own, experiment with baking soda and maybe one of the aforementioned sweeteners (just don't use sugar for obvious reasons).

Shampoo, Conditioner, Body Wash

Shampoo and body wash work equally well in hard and soft water, but they strip the oils out of your hair and skin. Hence the need for conditioner and lotion.

Natural soap is *way* better. The problems with soap are that it doesn't work as well in hard water, it requires actual scrubbing, and it's hard to rinse out of your hair. But, we can fix all that. Plus natural soap is not nearly as damaging as synthetic detergents.

You can buy a limited selection of natural soaps at any grocery or discount store. (Kirk's Castile and Ivory are about it.) However, there is a huge variety available online, at health-food stores, craft fairs, and farmers' markets. Natural soap should have a primary ingredient of "sodium some-kind-of-oil-ate." Sodium tallowate (made from animal fat), sodium palmitate (made from palm oil), sodium cocoate (made from coconut oil), sodium oliveate (you can guess that one) are all fine options. The sodium attracts the dirt and oil on your skin and hair and the fat or oil surround this dirt and allow it to be carried away in the rinse water. You can use natural soap as both shampoo and body wash.

Use apple-cider vinegar in place of conditioner. Vinegar on your hair! Insane, right? I kid you not, though, you can run your fingers right through your hair right after you use it. It pulls out any leftover soap and medicates a sensitive scalp. (I also use apple-cider vinegar for astringent, ear cleaner, and sunburn care.) Yes, its smells strong, but trust me, it's great stuff. And the smell dissipates quickly.

Now here's your new shower routine:

1. Wet a bar of real soap.
2. Rub the bar all over your head until you work up a good lather, especially attending to your greasy spots. Rub, rub, rub. Shampoo is made to strip as it slips through your hair. You don't have to scrub thoroughly for it to work. It just has to pass by your hair. Soap requires more attention. If you don't scrub over your ears, they will still be greasy when you're done. Leave the soap in your hair to allow it to continue working.
3. Wash the rest of your body with the bar or with handfuls of all that lather on your head.
4. Rinse your hair until it squeaks (that is, until you can't run your fingers through it easily and you're thinking, *Holy cats! What has Deanna done to me?*) This stiffness is caused by the acid in your hair reacting with the base in the soap. You also may have some hard water deposits in your hair.
5. Apply apple-cider vinegar to your freshly rinsed hair. Use ¼ cup apple-cider vinegar to 1 quart of water. I keep it in an old mustard bottle so I can "draw" on my head with it, instead of dumping it on.
6. Rub the vinegar around and rinse your hair again.

7. Notice that now you can run your fingers through it. Isn't that amazing? No conditioner.
8. Now, go shave your legs. You *so* don't want to do that before you rinse with the vinegar. Stingy, stingy!

LIQUID SHAMPOO/BODY WASH

You can try a liquid version if you like. Now, I have to tell you that I only make the liquid version for my hubby. I have no problem with scrubbing my head with a bar of soap, but he likes the body washes and the liquid shampoos. So, we use what makes him happy.

Incidentally, this is the same recipe you will see later for making liquid soaps for cleaning your home. Many homemade recipes have multiple uses around the house. They aren't as specialized as store bought, unless you want to make them that way.

Note this solution is perishable, so make a smaller amount to avoid spoilage.

Ingredients

1 bar of pure soap
hot water
a touch essential oil (tea tree, lavender, or rosemary), optional
a blender

There are two ways to make this liquid version

Option 1

1. Grate the soap.
2. Put it in the blender with just enough hot water to create a pudding-like consistency using the whip/liquify setting.
3. Once it's smooth, add enough water to get the consistency you want. Use like regular shampoo.

Option 2

1. Grate the soap.
2. Heat it in a pot over medium heat with 1 cup of water until the soap is transparent and melted.

3. Remove from heat, cool for a few minutes, and whisk in enough water to reach desired consistency. Use like regular shampoo.

Lotion Bars

DAISY What is a lotion bar? It is a soap-hard manifestation of moisturizer you can make yourself that doesn't go bad and doesn't involve:

- phthalates
- parabens
- formaldehyde
- PABA
- ethanolamines
- petroleum
- chemical sensitivity/allergies
- bisphenol A
- animal testing

Plus, lotion bars are child's play to create. The only somewhat exotic ingredient is beeswax, and that really isn't exotic at all, especially if you keep bees yourself. If not, ask your local beekeeper or find beeswax online or in some craft stores.

I have a Cadillac lotion-bar recipe, but I will lead with the, um, shall we say, Ford Escort of lotion bars.

EVERYMAN'S LOTION-BAR
Ingredients
    1 part vegetable shortening
    1 part beeswax
    1 part vegetable oil

1. Melt the shortening and beeswax in a double boiler, or a little pan in a larger pan of simmering water. Stir in the vegetable oil.
2. Pour the mixture into muffin tins or any baking/soaping mold you have around and let it cool for a few hours. As the bars cool, they should pull away from the sides of the mold. If not, pop

Spare the Scents

When I was an expectant mom, one of the worst parts of morning sickness was my superhuman sensitivity to smells. I could smell coffee breath from across the room and tell you whether it was a macchiato or a mochaccino. I could have gotten a job sniffing baggage at the airport.

The worst part was stepping into the shower. What was once a pleasure turned into a chore. I thought shampoo was the only way to get my hair clean. After standing green-faced in the shampoo aisle, unscrewing cap after cap, trying to find the least smelly brand, I realized that there's no such thing as unscented shampoo. In my state, I found them all hyper-scented—the florals, the fruities, the musks. Ugh. I got queasy just seeing the image of a flower on a label.

Daisy My quest for odorless shampoo helped me figure out that I could wash my hair with a bar of homemade soap either unscented or with a hint of peppermint (about the only scent that didn't bother me). During this time, I also discovered making my own lotion bars and deodorant because I found the scents of the commercial versions just as overpowering as commercial shampoos.

It seems like a small thing to be able to reclaim a lost sanctuary like the shower, and it is. But for me, it was a blessing. They say necessity is the mother of invention. In this case, that necessity was motherhood.

Next on the list: unscented coffee.

them in the freezer for an hour and they'll fall right out. (I personally always use the freezer to cool them.)

3. Pop a bar out of the mold and it's ready to use. The beeswax will fragrance the bars with a nice, light honey smell, or you can stir in a little essential oil (such as peppermint, orange, or lavender) before you pour the mixture into the molds.

To Use

Let the warmth of your hand melt a little of the bar and rub it into dry skin—hands, feet, elbows, etc.

Yes, it's oily at first. It's real oil, and it does absorb in. So use it sparingly and give the lotion a chance to absorb before you move on to your next activity.

LUXURY LOTION BARS

The oils and extracts are available through soap-making suppliers and some health food/nutritional supplement or craft stores. See the appendix for sources.

Ingredients

1 part shea butter
1 part beeswax
1 part avocado oil
1200 IU vitamin E (1 lg. capsule) per every 6–8 ounces other oils
essential oil (optional)

1. Melt the shea butter and beeswax in a double boiler, or a small pan in larger pan of warm water, on low.
2. Stir in the avocado oil, vitamin E, and essential oil (optional).
3. Pour into the mold(s) and allow to cool.
4. Pop out of the molds if desired, or leave in a dish and scrape off a little as needed.

Note: Shea butter can occasionally become grainy. To avoid this, use just enough heat to get your ingredients to melt. Once your ingredients are blended, cool your mixture quickly by pouring it into shallow container(s) in a cool room or by popping it into the refrigerator (not the freezer) to cool.

Lip Balm

DAISY If you read our lotion bars recipes, you can see that these are the same ingredients, only in different proportions, so no more ingredients to buy. And again, this recipe comes in two versions—economy and first class; everyday Jane and princess. (Accidentally switch them up and you may not be able to tell the difference.)

EVERYDAY LIP BALM

Ingredients

2 tablespoons vegetable shortening
1 tablespoon beeswax
3 tablespoons vegetable oil

1. Melt the shortening and the beeswax in a double boiler, or a small pan in a larger pan of barely simmering water.
2. Stir in the vegetable oil. If you like, you can add 3–5 drops of an essential oil such as peppermint. Lemon or lime is also a possibility, but use caution because citrus oils may increase sun sensitivity in some people.
3. Pour into mold(s) or tiny dishes or reuse clean, empty lip-balm tubes or pots. It is ready to use when it's cool.

LUXURY LIP BALM

Ingredients

2 tablespoons shea butter
1 tablespoon beeswax
3 tablespoons avocado oil
½ teaspoon calendula extract (optional)
3–5 drops essential oil (optional)

1. Melt shea butter and beeswax in a double boiler, or a small pan in a larger pan of water, warmed just enough to melt the oil and wax.
2. Stir in the avocado oil, essential oil, and calendula extract.

3. Pour into molds. Because shea butter can occasionally go grainy if it is overheated, watch it carefully over the heat and cool it quickly by pouring it into shallow containers in a cool room or by putting it in the refrigerator for a few minutes.

Sugar Scrub

DEANNA I have never been one for sugar scrubs. I have oily skin, and the idea of putting something with more oil in it, regardless of how "scrubby" it claims to be, is appalling to me. But after reading that sucrose in a "good" oil actually has alpha-hydroxy (chemical exfoliant) properties, I thought I might give it a try.

This scrub uses dried basil, but you can use any herb you have on hand (and are not allergic to). Calendula, lavender, and rosemary are good options. If your herbs are fresh, microwave them for a minute to dehydrate them. Buzz the dried herbs in a coffee grinder until they're powdered.

HERBAL SUGAR SCRUB
Ingredients
¾ cup of table sugar

¼ cup olive oil

1 tablespoon powdered dried herbs (1–3 different kinds if you like)

10–20 drops of your favorite essential oil

1 teaspoon vegetable glycerin (optional)

1. Combine the ingredients in a bowl and stir until blended. The mixture will be quite grainy, but trust me, it's awesome.
2. Store your sugar scrub in an airtight container and keep it by your sink or in the shower. If you are a slow user of this kind of thing, you may want to add a teaspoon of vegetable glycerin or make sure that you use an antimicrobial essential oil such as tea tree oil.

To use:
- Take a small handful and gently apply it to your face and neck. Don't wale away with it like you do with commercially produced scrubs—you'll scrub your whole face off. Be gentle.
- Leave on for two minutes.
- Rinse. Do a little icky-dance about the residual oily feel and rinse twelve more times.
- Realize that you're no longer beading up and the smooth feeling is actually your skin.
- Dry your face and hope that you don't wake up feeling like a greasy loaf of focaccia in the morning. (And I don't. Not greasy at all. Weird.)

Summer Skin Care

INSECT REPELLENT, SUNSCREEN, AND OINTMENT

DAISY In a competitive market, manufacturers of insect repellents aim for maximum efficacy. Understandable. Without being overly alarmist, I sometimes wonder whether the line between safety to humans and repellence to bugs is somewhat thin. The question for me becomes a matter of weighing the relative risks.

Before West Nile Virus, mosquitoes in my part of the world were mostly an irritation—itchy welts and possible allergies were the results of being unprotected. With West Nile, mosquitoes have become more than an inconvenience. The possibility of Lyme disease and Rocky Mountain spotted fever from ticks is another thing to worry about. Personally, I use this spray, cover my ankles, etc., and try to stay out of the worst parts of the yard during insect feeding-time (dusk to dawn).

This is an insect repellent for the skin. I'm not going to misrepresent this recipe. For me, it isn't the Holy Grail of natural repellents, which would last indefinitely and be 100 percent bug-proof. I keep a bottle in my back pocket and reapply it frequently, and I still get the occasional bite. I do like it, though. In a weird way, the fact that it fades after about half an hour can be an advantage because by the time I go back inside, the odor fades and I don't end up smelling like bug spray for the rest of the day.

If I'm out for longer, I just keep spraying if I see the need. With other sprays (or Skin So Soft bath oil), I had to wash it off immediately even if I was only outside for a few minutes.

You may find that this recipe performs better or worse for you depending on your body chemistry, the kind of bug conditions you face, and other factors.

HOMEMADE INSECT SPRAY

Ingredients

    1 cup vodka

    2 tablespoons aloe vera juice

    2 teaspoons favorite conditioning liquid oil (soybean, olive, castor, etc.)

    1½ teaspoons insect-repellent essential oil blend (usually named something obvious like "Bug-a-way" or "Bug-be-gone")

Combine all the ingredients in a spray bottle and shake before each use. These oils have less staying power than chemicals such as DEET, so they should be reapplied about every thirty minutes or as needed.

You can buy a blend of essential oils or create your own blend from these oils that have insect-repellent properties.

- catnip oil: mosquitoes
- cedarwood oil: lice, moths
- cinnamon oil: ants
- citronella oil: mosquitoes
- clove il: mosquitoes
- eucalyptus oil: mosquitoes
- geranium oil: flies, mosquitoes
- lavender oil: mosquitoes, ticks, chiggers, fleas, flies
- lemongrass oil: mosquitoes, ticks, chiggers, fleas, flies

- litsea cubeba: mosquitoes
- patchouli: gnats
- peppermint oil: lice, spiders, ants
- rosemary oil: fleas, ticks
- tea tree oil: mosquitoes, lice, ants

Although it's found in many lists of repellents, I avoid pennyroyal because of its potential toxicity. All essential oils are best used in dilution. Don't apply them directly to the skin in full strength.

SUNSCREEN

This recipe makes a sunscreen that contains emollient ingredients as well as zinc oxide. Shea butter and avocado oil also offer a small amount of sun protection factor (SPF 4–6). We don't know the SPF for this recipe, so use caution the first time you use it. Avoid prolonged exposure and reapply often. No matter what sunscreen you choose, follow the recommendations of the American Cancer Society for maximum benefit. Sun is serious.

Ingredients

    3 tablespoons shea butter

    1 tablespoon beeswax

    6 tablespoons avocado oil

    1 teaspoon soy lecithin

    1 capsule vitamin E

    1 tablespoon aloe vera gel

    2 tablespoons zinc oxide (available from www.essentialwholesale.com and other soaping/cosmetic suppliers)

    3–5 drops essential oil (optional)

1. Melt the shea butter and beeswax in a double boiler.
2. Whisk in the avocado oil, soy lecithin, aloe vera gel, zinc oxide, and essential oil. Also cut open a vitamin E capsule and squeeze the liquid into the boiler (I like to whir it in the food processing container of my immersion blender.)

This sunscreen leaves a white sheen on skin from the zinc oxide, but it is not opaque. It is moderately oily and very conditioning.

SKIN OINTMENT

This ointment is the consistency of butter at room temperature. Use it for minor skin irritations such as bug bites, blemishes, rashes, or minor burns.

Ingredients

    1 ounce shea butter

    1 ounce avocado oil

    ½ teaspoon beeswax

    ¼ teaspoon each calendula and rooibos extract

    1 teaspoon aloe vera gel

1. Weigh the shea butter and avocado oil using a kitchen scale.
2. Melt the shea butter and beeswax in a double boiler, or a small pan in larger pan of hot water. Take care not to overheat the shea butter and to cool it quickly after all ingredients are blended, or it may become grainy. If this happens, it won't ruin the ointment, it just affects the feel of it. The graininess melts at skin temperature. Remelting it at low temperature and quickly putting it in the fridge to cool will smooth out the grains.
3. Add extracts and aloe.
4. I like to whip this ointment in the processing attachment of an immersion blender, but this is not essential.
5. Pour into small dish or tin for storage.

Basic Soapmaking

FEAR AND SOAPING IN SUBURBIA

DAISY When I look back at the reading and research I undertook before making my first batch of homemade soap, I have to shake my head. I really over analyzed this one. I know I've said that before, about chickens particularly, but soap, I was petrified of it.

I read and reread all the books in the library about soapmaking. I joined soapmaking forums on the internet and begged the experienced soapmakers for advice. I visited soapmaking blogs and pored over the tutorials. And I still had yet to make my first batch.

But when I finally took the plunge and started making soap, I realized it wasn't anything to be afraid of. As I kept making soap, my methods got simpler and simpler until, these days, I consider making a batch of soap to be as intimidating as making pudding.

Looking back, I believe one of the reasons soapmaking seemed so scary is the extensive safety precautions stressed for working with lye. I've had many questions about whether or not soap can be made without lye from people who've looked into soapmaking and been frightened off by the prospect of dealing with this chemical. The short answer is no, you can't. While you can melt pre-made soap and alter it with scents and additives and approximate soapmaking after a fashion, you simply can't make soap itself without lye.

So just how scary is lye? I would say working with lye requires about the same level of caution as working with household bleach. If you can wield a jug of Clorox, you can work with lye.

Here it is, soapmaking without fear. I promise you'll wonder what the fuss is all about after you make soap for the first time.

CP, HP, DBHP, DHHP, DWCP, DOS, EO, FO, OHP, SAP. No, I'm not proposing a new slate of

government-aid programs. Those are soapmaking abbreviations and another of the reasons I felt so lost when I first began to learn to make my own soap.

Because I love simplicity, we are going to leave the alphabet soup behind and make soap the quick and easy way, no memorization of terminology required.

Simply put:

oil + (water & lye mix) = soap

That's it. You can learn about saponification values and the respective properties of babassu and kukui nut oil if you like, but if all you really want is a great bar of homemade soap, it isn't necessary.

EQUIPMENT

- scale (digital is nice, check overstock stores like Tuesday Morning and TJ Maxx for deals)
- immersion/stick blender
- medium to large non-aluminum pan (pans with tall sides are better than shallow, wide pans)
- large non-aluminum bowl or pitcher (can be hard plastic)
- long-handled plastic spoon
- household dishwashing gloves
- safety glasses
- old clothes or apron with good coverage
- old newspaper
- soap mold (can be an empty Pringles can, a washed milk carton, or special soap molds from the craft and hobby store)

THE SET-UP

The kitchen is the most convenient place to make soap because you will need access to a stovetop or microwave, running water, and counter space. I recommend soaping when there are no small children around, and it's a good idea to confine curious pets to another area while the soaping is in progress. You don't want cats leaping onto the counter trailing tails through any part of an ongoing soapmaking event.

Assemble all the equipment and ingredients. Put the number for poison control on your speed dial. Just kidding. Relax. Take a deep breath. It's going to be okay. Put on an apron or clothes you don't mind damaging and then put on your gloves and safety glasses.

Ingredients

36 ounces olive oil

6 ounces coconut oil

3 ounces castor oil

6 ounces lye

12 ounces water

2 ounces essential oil of choice, optional

1. Measure out 12 ounces of water and place it into the large bowl or pitcher. Water is the only ingredient you can measure by volume instead of weight, as these two measurements will be the same. Set the pitcher in the sink.

2. Weigh out 6 ounces of lye. Be sure to adjust your scale for the weight of the container you are measuring your lye in. I use a small, dishwasher-safe dish.

3. Carefully pour the lye into the water. Using the long-handled spoon, gently stir until the lye is dissolved in the water. A thermal reaction will be occurring between the water and the lye, and this solution will get very hot. It will also emit some fumes, so don't stick your nose over the bowl and inhale. Some people are more sensitive than others to these fumes. If you need to, open a window or turn on a fan. I don't generally have a problem with the smell.

4. Leaving the lye solution to cool a bit, turn to your oils. Weigh the olive oil, the coconut oil (this will be solid unless your room is quite warm), and the castor oil in any order and put them into the pan. Place the pan over low heat until the coconut oil is just melted, then remove it from the heat.

5. Test the heat of the lye solution by touching the outside of the container it is in. When it is comfortable to the touch and the oils are similarly warm but not hot, it is time to combine the two.

6. Plug in the immersion blender and have it ready within reach of your pan containing the oils.

7. Pour the lye-water solution into the oils and give it a few stirs with the long-handled spoon. Remove the spoon and set it in the sink. Without turning the blender on yet, immerse it in the mixture down to the bottom of the pan. Depending on the depth of your mixture, there may or may not be splattering when you turn it on, so be prepared for either case until you know how everything is going to behave. I like to do this with the pan in the sink or on a countertop covered with a few layers of newspaper. Make sure your safety glasses are on and you are wearing the gloves.

8. Turn on the blender and slowly circulate it around the circumference of the pan, getting a feel for it. Keep blending, watching the consistency of the mixture. It will soon begin to become more and more opaque and to thicken. Periodically cease blending and give it a stir with the blender in the off mode to check for what is called "trace." When the mixture is the consistency of runny pudding and part of the mix trailed across the surface leaves a visible "trace," you can stop blending.

8b. optional: If you have decided to add essential oil, now is the time. Pour it in and give it a final whir just to blend.

9. Pour your soap, because that's what it is now, into your choice of mold or molds. Scrape out the last bits with the long-handled spoon (rinse it first) and you're done for now.

Bad Soap

Occasionally, even experienced soap makers will end up with a truly horrible batch of soap. My most memorable disaster was my first attempt at hot process, which is usually a pretty dependable method.

To this day, I'm not sure exactly where things went wrong, but I turned out a spongy, oozing, brown, sudsless cake of crumbly nothing that was only good for burying in the yard—deep.

Egads, that thing was awful. I left it for awhile, thinking it might magically transform into a soap-like substance, but eventually it had to go. It was frightening the children. Shoot, it was frightening my husband.

To minimize the chance of bad soap:

- Perform the steps in your head or do a dry run with imaginary ingredients before you do it for real.
- Set out your supplies and measure every ingredient carefully before you mix anything together.
- Don't rush. Take your time and check and recheck your components against your recipe before proceeding.
- Make small batches the first time you are trying a particular recipe. If it doesn't turn out, the loss will be less expensive.
- Go easy on the add-ins, especially when you're a beginner. They're fun, but they're also famous for precipitating seizing and separating and mayhem in general.

10. Wash off your equipment and clean up any spills.
11. The next day, your soap should be firm enough to unmold and, if you used a large single block, such as a milk carton, from which individual bars need to be cut, now is also the time to cut the bars. Still use your gloves, as the soap is still fresh and may be a bit caustic. The bars don't have to be perfect—rustic bars are beautiful and chunky and look yummy. (You will want to take a big bite out of one of them. Don't.)
12. Leave the bars to cure for at least three weeks. Curing in this case simply means drying out and becoming harder and longer lasting.

As you become more adventurous, you will want to try other recipes and techniques and additives, but for now, savor the moment. You just made *soap*!

THE SCOOP ON LYE

Lye is 100 percent sodium hydroxide, NaOH in chem-speak. It's the essential chemical needed to saponify, or "soapify" oil to make soap. On our website, the most commonly asked soap-related question we get is how to find lye.

When I started to make soap, lye was available at the hardware store as a product called Roebic Heavy Duty Crystal Drain Cleaner, the one that said 100 percent sodium hydroxide on the label. Since then, it has all but disappeared from the shelves. The reason for this is that, like certain cold medicines, sodium hydroxide is used in the illegal manufacture of methamphetamines. While it doesn't seem fair to punish those of us with a soap-making habit or clogged drains, it's now a fact of life and we have to figure a way around it.

Lye is available online. The sellers I have used require buyers to "sign" an electronic form that says, basically, that the purchaser promises to use the lye for good, not evil, and then they will ship it to you. Some sellers have a form that you must print out, sign, and mail to them before the transaction can be complete.

Type the term "buy lye" into your search engine and choose from the many options available.

LARD SOAP
(a.k.a.) Piggie Soap, Grandma's Lye Soap

DEANNA Lard soap is a low-bubbling soap, which makes it especially good for laundry and scrubbing yucky stuff around the house. Additionally, it's cheap as all get-out to make. It's the only soap I've found that can beat Ivory on price.

However, regardless of how cheap and easy it is, piggie soap is an oft-requested present in our family. It's the only soap my father-in-law and uncle-in-law will use anymore. They were already hooked on Grandma's Lye Soap. It has three ingredients. Lard, lye, water. This is the same thing. Also, if your man likes to shave with soap or uses a lather cup, mold this soap in a Pringles can and it will fit the cup perfectly.

Yield: approximately 20 ounces. Cut bar sizes to your preference (the average bar of store-bought soap is 4.5 ounces).
Ingredients
> 1 pound lard (found in the shortening section of the grocery store)
> 6 ounces water
> 2 ounces lye

Wear clothing you don't mind messing up and put on rubber gloves (like those used to wash dishes) and safety goggles.
1. Melt one pound of lard in a saucepan over medium-low heat.
2. While the fat melts, put 6 ounces of water in a pitcher. Sprinkle in 2 ounces of lye, and gently swirl to dissolve.

3. Allow the melted fat and lye water to cool for a while, until you can touch the sides of each container without burning the snot out of yourself.
4. Pour the lye water into the saucepan. Place an immersion blender into the pan until it touches the bottom. Turn on the blender, watching for splashing (do this in the sink or put down several layers of newspaper). Blend until you see a "trace," which means until it's thick enough that you can kind of see where you've been and drips stay visible on the surface for a second or two. (This will take a while because of the lard.)
5. Pour into a Pringles can or a milk carton.
6. Let it sit a day or two, then peel off the can or carton, and slice it for curing. Let the bars cure for three weeks before use.

KITCHEN GREASE SOAP
(a.k.a. Bacon Soap)

DEANNA If you're saying to yourself, "Deanna, I don't wanna buy fat to make my soap. I have plenty of fat in my grease can," then this is the recipe for you. You can use fat drippings from any kind of meat and combine different drippings.

1. Render your fat
- Put half fat, half water in a pan and bring it to a boil.
- Remove from heat, stir, and add about half as much cold water as before cooking. (If I had a coffee cup of fat, and added a coffee cup of water to boil, I would add a half a coffee cup of cold water at this step.)
- Let it cool till the fat floats and you can scoop it onto a plate. (Fridge or freezer speeds it up. Just don't accidentally defrost your chicken breasts with the added heat in the freezer.)
- If it still seems a little iffy to you, repeat the process. I usually do.
2. Put on your soap-making clothes, rubber gloves, and safety goggles.
3. Weigh the fat and then melt it.

4. Use the weight of the fat to determine how much lye and water to use. For one pound of kitchen fat, you need 6 ounces of water and 2 ounces of lye. If I had ¾ of a pound (6 ounces) of grease after rendering, I would need 4.5 ounces of water (¾ of 6 ounces) and 1.5 ounces of lye (¾ of 2 ounces). Sprinkle the correct amount of lye into the water and swirl.

4 Wait until both the fat and the lye water are not smoldering hot, then pour the lye solution into the fat.

5. Blend with an immersion blender.

6. Stop when you can barely see where you've been.

6b. This is the time to put in the fragrance, if you wish.

7. Pour into an empty snack can or old milk carton.

8. Let it sit a day and peel off the carton, slice, and cure for a few weeks.

Volià! Soap. Any residual pork rind smells will be gone when it cures.

**Note to self, if the economy goes to heck in a hand basket, check crystal ball three weeks ahead so that soap will already be cured when the big one hits.

PURE OLIVE OIL SOAP

DAISY I heard the stories about 100 percent olive oil soap, that it was so gentle and mild, yet "slippery" and "low suds." I made up a batch and have been very pleased with it. Here's the deal on the "low suds" issue: It's true to some extent unless you use one of those scrubby plastic bath puffs. With the puff, it is unbelievably sudsy. It's also very sudsy as a shampoo bar. I love it.

This recipe uses a little less water than most, so the soap sets up very fast and gets hard as a rock in record time. Don't wait too long to unmold and slice into bars—eight hours or so is all mine needed, but check your batch and make the call depending on your best judgment.

Yield: approximately 24 4-ounce bars
Ingredients
　　100 ounces olive oil
　　12.6 ounces lye
　　30 ounces water

Wear clothing you don't mind messing up and put on rubber gloves (like those used to wash dishes) and safety goggles.

1. Measure 30 ounces of water into a pitcher. Sprinkle in 12.6 ounces of lye, and gently swirl to dissolve. Allow the lye water to cool for a while, until you can touch the side of the pitcher without burning yourself.

2. Measure 100 ounces of olive oil into a large bowl. Pour the cooled lye water into the olive oil. Place an immersion blender into the bowl until it touches the bottom. Turn on the blender, watching for splashing (do this in the sink or put down several layers of newspaper). Blend until you see a "trace," which means until it's thick enough that you can see where you've been and drips stay visible on the surface for a second or two. I bring mine to a fairly thick trace so I can make some swirls reminiscent of those made in the hot process.

3. Pour the soap into molds. Remove from molds as soon as the soap is set and cut into bars.

Let your soap cure for about six weeks for the hardest, mildest bars.

* I didn't add any essential oils to this batch, but a general guide for most essential oils is to add half an ounce of essential oils per pound of soaping oils.

For this recipe, you would need approximately 3.125 ounces of your favorite essential oil(s). Round up and use 4 ounces for extra oomph.

PEPPERMINT-ROSEMARY SOAP

DAISY I made this soap for presents this year. It's a little fancier than the soaps I usually do (I had never swirled before). I think I like it, though.

It's peppermint-rosemary with green clay and a smidge of ground rosemary on top. I used my standard olive, coconut, and castor oil blend for conditioning, hardness, and good lather. The scent is awesome.

Yield: approximately 35 4-ounce bars
Ingredients

> 72 ounces olive oil
>
> 12 ounces coconut oil
>
> 6 ounces castor oil
>
> 24–28 ounces water
>
> 12 ounces lye
>
> 2 ounces rosemary essential oil
>
> 2 ounces peppermint essential oil
>
> 4 tablespoons green clay powder
>
> 1 teaspoon ground dried rosemary

Use standard soapmaking procedures, including safety measures (see page 158). Upon trace, take out a small bit to a separate bowl, mixing the clay and the ground rosemary in with this small portion of the soap. Pour the bulk of the soap in the mold and then swirl in the clay portion.

Note: To make the ground rosemary, I whirled some dried rosemary leaves in a coffee grinder. A mortar and pestle or the like would also do the trick.

LAVENDER-ROSEMARY SOAP

This was a Christmas gift for some of my relatives. The basic recipe is adapted from Kathy Miller's web page (see appendix)

Yield: approximately 35 4-ounce bars
Ingredients

> 56 ounces olive oil
>
> 30 ounces vegetable shortening
>
> 9 ounces castor oil
>
> 12 ounces lye crystals
>
> 28 ounces cold water
>
> 3 tablespoons lavender oil
>
> 1 tablespoon rosemary oil

Wear clothing you don't mind messing up and put on rubber gloves (like those used to wash dishes) and safety goggles.

1. Sprinkle the lye crystals into the measured amount of water for the recipe. Swirl gently with a long-handled spoon. Allow it to cool enough to where you can touch the side of the container.

2. While the lye cools, weigh out the shortening and melt it in a large saucepan over medium-low heat.

3. Pour in the other oils.

4. Add lye (if it's no longer screaming hot) and mix with immersion blender to a light trace.
   The first time I did this, I took it to "trace" before adding the oils. Then, I blended again. This went to super trace, which I do not recommend, as it's like spooning mashed potatoes into the mold. So just blend to barely trace before proceeding to the next step.

5. Add 3 tablespoons of lavender oil and 1 tablespoon of rosemary oil. Blend to trace.

6. Line your molds with freezer paper. Fill them and cover them with a towel. (If you make a smaller amount of soap, you can use empty milk cartons or snack cans for your molds.

7. Cut into bars in the next day or so and allow to sit for at least a month. The first time, I only cut them into big bars to be divided later. It was not easy to cut those babies after they cured for a while. Go ahead and cut them to the final size.

Also, to make sure they were as dry as possible come wrapping time, I set them in the dehydrator for a few days. That's not typical soaping behavior as far as I know, but it worked well for me and my house smelled awesome.

HAND-MILLED GARDENER'S SOAP

DAISY I wanted to include a homemade soap for the gardener and came up with this one. It's hand-milled from my base soap of olive, coconut, and castor oils, and superfatted with almond butter for a bit of extra conditioning. I added oat flour for a little oomph and soothing, plus a "bug-away" blend of essential oils—because gardeners always go back out into the garden after they have washed their hands just to wander around and moon over the work they just accomplished (not just me, right?)

Yield: 2 4-ounce bars

Ingredients

   8 ounces grated homemade soap
   1 tablespoon oat flour (make by whirling oatmeal in the blender or a coffee grinder)
   1 teaspoon almond butter (or other conditioning fat)
   1 teaspoon essential oil (a blend of eucalyptus, citronella, catnip, cedarwood, et al.)

1. Melt the soap using your preferred method. This time I used a double-boiler. Because I chose not to add any water to my soap to hasten drying time, the soap only melted to the consistency of a soft clay.
2. One at a time, stir in the oat flour, almond butter, and essential oils. When I did this, it was like adding color to homemade Play-Doh, but it all blended in eventually. It helped to keep it over the hot water bath as long as possible.
3. Smush the soap-dough into the mold.
4. When cool, remove from mold and allow to dry several days until hard.

8

MY HOUSE WAS NEVER SO CLEAN

Many cleaning products on the market contain toxic chemicals. Fortunately, there are also plenty of recipes for nontoxic homemade cleaners out there, but you have to be careful about the ingredients. The "frugal" crowd and the "green" crowd aren't always the same crew. Frugal recipes for homemade cleaners can involve plenty of bad stuff like ammonia or bleach, both of which are horrid for your body. We like to avoid these two ingredients entirely.

Why Make Your Own Cleaning Products?

DEANNA Health concerns aside, do homemade nontoxic cleaners work as well as their toxic commercial counterparts? To be honest, the answer is yes and no. To explain why, let's start with a little lesson on the chemistry of cleaning.

The acronym to remember is TACT.
- Temperature
- Agitation
- Chemistry
- Time

These are the four factors that determine how well some thing cleans:

1. The warmer the water, the better something cleans.
2. The more agitation (read: elbow grease) the better something cleans.
3. The stronger the chemistry involved, the better something cleans.
4. The longer you let the product sit or soak, the better something cleans.

These days, most of the products on the shelf are meant to work:
- at cold or room temperature
- with little or no elbow grease
- with little or no wait time

So, when you void three of the four factors, what does that leave? Chemistry. The stuff in the store is effective because it contains very strong chemicals! The stuff you make at home won't have all those chemicals, so, no, the homemade versions won't work as well as store bought if your goal is to rip the hide off your walls at room temp, with no scrubbing, and no wait time. But, if you just want to *clean* the surface, we can do that.

All of our recipes have the chemistry necessary to clean, but you can boost a recipe's effectiveness any time by using hotter water, more elbow grease, or letting it sit for a few minutes before you scrub it off.

General-Cleaner Formulas

DEANNA Some cleaners require a recipe, while others don't. The following cleaning products require no measuring, so to call them "recipes" would seem over the top. So we call them formulas. Here are a few:

SCOURING POWDER
Baking soda or borax and a scouring pad

TILE AND GROUT
Equal parts salt and baking soda with enough liquid soap to make a paste

TOILET CLEANER
- full-strength vinegar or
- vinegar with baking soda or
- lemon juice with baking soda or
- borax

DAILY ALL-PURPOSE CLEANER
Equal parts white vinegar and water. Add a few drops of soap for more power.

FLOOR SOLUTION
For kitchen floors: undiluted vinegar splashed all over and wet mopped.

For laminate/wood floors: 1 cup of vinegar in a gallon of hot water and wet mop. (Also works for bathroom floors.)

For bathroom floors: scour with baking soda, then wet mop, or use hot soapy water.

Tip: If you love your self-spraying mop, but hate buying that solution, simply run the top of the empty bottle under hot water until you can pop it off and refill it with your favorite homemade cleaning solution. We've also found

Simplify Your Cleaning

We've found that there are several habits that greatly reduce one's need for strong cleaners and greatly reduce the workload on cleaning day. What it basically amounts to is lazy cleaning every day or every other day.

- When you're getting ready in the morning, swish the toilets with a brush to loosen dirt and hard-water deposits. Scrubbing days will be much farther between and take less time.
- While you're in the shower, wipe down the walls with your washcloth.
- Every other day or so, splash vinegar all over your kitchen floor and scoot around on it with a towel. Then real cleaning days are mostly about edges.
- Put your children to work for most of this. Even a poor job, done daily, greatly reduces the workload on super-cleaning day.
- Scrub your tub with your broom. It cleans the broom and the shower, while saving your back.
- Use cast iron for cooking. Clean up is a snap. Scrub with salt and oil and wipe with a paper towel.
- Run a load of laundry every morning. Put a load away every night. It takes a few minutes and you'll eliminate laundry day.

that microfiber cloths cut to size stick to the bottom of those mops just as well as the disposable pads.

BAKING SODA AND VINEGAR TOGETHER
People love this combination because its vigorous reaction makes you feel like you're really doing something! Plus, it's a great drain cleaner because it expands to reach the walls of your pipes rather than just running along the bottom like any other liquid.

The reaction does lift dirt away and helps prevent re-depositing, which can make your cleaning more effective, but vinegar and baking soda are more powerful on their own.

The vinegar/baking soda combination is *not* strong chemically. Vinegar and baking soda combine to make carbonic acid, which is basically club soda. As an acid, it will clean, but not nearly as well as vinegar alone.

Plus, after the momentary appearance of carbonic acid, vinegar and baking soda quickly break down into carbon dioxide and water. That means if you combine them in a bottle,

once the initial reaction is over, you're just cleaning with water.

So, if you love that reaction, here's how to use it effectively.

1. Scrub your surface with either full-strength vinegar or baking soda.
2. Splash or sprinkle on the other chemical.
3. Rinse during the delightful fizzy reaction to lift away dirt that was loosened or dissolved in Step 1 and to make you feel like you really "did something."

The Economic Dishwasher

Unfortunately, I have yet to find a satisfactory homemade dishwasher detergent. All of the home-made recipes leave a white film on my plastics no matter how little I use, which may not seem too problematic until you consider that the usual ingredients (borax) are poisonous to pets and children in amounts over one gram.

However, you can cut the amount of detergent you use (saving money and phosphates) by cutting store-bought detergent with baking soda. Use equal parts detergent and baking soda.

For a cheap and effective rinse solution, use vinegar in the rinse compartment.

Kitchen Cleaners

SUPER DISINFECTANT SPRAY

DEANNA This simple disinfectant recipe is more effective than bleach. It kills salmonella, E. coli, all that bad stuff! A study was done at Virginia Tech a while back that found that misting a countertop (or food) separately (and in either order) with store-strength vinegar and hydrogen peroxide was ten times more effective at disinfecting the surface than either product alone.

Ingredients
> undiluted white vinegar
> 3 percent hydrogen peroxide
> 2 spray bottles

1. Using a spray bottle, mist the surface with undiluted white vinegar.
2. Immediately spray the same area with 3 percent hydrogen peroxide from another spray bottle.
3. Wipe the area clean or rinse with water.
   Note: Use two separate sprayers. Don't try to mix them in the same bottle. It's not the same.

DAISY'S HOMEMADE VEGETABLE AND FRUIT WASH

This solution removes supermarket yuck from store-bought produce and cleans off dirt and bugs from your garden harvest. The acid in the vinegar helps trash bacteria and the salt sucks the life out of soft-bodied insects (remember osmosis from freshman Biology?) I imagine the vinegar doesn't do the bugs any favors, either.

Ingredients
> ¼ cup vinegar
> 2 tablespoons salt
> basin/bowl of clean water

Stir the vinegar and salt into the water and soak your produce for several minutes. Scrub and rinse as usual and eat.

For a simple vegetable/fruit spray, try a solution of 1 part vinegar to 3 parts water. Keep in a spray bottle, spray your produce, let it sit, then scrub as usual and rinse.

The Super Disinfectant Spray can also be used safely on produce, but it never occurs to us to use it for that.

TOUGH MULTI-PURPOSE CLEANER

DEANNA We spray all kitchen surfaces with diluted vinegar daily or every other day. However, sometimes things need a serious scrub down.

Ingredients
> 2 tablespoons vinegar
> 1 teaspoon borax
> 2 cups hot water
> 2 tablespoons to ¼ cup Castile soap (depending on the severity of the mess)
> 10–15 drops essential oil

1. Combine the vinegar, borax, and hot water in a spray bottle and shake like the dickens until the borax is dissolved.
2. After the borax dissolves, add the soap and essential oil and swirl.

LIQUID DISH SOAP

DEANNA
Ingredients
Half bar of soap, grated (homemade or Ivory is fine)
1 quart water

1. Melt the soap in water over medium heat.
2. Cool and place in a cleaned-out used pump bottle.
Use like regular dish detergent.

As a side note, I don't use liquid dish soap. I rub a round scrub brush across a bar of soap and then scrub my dishes. If I want a sink full of bubbles, I stick the bar under the running hot water. This is truly the easiest and most economical solution I've found for dishwashing.

Air Fresheners

DRY CARPET FRESHENER

DAISY
I gaze in horror at the TV ads for spray fresheners. The lady of the house spritzes away like a madwoman, then sticks her nose right in the middle of it and inhales deeply. She goes after it all: sneakers, beds, clothes, everything. Why, I wonder, don't they just clean the stinky things? If my bed emanated a palpable odor, I think choosing the right deodorant spray would be the least of my concerns.

That said, I have a terrier. Dip him in a vat of peppermint and he'd smell like terrier two minutes later. It has an effect on the vacuum-cleaner bag, turning it into an odor-dispersal system. Not the ambiance I'm going for right before company shows up.

Bonus: This also makes a great scouring powder for sinks and tubs. Then when you've finished cleaning house, sprinkle some into a nice hot bath.
Ingredients
2 cups baking soda
essential oil(s) of choice

With a fork, stir in your favorite essential oil by drops until your nose tells you it's enough. I use about a teaspoon or less. It's best to let the oils permeate for a while before first use. I use the baking

Easy Air Freshener

Here's a little trick that makes the entire house smell fresh. I accidentally discovered the power of vacuum-bag scent dispersal when my babies dumped a bottle of cumin on my bed and I removed it with a vacuum. For the next two weeks, the house smelled like tacos every time I ran the vacuum. Here's how you do it on purpose:

1. Place drops of your favorite essential oil on a paper towel.
2. Tear out the scented portion.
3. Throw it on the floor.
4. Suck it up in your vacuum cleaner and vacuum the house.

soda by itself with good results, but the essential oil is a treat. Oils, such as peppermint, eucalyptus, and rosemary, are invigorating and fresh. Lavender is soothing.

Store in an empty shaker bottle, such as a clean Parmesan cheese container.

To use
Sprinkle on carpeting and let it sit for a couple of hours or overnight, then vacuum.

CHILD-LABOR HOMEMADE CAR-AIR FRESHENER

 My car doesn't smell bad to me, but someone was making a stink-face every time we had to go somewhere. Enter child labor.

1. On a piece of paper, draw (or have someone draw) a simple-shaped motif. My kids like stars. Cut out the motif and transfer it to a piece of craft felt. Cut out the pattern on the felt. Make two.

2. Pin the pieces of felt together and hand-stitch around the edges with colored thread, leaving an opening.
3. Soak a cotton ball (or dryer lint) with essential oil, ½ to 1 teaspoon, and stuff in the center of the freshener-to-be.
4. Sew closed.
5. Sew on a favorite bit of ribbon to serve as a hanger.
6. To refresh, slip a dropper in between the stitching and squeeze in some more essential oil, or just pour some directly on the felt.

Surface Cleaners

HOMEMADE FURNITURE CLEANER

 Dry dusting is always your best option for cleaning your furniture surfaces. Use this polish occasionally to condition the surface of wood, vinyl, and leather. Always dry dust before applying

this cleaner. This stuff is the real deal. Read: greasy. But, your wood will soak it up like a sponge. I also use it on the leather and vinyl in the minivan.

Ingredients

½ cup olive oil

2 tablespoons lemon juice or vinegar

several drops essential oil(s) of choice (optional)

Combine in a jar or bottle with a tight-fitting lid.

To use

Dry dust first, then shake well before each use. Pour a little on a dry soft-cotton rag and rub into wood. (Deanna likes to use a spray bottle instead.) Buff gently with a clean, dry cloth to remove excess polish (too much left on the finish will attract dust).

A small dowel sharpened in a pencil sharpener and wrapped in a cleaning cloth can help get the grunge out of intricate carvings.

SUPER GLASS CLEANER

DEANNA We use vinegar and water for daily cleaning, but once in a while, we really need to get the windows clean!

Ingredients

2 cups water (the warmer the better)

½ cup vinegar

¼ cup isopropyl rubbing alcohol

Combine all ingredients in a spray bottle and swirl. Use with newspaper or a lint-free cloth. Be sure to obey the dilution on the vinegar. It can etch the glass if it's too strong.

BATHROOM MOLD KILLER

DEANNA Online, you'll find recipes for bathroom-tile cleaners involving a great deal of vinegar. Vinegar dissolves mineral deposits. Guess what your grout is made of? Over time, you will need to re-grout. So, I use only diluted vinegar or none at all. I have two options for bathroom mold prevention and mold killing:

Option 1

2 teaspoons tea tree oil

2 cups of water

Combine in a spray bottle.

Option 2

Combine equal parts water and hydrogen peroxide in a spray bottle.

Keep your spray bottle in the shower to use after bathing.

To use either option on an existing mold problem, use TACT:

- Use hotter water.
- Spray on and leave for a while.
- Scrub hard.
- Tea tree oil will kill mold, but peroxide bleaches the stains left behind. I like to use a combination of both.

BEESWAX WOOD POLISH

DAISY **Ingredients**

2 ounces beeswax

8 ounces oil (olive, jojoba, or food-grade linseed)

1 teaspoon lemon essential oil

1 teaspoon vitamin E

1. Melt the beeswax in the oil over a double boiler or in the microwave, stirring to combine.
2. Remove from heat and cool slightly until the outer edges have begun to thicken.
3. Stir in the lemon essential oil and the vitamin E. Continue to stir periodically until the mixture is thickened, creamy, and room temperature.
4. Store in a lidded jar for up to one year or two years if refrigerated.

To use

Rub a small amount onto a soft, clean rag and rub into wood. Buff lightly with a clean, dry cloth.

Homemade Laundry Solutions

To make low-bubbling detergent for both high-efficiency and traditional machines, you need four ingredients: borax, washing soda, soap, and water. Essential oils are a bonus.

Borax and washing soda can usually be found in the laundry aisle of any good grocery store. Do not confuse washing soda with baking soda. Baking soda will work, but it has about half the effectiveness of washing soda.

Pretty much any soap is suitable for laundry use; however, some soaps are so *good* or so *expensive* that it would be silly to buy them for laundry. If you make your own lard or Crisco soap (see chapter seven for recipes), that works great. If you're not into soapmaking, another economical option is to use the leftover bits of old bars of soap. If you need to actually go out and buy soap, Ivory is your best bet for versatility and price. Fels-Naptha and Zote are also fine options. Zote may be as economical as Ivory or homemade because it comes in such a large bar, but I haven't found it in my area.

POWDERED LAUNDRY SOAP

DEANNA

Ingredients
2 cups finely grated soap (Ivory, Fels-Naptha, Zote, homemade, or a combination)
1 cup borax
1 cup washing soda

Mix and store in a sealable container of your choice. I recommend an old coffee can.

If you intend to use this detergent dry, buzz it in a coffee grinder or food processor to get the soap really fine and/or use hotter water in your washer. I can't stand to see undissolved soap floating at the top of my washer.

To use
Add 1–2 tablespoons per load.

There is a great degree of debate about this laundry powder and others like it. Some find that the laundry comes out clean as a whistle using the usual 1–2 tablespoons per load.

Others find that their clothes come out dingy. In my experience, dinginess is caused by soap deposits, especially in hard water (harsh commercial detergents prevent things from re-depositing even in very hard water), but it may be the soil level on your clothes.

Dinginess can be solved in several ways. Remember TACT (page 168)? If you have any trouble with this detergent, try one or more of the following:
- Raise the temperature of your water.
- Use more detergent (up to ½ cup).
- Put it on the pre-wash soak cycle.
- Use vinegar in the rinse cycle (this and temperature are probably the best solutions if you have soap deposits).

Depending on why you are choosing to make your own laundry soap, dinginess may or may not discourage you from continuing to use it. It won't affect you if, for example, you are doing it for the environment, to be more self-sufficient, to reduce chemicals in the home, or because you hate shopping.

However, if you are doing this solely for the purpose of being frugal, you may find that your perfect amount of powder exceeds the five-cents-a-load cost of detergent that you can squeeze out of a wholesale-club bulk buy.

Now, onto the liquid. I prefer to use the liquid version of this recipe because I'm obsessed with undissolved particles. If you plunk a wad of the dry soap in a bucket and stir it for a while, you will notice that it doesn't all dissolve. That bugs me. So, I pre-dissolve it.

The Cult of the Clothesline

When I posted on our website about the benefits of line-drying laundry, I was amazed by the passionate responses from our readers. Readers waxed rhapsodic about the meditative quality of the act of hanging clothes on the line, about the smell and feel of sleeping on sheets dried in the sun and air, and about the great memories it brought back of childhood and family.

I was also impressed by the lengths they would go to in order to line-dry, hiding it from homeowners' associations in garages and on secluded patios, or else thumbing their noses at prohibitions by boldly displaying clotheslines even in areas where it was a no-no.

Many residents in communities that outlawed clotheslines have successfully fought to have ordinances amended to allow line-drying. If you are living under such a prohibition and you would like to fight it, you can find support at Project Laundry List (www.laundrylist.org), an online organization that promotes solar drying. It features a cost calculator that can help you estimate how much you can save by ditching the clothes dryer, and you can find out how to become involved in promoting "Right to Dry" legislation in your part of the world.

Here are a few line-drying tips from readers of our blog:

"To avoid T-shirt sag and peg marks, I hang them double-folded over the line at a bit above breast height. The peg marks disappear in your armpits, and you save a lot of time and energy because you don't have to press/iron. You just fold them nicely and put them in the bottom of the stack, and by the time you take a shirt to use it, it's been nicely pressed by the weight of the shirts that were on top." —Cipollina

"My mom discovered that most articles of clothing dry with less distortion upside down. This works for pants, blouses, T-shirts, and more. You also don't get pinch marks on the shoulders. Long sleeves are tricky. Hang them upside down and pin up the sleeves, too. For knits, my mom had a special rack that was polymesh on a slight incline." —Synj

"I hang things out every time I can. Things are softer when the wind is blowing, not enough to send your things over to the next county though. I give things a good shake before hanging them just to help soften them. The smell is so great and lasts so much longer then the store-bought softener. In the winter, if it is too cold or wet to hang clothes outside, I have a wooden rack by the wood stove and some hooks in the ceiling to hang clothes from. The shower rod makes a good hanger for some things, too." —Alice

"To save your money on the clothespin holder, clean a plastic milk jug and cut a chunk out of it (on the top half opposite the handle). Cut the handle near the bottom where it rejoins the jug just enough to slip it over the clothes line. Cut a couple little holes in the bottom to drain rainwater if you plan to hang it outside. Hook the handle over your clothesline. It's cheap as dirt and will last." —Stephanie

LIQUID LAUNDRY SOAP

DEANNA **Yield: enough for 64 loads**
Ingredients

2 cups finely grated soap
1 cup borax
1 cup washing soda
2 gallons water
water (less than 2 gallons)
5-gallon pail

1. In a saucepan, melt the soap over medium in a gallon of water.
2. Remove from heat and immediately add the borax and washing soda. Stir to dissolve the dry ingredients.
3. Pour in the pail and add another gallon* of *hot* water. Stir well and often. I stir it with my stick blender a few times over the next 24 hours.
   * The exact amount of water you add is not important. You can make it stiffer or soupier. If you use the exact amounts of powders and soaps I recommend, then you have sixty-four loads. Just divide accordingly. I like the two-gallon mark, because adding a good ½ cup makes a satisfying *whop* in the washer and I really feel like I'm adding something. Two table-spoons in forty gallons of water just doesn't feel like I'm cleaning anything.
4. Let set up overnight.
5. Stir. It will be a soupy gel.
6. Use ½ cup per load.

This stuff also works well as a pre-treater. I've also used it to scrub the bathroom and in place of dishwasher detergent.

FABRIC SOFTENER

DEANNA **Ingredients**
½ cup white vinegar

Instead of adding a fabric softener sheet to the dryer, just use vinegar in the washing-machine rinse cycle. Add ½ cup of white vinegar to the liquid fabric softening dispenser. This will reduce cling and remove hard-water and soap deposits.

NONCHLORINE BLEACH

DEANNA I use this especially on whites. We are super hard on whites in my house so, I use every part of TACT (page 168): Add a soak cycle to a normal wash setting (Time & Agitation), detergent (Chemistry), hot water (Temperature), vinegar in the rinse cup (more chemistry), peroxide in the bleach cup (more chemistry). The clothes come out white as snow!
Ingredients

homemade Liquid Laundry Soap (see recipe in left column)
hydrogen peroxide

To bleach

use ½ cup to 1 cup hydrogen peroxide in the bleach cup.

There are some oxy-cleaning recipes on the Internet using baking soda and hydrogen peroxide, but these are incorrect for two reasons:

1. Oxy-powders are supposed to be washing soda and hydrogen peroxide, not baking soda.
2. There's no reason to try to make the powder version because as soon as the mixture hits the water, it breaks back down into hydrogen peroxide and washing soda—a bleach and a booster.
   You can achieve the same effect by using home-made detergent and bottled hydrogen peroxide. If you want it to be just like store-bought, add a bit more washing soda to the load.

SPRAY STARCH

DEANNA This stuff can go rancid. (Any cleaner with water requires a preservative to prevent rancidity. Add in the starch element and you have a perfect micro-buggy growing solution.) However, I've never had that happen. I use it up too fast. If you are concerned, add a few drops of tea tree oil or just keep it in the fridge, but really, it's so easy that you could mix it up every time.

Ingredients

　2 teaspoons corn starch
　Spray bottle full of water

　Shake before use. If you get flakes when you iron, don't be discouraged, it simply means you have too much starch in the bottle. Pour out half the mixture and refill with plain water.

Cloth-Diapering Basics

DAISY　I had a horrible fear of cloth diapering before I tried it. I have a huge problem with the unknown. What if I bought all the gear and then couldn't make it work for me? Cloth diapering requires a larger up-front cash outlay than a couple of packs of disposables. What if I had to go crawling back to disposables after finding cloth diapering made an already exhausting time in our family life just that much more exhausting?

　Plus, there were so many choices in diapers, so many contradicting opinions regarding laundering methods and accessories. How was I to decide, without trying them all out, which was going to work best for me, my husband, and my kids? What if I made the wrong picks? I would be stuck.

　In the end, I made the leap, and I wish I hadn't waited so long. It's actually very simple, very doable, and I can't tell you how fun it is to swan past the diaper aisle in the supermarket without giving it a second glance. I can just hear my pocketbook sigh with relief.

　The consensus is that cloth diapering is much less expensive and a huge improvement over disposables from an ecological perspective. It's possible to save thousands of dollars over the approximate three years your child will be in diapers. Not bad. And you're saving about two tons of landfill space, per kid.

And as a bonus, you'll never have to make a late-night run to the store because you ran out of Pampers. The online resources for cloth diapering are comprehensive. I recommend www.diaperpin.com for comparisons and reviews of cloth-diapering products and advice forums to answer all your cloth-diapering questions.

Baby Wipes
MATERIALS

DEANNA　There are two camps on homemade baby wipes: The disposable and the nondisposable. For the disposable option, you can use paper towels. Cut the roll in half along the width and again along the length. Use one-fourth of a roll per batch of solution.

For the nondisposable, you can use cut-up T-shirts. (Daisy uses *gorgeous* hand-sewn flannel rags, but I'm just not as fancy.)

I have to tell you right off, that my preference between cloth or disposable homemade wipes has little to do with my feelings about the planet or my wallet. It has more to do with how I feel about "the mess" I'm cleaning up. I find cloth works fine for very young babies that are milk-fed or starting on baby food. After babies graduate to solid food and begin eating regular diets, their waste becomes much messier and more unpleasant, and I find it easier to throw away that mess instead of trying to wash it out of cloth.

Cut your wipes (either cloth or disposable) and stack them in a plastic container. Don't worry about making the wipes uniform in size. They're *bum wipers* for crying out loud.

CLEANING SOLUTION
Every cleaning solution has one or more of a few basic components. However, you can add a myriad of things depending on your preference and resources:

1. water (necessary)
2. cleaner or soap (almost necessary): baby soap, homemade soap, no soap, baby shampoo
3. something lotiony (perk): calendula oil, lavender oil, aloe vera gel, juice from an aloe plant, baby lotion
4. something a bit antibacterial/antifungal (perk, especially if you pre-wet your wipes and let them sit): a bit of vinegar, tea tree oil, or other essential oils are good preservatives that also fight infection.

BASIC SOAPY BABY WIPES
Ingredients
- 2 cups water
- ½ tablespoon soap
- 2 tablespoons aloe juice (or lotion)
- 5 drops tea tree oil

BASIC NO-SOAP BABY WIPES
I don't put soap in my baby wipes because we have über-sensitive skin in my house.

Ingredients
- 2 cups water
- 2 tablespoons squished up aloe juice (I have a plant in the house)
- 5 drops tea tree oil

WET OR DRY?
The next decision is between always-wet wipes and wetted-at-the-time wipes. I tend to use wetted-at-the-time for my cloth wipes, but after baby has graduated to the aforementioned "advanced mess," I do the wetted-all-the-time disposable wipes.

As I said, I use cloth wipes only on young babies, and they don't need a lot of wipes. And always-wet wipes start to turn icky before I use them all. That, and I like the idea of *fresh* wipes on a baby booty. I keep the solution in an old mustard bottle and wet the wipes as needed.

I've put together a few of what I call "extras" that can be used whether or not you choose to use cloth diapers. They go great in a new-baby gift basket.

WIPE-SOLUTION CONCENTRATE

DAISY

Ingredients
- ½ cup olive oil
- ¼ cup liquid Castile soap*
- 1 tablespoon lavender essential oil
- 1 teaspoon tea tree essential oil
- 1 teaspoon calendula extract

* You can make liquid Castile soap out of grated bar soap and water. Just grate about ⅛ cup of soap, add water to cover, and let sit overnight to dissolve.

Combine ingredients in a bottle with a tight cap. Shake well.

Handmade Flannel Wipes Set

Flannel wipes are simple to make. If you have a serger, measure and serge 7.5-inch (19cm) squares from pre-washed, 100-percent-cotton flannel. In the absence of a serger, the edges can be cut with pinking sheers to the same dimension or finished with a zizzag stitch.

Wipes this size store easily in disposable-wipes boxes.

To use

Put 1 tablespoon of concentrate in a spray bottle or drinking-water bottle with a pull cap. Add 2 cups of water. Shake well.

Dribble or spray onto a cloth at each use. You can also pour over folded cloth wipes in an old, clean disposable-wipe box to saturate the wipes and use like disposable ones (just toss in the diaper pail with the diapers).

DIAPER-PAIL FRESHMAKERS

DAISY **Ingredients**
2 cups baking soda
1 teaspoon peppermint essential oil
distilled water
cupcake liners

1. Stir the essential oil into the baking powder.
2. Drizzle the water over the baking soda, stirring gently until it forms a very thick paste.
3. Pack into the cupcake liners about ½" to ¾" (12mm to 2cm) deep. Allow to dry. Store in an airtight container or bag.

To use

Place in the bottom of the diaper pail. Toss into the wash each time you launder the load of diapers.

CALENDULA DIAPER CREAM

DAISY **Ingredients**
3 tablespoons shea butter
1 tablespoon beeswax
6 tablespoons avocado oil
1 teaspoon soy lecithin
1 capsule vitamin E
2 tablespoons zinc oxide
1 teaspoon calendula extract

1. Melt the shea butter and beeswax in a double boiler over low heat. Promptly remove from heat as soon as it is melted.
2. Whisk in the avocado oil, soy lecithin, vitamin E, zinc oxide, and calendula extract.
3. Store in any lidded container or jar you have handy.

9

I MADE IT MYSELF: GORGEOUS GIFTS APLENTY

Gift baskets are an awesome way to show someone you are thinking of them. The beauty of handmade baskets is you can customize the items to the recipient's taste for no extra charge. Want monograms or specific colors, fragrances, or shapes? No problem—you're in control. This chapter will show you how to create these great themed gift baskets: The Pedi, The Pet Lover, The Gardener, The Spa, and The Tushie. Keep the makings on hand so you're ready whenever you need to give a gift. The "I" in this chapter refers to me, Daisy.

Finding Ingredients

DAISY Several of the skincare-product recipes in this chapter require ingredients that aren't available from your local market.

Some, like beeswax, are carried in hobby and craft stores, or you could purchase beeswax from a beekeeper or harvest it from your own hive, but most of the ingredients will need to be ordered online. Sellers of soaping supplies are your best bet. They will have all the oils, including avocado and castor oil (called carrier oils), butters, herbal extracts, and essential oils, as well as lye for making your own soap. Just search "soapmaking supplies" online.

Baking soda and kosher salt are sold in large, recloseable bags at members-only bulk stores, and Epsom salts can be found at any drugstore.

A kitchen scale or a scale used for soapmaking will help you weigh the ingredients. See the soapmaking resource page in the appendix for ideas of where to find the necessary ingredients and equipment.

Containers

You'll need to find containers for the bath salts and scrubs you make. These containers can be slippery when handled with wet hands so I prefer reusable plastic containers instead of glass jars because plastic reduces the risk of breakage.

It's also a good idea to store these salts and scrubs in dry areas, which means not in the immediate tub and shower area. Moisture will cause them to become either soupy or to solidify into chunks. Keep them where they won't get sprayed with water and don't dip into them when your hands are wet.

The Pedi Basket

I know I take my feet for granted. In a busy week, foot care is so far down the list that it nearly always gets knocked off entirely. What makes this a good gift is that it compels the recipient to put a home pedicure back on the list and make it stick.

CONTENTS
- Lavender Foot Soak
- Exfoliating Peppermint-Avocado Foot Scrub
- Calendula and Shea Butter Lotion Bar
- Knitted Scrub Mitt (or sewed version)

LAVENDER FOOT SOAK
This soak is very relaxing and an ideal prep for exfoliation and moisturizing.

Ingredients

- 1 cup Epsom salts
- 1 cup baking soda
- ½ cup kosher salt
- ½ teaspoon lavender essential oil

Combine all ingredients and stir well to combine. Store in an airtight jar.

To use

Fill a large basin with warm water, stir in ½ cup of the mixture, and immerse feet.

EXFOLIATING PEPPERMINT-AVOCADO FOOT SCRUB

Sloughs away calluses; moisturizes and deodorizes.

Ingredients

- 1½ cups kosher salt
- ¼ cup avocado oil
- 6 drops peppermint essential oil

1. Combine salt and avocado oil, blending until the mixture holds together like wet sand.
2. Stir in the peppermint essential oil.
3. Store in an airtight jar.

To use

Rub into feet, especially heels and soles. Rinse with warm water and dry thoroughly.

CALENDULA AND SHEA BUTTER LOTION BAR

Rich conditioning plus healing and antifungal.

Ingredients

- 2 ounces shea butter
- 2 ounces avocado oil
- 2 ounces beeswax
- I large vitamin E capsule
- 1 teaspoon calendula extract

1. Over low heat, melt shea butter and beeswax in a double boiler or small pan in a larger pan of water.

2. Stir in the avocado oil, calendula extract, and vitamin E (split the capsule open and squeeze out the content).
3. Pour into mold(s) and allow to cool. Any mold will do, even a muffin tin. You can also pour the mixture into a cute saucer or dish. Leave the hardened lotion in the saucer and scrape off a little as needed.

Note: Shea butter can occasionally become grainy. To avoid this, use just enough heat to get your ingredients to melt. Once your ingredients are blended, cool your mixture quickly by pouring it into shallow container(s) in a cool room or by popping it into the refrigerator (not the freezer) to cool.

KNITTED SCRUB MITT

These are fingertip wash mitts. Compared to big, luxury mitts, they dry more quickly and don't drip as much while washing at the sink—you know that drip down the elbows? The textured stitch makes for good scrubbiness. They measure about 4" (10cm) tall and 3½" (9cm) wide at the top, flaring out to 4" (10cm) at the ruffled bottom edge. This is a very quick knit.

Materials

worsted-weight yarn in two colors
size 6 circular or straights needles

Pattern

CO 63 sts
Row 1: (RS) Using color A, K3, *bind off 3, K3, repeat from * to last 6 sts, bind off 3, K1, K2tog. You should now have 32 sts on needle.
Rows 2–3: K
Row 4: P
Row 5: K
Row 6: Change to color B; P
Row 7: K
Row 8: Change back to color A; P
Row 9: K
Row 10: Change to color B; P
Rows 11–12: K
Row 13: *K3, sl 1, rep from * to end
Row 14: *sl 1, P3, rep from * to end
Row 15: As row 13
Row 16: K
Row 17: *K1, sl 1, K2, rep from * to end
Row 18: *P2, sl 1, P1, rep from * to end
Row 19: As row 17
Row 20: K Repeat Rows 13–20.
Fold over and knit together the edges of the mitt using your preferred method. One way is simply to sew the top and side edges. Another way is to use the three-needle bind off for the top edge and sew together the side with a tapestry needle.

Abbreviations: K=knit, P=Purl, K2tog=knit two together, CO=cast on, RS=right side, sl=slip stitch

The Pet Lover

This basket makes a welcome gift for the new or the veteran dog owner. Dogs love to graze on the fresh wheatgrass as much as cats, and it's fun to grow your own.

CONTENTS
- Conditioning Pet Soap
- Pet Greens Grow Kit
- Cheddar Oat Dog Biscuits
- Fleece Rope Dog Toy

CONDITIONING PET SOAP

This soap is very mild. The neem oil is renowned for its healing properties for irritated skin as well as for being pest-repellent. The essential oils are chosen to chase away both pet odor and insects.

Ingredients

    30 ounces olive oil
    12.5 ounces coconut oil
    4 ounces neem oil
    3.5 ounces castor oil
    6.925 ounces lye
    15 ounces water
    ½ ounces each peppermint, eucalyptus, tea tree,
        and rosemary essential oils

Follow the instructions for Basic Soapmaking that begins on page 158.

PET GREENS GROW KIT

Copy or explain these instructions to the recipient. It's simple, really—just wet the dirt and plant the seeds.

Materials

    organic wheatgrass seeds (available at health-
        food stores)
    soil mix in a resealable plastic bag
    plant tray (recycled plant trays work perfectly)

1. Add warm water to the soil in bag a little at a time. Seal the bag and squeeze the contents to mix in the water. Continue this process until the soil is thoroughly moistened but not waterlogged.

2. Pour the moistened soil into the plant tray, reserving about a cup for covering the seeds later. Gently press the soil into the tray and even out the top surface.

3. Evenly sprinkle the wheatgrass seeds onto the surface of the soil about ¼" (7mm) apart.

4. Sprinkle the remaining soil over the seeds and gently pat down to cover.

5. Cover loosely with plastic wrap and put in a sunny window. After a few days, the seeds will begin to sprout. Remove the plastic wrap. Keep the soil moist. When your wheatgrass is about 4–5" (10cm–13cm) tall, snip a little at a time and add to your pet's food or allow him periodic nibbling access to the growing grass.

CHEDDAR OAT DOG BISCUITS

Brewer's yeast is rich in B vitamins, omega fatty acids, and antioxidants, and is said to boost immunity, improve pet skins and coats, and repel fleas.

Ingredients

   1½ cups whole wheat flour

   ½ cup oatmeal

   ¼ cup brewer's yeast

   ½ cup shredded cheddar cheese

   2 tablespoons olive oil

   ½ cup chicken stock

Preheat oven to 350°F (175°C).

1. Combine the dry ingredients.
2. Stir in the cheddar, the oil, and the stock until the mixture forms a soft dough.
3. Roll out a scant ½" (12mm) thick on a lightly floured board and cut into shapes with a bone-shaped cookie cutter or with a knife.
4. Bake at 350°F (175°C) for 10–12 minutes or until lightly brown on the bottom. Turn off the oven and let the biscuits sit inside the oven until they're cool.

Store in airtight containers. They will keep for several weeks.

FLEECE ROPE DOG TOY

This toy is colorful and easy to make.

Materials

   fleece remnants in three colors, combined size about ⅓ yard (⅓m) per toy.

   scissors

See the instructions on the next page.

1. Cut perpendicular to selvage into three 4" x 36" (10cm × 91cm) strips per rope.

2. Stack three strips, one of each color, and tie the three strips into a knot near one end of the strips.

3. Very tightly braid the three strips together, starting at the knotted end.

4. Stop braiding a few inches (several centimeters) from the end, leaving enough to tie another knot right at the end of the braiding.

5. Trim selvages from both ends and cut a fringe into the remaining unbraided fleece.

    Tie an additional knot or multiple knots in the center of the braided section for Doggy to sink his teeth into.

The Gardener

Gardeners live and breathe their gardens. One of the best things about making this basket is making enough to keep some for yourself! For a beginning gardener, add a few seed packets and make corresponding plant markers.

CONTENTS
- Homemade Insect Spray (recipe in chapter 7)
- Twig Plant Markers
- Gardener's Lotion Bar
- Poppyseed Scrub-up Soap
- Homemade Dibble

TWIG PLANT MARKERS

These can be as basic as segments of whittled twigs written on with a permanent marker, or a bit more elaborate when printed with stamps and dipped in spar varnish to prolong their longevity.

Give blank ones, too, and include in the gift a waterproof marker so the gardener can customize the twigs to her garden.

GARDENER'S LOTION BAR

The rooibos and calendula in this bar sooth and heal raw, chapped hands.
Ingredients
    ½ teaspoon rooibos extract
    ½ teaspoon calendula extract
    ½ teaspoon rosemary essential oil

Follow the recipe for the Everyman's Lotion Bar on page 154, adding the rooibos, calendula, and rosemary essential oil when you stir in the vegetable oil.

POPPYSEED LEMON SCRUB-UP SOAP

The poppyseeds help exfoliate and remove garden grime while the lemon refreshes and uplifts.
Ingredients (per pound of soap)
    3 teaspoons poppyseeds
    2 ounces lemon essential oil
    2 ounces litsea cubeba essential oil

Use the Basic Soapmaking Recipe (page 158) and add the extra ingredients at the end of step 8.

HOMEMADE DIBBLE

A dibble is a traditional gardening tool used to make depressions in the soil for planting seeds.
Materials
    12-inch dowel
    whittling knife
    ruler
    permanent marker
    paint or markers
    twine

1. Cut the dowel to your desired length. Mine are typically 12" (30cm) long.
2. Whittle one end to a blunt point. This won't take long.

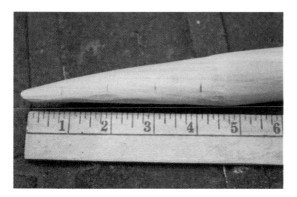

3. Line the dowel up next to a ruler (blunt end at the 0 mark) and place 1-, 2-, 3-, and 4-inch (2.5cm, 5cm, 7.5cm, and 10cm) markers on the dowel using the permanent marker.
4. Paint or decorate the dibble as desired. Attach the hanger material to the opposite end of the dibble. If desired, drill a hole for a hanging cord.

The Spa

Everyone on your gift list will appreciate the pampering associated with a home-spa experience. If you aren't a knitter, substitute a loofah (maybe you grew it yourself!) or a pretty terry washcloth.

CONTENTS
- Honey Conditioning Soap
- Oatmeal Bath Milk
- Body Butter
- Hugs-and-Kisses Hand-Knit Face Cloth

HONEY CONDITIONING SOAP

With extra shea butter for conditioning, olive oil for mildness, and a dollop of honey, this rich amber soap is a complete luxury. The the soft floral fragrance of the litsea cubeba combines with the lemon essential oils and complements the scent of the honey and beeswax.

Yield: about 12 bars

Ingredients

    24 ounces olive oil

    8 ounces coconut oil

    2 ounces shea butter

    2 ounces beeswax

    10 ounces water

    4.76 ounces lye

    2 ounces honey

    1 ounces litsea cubeba essential oil

    1 ounces lemon essential oil

1. Mix lye and water, allow to cool to about 120°F 49°C).

2. Combine olive oil, coconut oil, and beeswax in a large, non-reactive pot and warm over low heat until coconut oil and beeswax are just melted. Add shea butter and allow to melt, stirring. Remove from heat.

3. Pour the oil and wax mixture into the lye and water mixture stirring constantly with a stick blender until tracing occurs. The mix will thicken rapidly.

4. Stir in the honey and essential oils with the stick blender and pour the mixture into molds. Unmold the next day. Cut into bars. Let cure for three to six weeks.

OATMEAL BATH MILK

The milk is moisturizing while the oatmeal helps soothe and condition skin.

Ingredients

3 cups dried milk powder
1 cup oatmeal, whirred fine in a blender
½ cup kosher salt
1 teaspoon essential oil of choice

Blend well. Store in an airtight container.

To use:

Add 1 cup to running water as the bath fills.

BODY BUTTER

Super-emollient shea butter combines with avocado and coconut oil for a decadent slather for dry skin. Scent with your favorite essential oil.

Yield: 1 cup

Ingredients

1 ounces beeswax
2 ounces shea butter
1 ounces coconut oil
4 ounces avocado oil
1 vitamin E capsule
6–8 drops essential oil of choice (optional)

1. Melt the beeswax, shea butter, and coconut oil in a double boiler.

2. Add the avocado oil. Whip with an electric mixer, slowly, for several minutes as the mix cools and takes on the consistency of whipped cream. Blend in the essential oil, if you choose. Scoop into prepared jar(s).

HUGS-AND-KISSES HAND-KNIT FACE CLOTH

A good beginner's first cable project. It looks harder than it is. I love the sweatery-ness, and the X's and O's make me smile.

Materials

worsted-weight yarn (example is Lily Sugar 'n Cream in ecru)
size 6 circular or straights needles
cable needle

Pattern

As you begin your pattern stitches, begin and end each row with 4 knit stitches for a garter stitch border, indicated by MB in the pattern stitch section.

C4B: Slip two sts onto the cable needle and hold to the back of the work. Knit two stitches. Knit the two stitches from the cable needle.

C4F: Slip two sts onto the cable needle and hold in front of work. Knit two stitches. Knit the two stitches from the cable needle.

Cast on 35 sts.
Ribbing: (first 6 rows and final 6 rows) K2, P2 across—because there is an uneven number of cast-on stitches you will end up with one orphan at the end of a row. That's okay. Just keep to your ribbing on the wrong side, knitting the knits and purling the purls. There is no garter stitch border on the ribbing section.

Row 1: MB, K11, P1, K3, P1, K11, MB
Row 2: MB, P8, K1, P1, (K3, P1)x2, K1, P8, MB
Row 3: MB, C4B, C4F, (K3, P1)x2, K3, C4B, C4F, MB
Row 4: As Row 2
Row 5: As Row 1

Row 6: As Row 2

Row 7: As Row 3

Row 8: As Row 2

Row 9: As Row 1

Row 10: As Row 2

Row 11: MB, C4F, C4B, (K3, P1)x2, K3, C4F, C4B, MB

Row 12: As Row 2

Row 13: As Row 1

Row 14: As Row 2

Row 15: As Row 11

Row 16: As Row 2

Repeat these 16 rows 1 time.

K2, P2 six more rows of ribbing.

Cast off.

Abbreviations: K=knit, P=purl, MB=make bobble,
C4B=cable four back, C4F=cable four front

The Tushie

Encourage a friend who's going the cloth-diapering (CDing) route with these tried-and-true CDing helpers.

The salve is approved for cloth diapers. The Wipe Solution Concentrate is effective and easy to use, and the Freshmakers help keep diaper-pail odors under control. The recipes and the flannel wipes instructions for this basket are found in Cloth Diapering section of chapter 8.

CONTENTS
- Calendula Diaper Cream
- Diaper Pail Freshmakers
- Diaper Wipe Solution Concentrate
- Homemade Flannel Wipes Set

10

SMALL TOWN IN THE CITY

While it's true that good fences make good neighbors, never stepping foot outside your privacy fence is a recipe for turning good neighbors into perfect strangers. You can set up baby-sitting and meal co-ops with friends far and wide, but you'll save yourself a lot of time and gas money working with like-minded people in your own neighborhood. The "I" in this chapter refers to Deanna.

Baby-sitting Co-Ops

DEANNA Most companies give their employees personal days for those pesky tasks that can only be completed during business hours—medical and dental appointments, volunteering at your kids' school. But what do you do when your job is to care for your young children?

If you dare to have more than one child—or like me, Daisy, and all our friends, to have *four* children—you might be applying for social security before you have your next checkup!

Here is the solution—a baby-sitting co-op. A baby-sitting co-op is a group of families who agree to take turns sitting for each other's children in order not to be chained to the house. Instead of paying with money, members pay with the points or tickets they earn from sitting other members' children.

We created our co-op to give everyone a chance to take care of business that can't be accomplished with young children in tow. The first few months of sits were almost exclusively doctors' appointments. My teeth and those of my children are cleaned and checked every six months! I know that's normal for the rest of y'all, but for mothers of three or more children, it's as rare as a monthly pedicure.

Trust me, teachers look at you like you have horns when you ask if you can bring your toddler with you when you come to read in your older kids' classes. I guess we're supposed to *hire* a baby-sitter for that kind of thing, or just be the useless, slacker mom in the class, which was my choice before the co-op. "Sorry. Unless baby-sitting is provided, you can't have me."

That didn't go over very well. So, being in a co-op helped me to get off the slacker-mom list at my children's school.

Some co-ops are for date nights. In our group, I don't think we've had ten sits in four years that were after six PM. We just aren't a date-night crowd. We even have it written into the rules that night sits "cost" more than day sits. But, if date night is your thing, then a co-op will save you money. *Lots* of money. Baby-sitting these days is super expensive!

ADVANTAGES AND DISADVANTAGES
Other advantages to a baby-sitting co-op are having:

- The option to basically handpick your child's best friends.
- A base of girlfriends who know your family well enough to relieve you of children and bring you food when there's a crisis in your life.
- A pool of children from which to borrow when you need your kids spontaneously occupied ("Can I borrow Johnny for a hour to entertain Bobby while I clean?").
- The freedom to go walk mindlessly around a mall with a cup a coffee for an hour, whenever you need it.

Disadvantages of joining a co-op:

- You might end up with a few people you don't like.
- You have to baby-sit for other people and sometimes it's not convenient.
- You have to take a turn being the person everyone calls for sits.
- You have to deal with other moms' picky rules about their kids.
- You have to deal with others not loving your picky rules about your kids.
- Some kids are naughtier than others and require more supervision.

However, for the most part, the benefits significantly outweigh the annoyances. I have never once thought, *I want to quit my co-op*. I have, from time to time, thought, *Gosh, I wish she'd quit our co-op*, but those little personality clashes usually aren't enough to get someone to give up free baby-sitting, right?

GATHERING YOUR GALS

Know thyself. This is the most important step in an enjoyable co-op experience. As you begin to form your co-op, have a clear idea of who you are and what kind of people you get along with, or, more importantly, what kind you don't get along with! Co-ops have personalities, and you want to make sure you join or form one that isn't schizophrenic. Otherwise, your group will spend too much time mediating personality clashes.

You may be a stickler for this or that or only want organics around your kid or any number of niche personality quirks that may make or break your co-op happiness. However, the most important distinction we've found is *how you feel about rules.* Are you a By-the-Book-Mom or an I'm-So-Over-It Mom?:

By-the-Book Moms: These ladies have their rules and everyone abides by them without question.

- They bring their emergency contact cards to every sit.
- They bring the food they intend their children to eat.
- They attend group meetings and play-dates.
- They specify what TV is and is not okay.
- Everyone's insurance is up to date.
- They always give twenty-four hours notice for a change in plans.

I admire these people. They have beautiful co-ops that flourish and last for decades. And I'm not one of them. I couldn't find my emergency card if I had to.

I'm-So-Over-It Moms: We just want to get out of the house and do our errands. We respect co-op rules and therefore always try to ask permission when we want to break them. We're all scatter-brained, and we're okay with that.

- We don't have meetings.
- We rarely have group playdates and even then, half of us won't make it.

- We don't supervise closely. Your kids will get bruises on the play equipment.
- We let the kids run around upstairs and in the backyard and listen for screams of pain. All other arguing screams and tiffs are left up to the children to work out themselves.
- We almost never bring our emergency contact cards.
- We don't care if we sent healthy food and you fed them microwave popcorn and Fruity Pebbles. We like to know that it's a possibility when we drop them off, but a "Hey, I'm tired. Do you care if they eat junk and watch cartoons while you're gone?" is plenty enough courtesy for us.

We do, however, have a few "good moms" in the group that tolerate the rest of us fabulously. They exercise and shower regularly and always look like they've brushed their hair recently. When our kids go to their houses to play, they aren't coming home with scrapes on their knees, mud under their nails, or Cheetos dust around their mouths. They may have colored something beautiful with washable markers, read books, or (if mom was really tired) watched something ridiculously educational on TV for twenty minutes. Our children have a beautiful, enriching time at their homes. They're probably By-the-Book Moms at heart, but they don't seem to mind the rest of us. So regardless of which type you are, if you aren't too solidly committed to one category or the other, like our "good moms," you have options.

I don't have options. I'm a stubborn I'm-So-Over-It Mom. I've realized, over the years, that I have a poor relationship with rules and the people who love them. I think rules exist to protect us from people who would abuse us and are otherwise totally optional. If I've proved I'm a kind, well-intentioned, and dependable, then flexibility is my reward. Thereafter, rules are insulting. Tried-and-true

By-the-Book Moms would kill me. And the few we've had pass through our group were really unhappy with me.

If you're starting a group from scratch, mine your friends and your friends' friends for co-op members. That's the fastest way to keep the group homogeneous and happy. And before you join a co-op, get to know the character of the group!

CHOOSING YOUR RULES

The appendix includes a full sample set of co-op rules and bylaws. You will find many more examples online. These are the important issues we have found in our group along with what works for us:

Set a minimum and maximum number of families: Six is almost too few. Twelve is likely too many.

Establish locational boundaries: How far are you willing to drive? Our boundaries are basically the incorporated parts of our town. However, we know of other co-ops that only encompass a couple of neighborhoods. You must live inside the boundaries to join. For our co-op, we put it to a vote. When one of our near and dear moved outside the boundaries, we made an exception. But a new girl? Not likely.

The appendix includes a sample purpose and administration duties sheet that outlines rules for:

- purpose
- payment requirements
- requirements of new members for entry into Co-op
- exiting the co-op
- president's duties
- voting and administrative changes

AS THE CO-OP AGES

As the co-op ages, or rather, as the children in the co-op age, things change. Knowing this ahead of time can help you see where your co-op is heading and changes you might want to make before people outgrow the group.

Members who have all their children in school start only wanting night sits or may leave the group entirely. In our experience, the relationships remain, and should a member have an extreme emergency (death in the family), these people still rise to the occasion. But for the day-to-day sitting, they are out of the loop.

Members who have most of their children in school and only one is at home generally have trouble remembering to use their minimum points in a month. They may need a reminder if the secretary wants to avoid an end-of-the-month pileup. (We commonly have three or more sits scheduled in the last two days of the month.)

Relatives age and pass away. We've had two significant parental deaths in our co-op. One was sudden and completely unexpected. The other involved six months of hospital stays prior to the passing. We found that we needed to establish a bank of emergency points for people who needed a lot of sits and weren't going to be able to pay them back anytime soon. "Mrs. Pot" pays members to keep kids for people in crisis. The president activates her when she sees fit. Our pot is generally 60 points. But bleeding hearts that we are, we'll just start taking sits under the table for someone in crisis if Mrs. Pot is getting too poor.

Members' families may grow. This isn't the same as a death-in-the-family emergency, but if the co-op has already discussed how to handle new babies, then everyone knows the plan before someone calls for two weeks of sits they can't afford because "Someone-has-to-take-these-kids-for-an-hour-so-I-can-nap!" In our co-op, new mommies may have access to Mrs. Pot, but unless the Blues have set in, the amount of emergency points supplied is about half.

Any co-op that lasts for several years will run into these issues. The more prepared you are, the more you will avoid hurt feelings and awkward situations.

YOU HAD ME AT "FREE BABY-SITTING"
Baby-sitting co-ops free you to impersonate the well-pulled-together mom you gave up on being a long time ago. You, too, can do your hair, put on that adorable white sundress and those impractical high-rise sandals and leave your babies at the home of some shoeless friend in holey black yoga pants with peanut butter in her hair and pretend, for a few hours, you aren't her twin every other day of the week. Get your oil changed. Get your teeth cleaned. Actually *wait* in waiting rooms, not run a miniature day-care center in a place that was designed for silent magazine-reading. (Heck, you've missed a lot of *People* magazine issues that way. How else are you supposed to know who's married to whom?)

Or do something outright fun. Go to lunch. Get your hair colored. Get a pedicure. (But maybe not a manicure. You do have to go back and get the kids eventually and heaven knows, you'll wreck your nails before you even get them buckled in those 700-point safety straight jackets.) I have one friend who took herself out to see a three-hour matinee . . . alone.

Regardless, baby-sitting co-ops are a lifesaver for today's mom. They save money. They save sanity. They forge lifelong friendships.

Meal Swaps

Cooking co-ops are a natural extension of neighborhoods, churches, and friendships. Each one has its own personality and has the potential to build lifelong relationships. You save time, money, and sanity while getting to know your friends better.

BENEFITS
- time savings
- financial savings
- simplified trips to the grocery store
- no more stressing about what to make for dinner
- builds community and a network of people who know and care about you
- creates friendships that last even after families have left the co-op
- one day of cooking equals one week's worth of meals
- you get to try something new—new recipes and new ways to cook old standards (My kids won't touch my lasagna, but *love* Jackie's. Go figure.)
- home-cooked quality meals with next to no effort

BUT NO ONE COULD COOK FOR
MY FAMILY
Pickiness and varied diet requirements are the biggest obstacles for most people. I know entire co-ops that don't even list ingredients and make do with whatever arrives. If you're one of these families, skip to the next section.

If your family is like my family, we can't "make do." But, if your friends are willing to be flexible, even the pickiest tastes can be accommodated. I have medical issues that prohibit me from consuming any milk, starch, or sugar. My son is allergic to soy, almonds, and anything with "pea" in its name, yet with understanding friends and communication, even my family can participate in a co-op. And far from driving my friends crazy, their intimate knowledge of our health issues has brought us closer.

The other members of our group have their own preferences as well. One member hates broccoli, has a meat-and-potatoes husband, and her children turn up their noses at anything with too many ingredients. Another member keeps everything very lean and prefers ground turkey to ground beef. The fourth member's family will eat anything, but she avoids high fructose corn syrup. The fifth member has no preferences or allergies at all.

Like preparing lunches for my children (no grapes for this one, no crusts for that one), it's no trouble remembering everyone's preferences. I toss extra onions in one meal, exclude the broccoli in another, and substitute ground turkey in another. If I were cooking for ten families, it might be a nightmare, but for our little co-op of pickiness, it's not trouble at all. I enjoy preparing things my friends enjoy.

There are two groups of swaps—hot swaps and or freezer swaps.

HOT SWAPS

In these groups, each member prepares meals on a designated day of the week, then delivers the meal to the other members. If she delivers at dinner time, the meal is hot and ready to serve. If she delivers the morning of, it is accompanied by cooking instructions. This option is high on social contact, but not as convenient as some of the other options. You see your girlfriends almost daily and really get to know their lives, but scheduling can get complicated when people aren't home at delivery time.

Make, Freeze, and Bring. In these groups, everyone prepares and freezes many portions of one recipe at home. The group meets at a central location to swap meals. This option is high on convenience, but low on social contact.

To increase social contact, swap meets can be extended into playdates or members can choose to deliver meals to other members' homes.

Make Together and Freeze. In these groups, the members meet at a central location (a church kitchen or a member's large kitchen) and cook meals together. At the end of the session, they box/bag up the food and take it home to freeze. Members can bring their own ingredients or combine shopping and split the bill.

This option is best for people who want to socialize and get to know their friends better. It's also good for people who aren't confident about their cooking skills and want to learn from experienced members.

FREEZER SWAPS

The following swaps are types of freezer swaps. They can be Make, Freeze, and Bring *or* Make Together and Freeze groups:

Once-a-Month Cooking: All food is cooked before freezing. Meals are thawed and reheated at dinner time.

Chop and Swap: All food is assembled in freezer bag kits, *uncooked*, ready to be tossed in a skillet at dinner time. Your diced chicken is in one bag, your olive oil and seasonings in another, your onion and peppers in another, your dry pasta in another. Then all is bagged in one big freezer bag and labeled. This options works really well for varied diets and picky eaters because it's not already cooked together. (It's really hard to get the sauce out of a dish when it's already cooked.) For those unfamiliar with this type of freezer cooking, I highly recommend purchasing a few freezer menus from www.savingdinner.com.

HOW TO ORGANIZE IT

Once you've found four or five like-minded friends or neighbors (similar diets, budgets, food preferences) to join forces with you, it is time to lay down some ground rules.

- *Meeting Location/Schedule:* Will you be a weekly group or monthly? Who's going to organize each swap or will you rotate? Will you meet in person to choose recipes or communicate primarily by e-mail? Will the swap be grab-and-go, party/playdate, or delivered to your door? If you meet, will the swap happen at the same location or will it rotate?

- *Portions and Meal Components:* Choose a standard portion number. Four to six is common. You may want to discuss what that means for your group as people have varying opinions on portion size. If you're cooking five servings, how many pounds of ground beef is that to you? How many chicken breasts, tenders, or meatballs? How many cups of soup/chili?

- *Meal Components:* Decide what a "meal" means. For example, some groups make and freeze complete dinners with side dishes, while others just focus on a main dish.

- *Cost:* Agree on a budget. Do you want to take the total grocery bill and divide it by the number of group members or set a cap amount per meal? If our group agreed on $7 a meal, then I should top out around $35 cooking for the five of us. Feel free to spend more, but $35 is the standard. And if you use something you already have on hand (like garden produce), count that the same as if you were to buy it.

- *Variety:* How will your group ensure that you aren't eating lasagna every night? In some groups, an organizer assigns a food category to each member for that round (soup/chili/stews, breakfast for dinner, Italian, Mexican, American, Asian/Indian). Others may rotate meat categories to help even out expenses (beef, chicken, fish, turkey, etc.)

- *Recipes:* Do you want to meet to discuss recipes, e-mail, or do you want to just wing it? Some groups have members e-mail in only the name of the recipe and a "master coordinator" makes sure there are no repeats. Some groups send in three recipes and members vote on what they want. Others bring their top two or three to the swap and everyone votes when they pick up their bags, which then sets the menu for next month (whatever wasn't chosen will come back). Some groups have a standard list of recipes that all members have agreed will work. Others use a single cookbook and you can cook anything out of that book.

- *Pickiness and Allergies:* Are you meat-and-potatoes people? What is your definition of *healthy*? Is cream-of-chicken soup allowed? Are your kids picky? Allergic? How much is your group going to cater to those traits? For example, I know one mother who hates beef, but it doesn't affect the co-op because she just saves those meals to serve to her family when she won't be home that night. Another mother has picky children, but they are accustomed to making their own P B & Js if they don't like what everyone else is having for dinner. My little group caters to everyone, but that's only four families, so it's not a stress to leave broccoli out of one dish and put extra onions in another.

- *Containers:* Will you use disposable or reusable? If you choose reusable, will you use your own containers (and swap them back the next round) or buy a group set of containers? Container agreements are especially important for freezer groups, as awkward sizes can eat up limited freezer space.

- *Clean Up:* This is especially applicable for the ones who cook together. If you cook together, clean together. No leaving a hostess with a mess!

TIPS AND WARNINGS

- *Start small.* Cooking for ten families your first time is exhausting! You might find you wish to keep the co-op small. My group did.
- Choose people who live within reasonable driving distance of each other.
- Choose a date for the exchange two to four weeks out to allow members to wait for the best price on their ingredients.
- Disposable trays may be the best choice, especially in a Make, Freeze, and Bring group, as members may vary from month to month and you may never get your casserole dish back.
- Be sure to set a budget. Our swap ended mostly because it got too expensive. Some people felt obligated to make their best meals (which is also their priciest).
- Meals should take only two to three hours to prepare and package.
- On the day of the freezer swap, it is helpful to bring a cooler to store your meals for the ride home.
- Label all packages!
- Consider having a main set of recipes like Fix, Freeze, Feast, or Don't Panic Dinner's in the Freezer or the Freezer Menus from www.savingdinner.com. Everyone buys a copy and shares notes if a recipe is too spicy or worked better with substitutions.
- Recipes should be able to be cooked or reheated by broiling or by using a stovetop, crock pot, microwave, or oven. Not everyone has a grill.
- Pick a constant date and place each month to swap meals.
- Bring prepared meals already frozen.
- Cooking instructions should be included in the bags or printed by the coordinator.
- Make it possible for people to bow out for a session or two if they aren't interested.

Life-long meal swapping may not be your thing—it isn't for most people. But everyone should try it for a few months. It sure whacks a lot of time off the cooking schedule! But most importantly, food is an important bond. People sharing the same meal, even though they're not at the same table, share a connection that I can't explain.

The relationships I have from meal swapping are some of the closest, and most rewarding in my life. And in each case, it's not just the moms who know each other. Husbands and children, who in the first few weeks call people by the dishes they cooked, "Is this from pineapple-chicken lady or couscous lady?", slowly move to knowing actual names and can soon carry on whole, relevant conversations with someone whom they would never otherwise have known. Meal swapping creates relationships between families, not just wives.

And the dinners are pretty yummy, too.

Barter and Other Swap Systems

In the previous two sections, we've shown you in grand detail how meals and baby-sitting can be traded. These barter systems build community and friendships. But what if you love to cook every night and you don't need any baby-sitting? That doesn't mean you can't join a group and get to know your friends or neighbors better, because *anything can be traded.*

My tenth-grade social studies teacher made us write in the front of our books, "Trade makes the world go round." But, doesn't love make the world go round? Yes, but I think those of us in the burbs are used to having it all, so why not build caring relationships through trade?

That's what swaps and barter systems do for you. Yes, you get things done, but more importantly, you build community! So let's explore other ways to build interdependence that don't rely on dinners and baby-sitting.

BARTER SYSTEMS

This type of co-op works just like the baby-sitting co-op except points are flexible, rather than standardized, by the hour or number of children.

In our swap, we often don't even use points at all if there's just a one-to-one trade happening. For example, my friend Lisa makes wonderful bread, and I have chickens. I trade her eggs for loaves of homemade bread. The number of eggs I give her varies on how much the chickens are laying at the time, but we work it out between ourselves.

Points become necessary when a one-to-one trade isn't possible. Let's say Lisa wants eggs, but I don't want bread. Maybe I want Margaret to hem some pants for me. And Margaret wants bread from Lisa. In that case, it works more like the baby-sitting co-op.

- Lisa and I agree on a number of points for eggs.
- Margaret and I agree on a number of points for the sewing.
- Lisa and Margaret agree on a number of points for the bread.
- Once the trades happen, we call the monthly secretary and report the points.

Sometimes a member may want something that anyone could do. In that case, the monthly secretary would alert the group by e-mail and see who is up for the job. Maybe someone's mother needs a ride home from the doctor. Maybe someone wants help painting a room.

The most stressful part of a barter group is adjusting to the flexibility of the points. It doesn't work like money in the real world. For example, I made twenty-seven dollars an hour tutoring high-schoolers. Margaret probably couldn't claim twenty-seven dollars an hour for hemming pants. But, more than likely, we'd make that a one-to-one swap. I'd tutor her daughter while she was hemming my pants. She's be measuring and what not, while I'm explaining trigonometry.

In another case, if I need a bunch of dresses done for my daughter and Margaret is really pressed for time these days, her point charges might go up.

Or maybe I have a bumper crop of organic zucchini this season. In the past, I may have charged more points because I had less zucchini and sharing would have cut into what my family would have normally consumed.

But regardless, if you're willing to suffer through the initial awkwardness, bartering with friends can be really fun. In this system, a deal almost never falls through because prices aren't set. You can almost always work it out! But if bartering isn't for you, don't worry. We have even more swap ideas!

PROCRASTINATION SWAPS

We all have those big chores lingering in our minds that we may never get to. Clean the garage. Empty the attic. Get all those pictures in the albums. Put together all those bookshelves you ordered six months ago.

The problem is, without a firm deadline, most of us will never get to it. Enter the Procrastination Swap.

Here's the basic plan:

1. Contact some friends and see if they have any big jobs on their mental to-do lists: attic/garage purging, picture albums, spring cleaning, garage-sale preparation, freezer cooking, what have you.
2. Invite interested friends to a party at your home.
3. Let everyone know the chore, so they can bring any special equipment they have on hand for the job.

4. You provide the basic supplies and refreshments. They provide the elbow grease.
5. During the party, decide who's hosting next month and what you'll all be doing.

PROCRASTINATION SWAP EXAMPLE 1: SCRAPBOOKS

When I was about to have my third child, Daisy threw a scrapbook baby shower for me. But, it had a really unique twist. Rather than preparing new pages for the baby-to-come, I was to bring all of the pictures from the last couple of years that weren't in books and all my friends would catch me up. Guests were invited to donate five dollars to supplies rather than bring baby presents. Of course, many still brought presents anyway, but the supplies were covered and I went home with a big thing checked off my mental to-do list!

That was five years ago. Several of my current friends didn't even live here yet. When I was telling them about it one day at a playdate, we all decided that we should make that idea into a swap group. Each month, or every other month, we'd gather at another person's house and do a bunch of their pages for them. The hostess would provide the pictures (organized, hopefully) and supplies, while guests brought the elbow grease. Pot luck or hostess-provided refreshments were up for negotiation.

PROCRASTINATION SWAP EXAMPLE 2: CHORES

After my good friend's mother passed away, a bunch of gals from her Mothers Of Preschoolers (MOPs) group showed up to clean her house. They didn't just dust and vacuum. They polished the banister, the baseboards, everything they could get their hands on. My friend couldn't remember the last time she had cleaned many of the surfaces and areas her friends tackled.

That's where the idea for the chore swap started. This can be done as a monthly "spring-cleaning" type swap focusing on one member a month, or it can be more like a regular cleaning crew. A spring-cleaning-type party would operate just like the aforementioned swap parties, but for weekly cleaning, the format would change a bit.

1. Gather four like-minded gals.
2. Agree on a certain day of the week as Cleaning Day.
3. Each week, meet at a different member's home* and scrub it up!

*For more regular cleaning, members could do two houses per meeting so each person gets the tubs scrubbed twice a month!

SWAP MEETS

I don't know about you, but garage sales are a lot of work! Plus storing all that useless paraphernalia in my garage until the weather warms up drives me crazy. Worst of all, on the day of the sale, there's no one fun to hang with unless your friends happen to live in your neighborhood and want to join the sale.

Why not save time, money, and your sanity while getting to know your friends better by hosting a Swap Meet?

How to host a Swap Party:

1. First ask around and see if your friends have items they would like to swap. Possibilities include: children's clothes, home décor items, books, baby gear, etc.
2. If your friends are interested, ask them what they will bring and roughly how many items they will bring. For a good swap, everyone needs to bring at least five items each. Ideally, for a home swap meet, you would have no less than three guests and probably no more than ten.
3. Food and beverage is a must for a fun swap, so either plan to serve finger foods or encourage the guests to bring their

own dishes for a potluck-style brunch. Be sure to have plenty of tables to lay out items and inform your guests of two times: the Party Time (eating and chatting) and the Swapping Time (getting down to business).

4. At some swaps, everything is free and there is no limit on how much you can take home, but many folks find that unfair. If Jenny brought a garbage bag full of clothes and Amy brought only a few items, it may be wise to try to give Jenny a shot at the bulk of the items before Amy sweeps away the whole table. One really fun solution to this problem (from www.ehow.com) is to print your own Swap Dollars or use Monopoly money. When guests arrive, arrange their items neatly on a table and give them their money in Swap Dollars. All items should cost the same, one Swap Dollar.

5. Once everyone has arrived, eaten, and Swap Dollars are handed out, the shopping can begin. Be sure to provide plenty of bags and tag them so that partying can continue after the shopping is over.

6. If there are items left over after everyone has spent all of the Swap Dollars they have (or less, if for example, they brought 15 items and only wanted to take home 10), let guests take whatever else they want and donate the rest!

Swap meets are a fun way to get rid of your unwanted items, to get something you want in return, and to get to know your friends better over some yummy treats.

Barter systems, procrastination swaps, swap meets—all great ways to get stuff you need and get rid of stuff you don't want. And they're free!

They're also a great way to bring a smile to your face, even after the party. Hearing someone brag about your bread or go on about those delicious eggs you sent—it makes you feel all happy inside. I have a neighbor who ended up with all the dress shirts from my old life. (The one where I wasn't covered in hoof prints and baby burps.) Every time I see her in one of them, it makes me smile. I can't explain it. It's like running into a friend you haven't seen in ages.

But the most important thing is that barter systems and swaps create interdependence, a little, old-fashioned town in your thriving burb. People aren't just there for companionship, you depend on each other for practical help: You help in my garage now and this spring I'll be helping you stain your shutters.

So, find a few friends and try it out. Pick a system that sounds good to you, get out there, and swap!

11

IT'S HARD TO COMPLAIN WITH A MOUTHFUL OF COOKIES

We live in a community with our family, our neighbors, and our city or town, and when we alter the status quo of that community, we make ripples. For a while, it seemed like Deanna had triggered a tidal wave when she brought a couple of baby goats to live in her backyard.

DAISY Doing things differently isn't always easy. When you're the first person in your town to keep pet goats, or bees, or chickens, or to plant vegetables in your front yard, the reactions can run the gamut from curious looks to pointed comments all the way to legal action or even mischief.

Some believe that as long as one is within the law, one has the right to behave however one sees fit. Technically this is true. In the real world of day-to-day interactions, however, we submit that there is a right way and a wrong way to be right. To put it another way, you can be fully compliant with all laws and regulations, but if you have to battle the members of your own household over your desire to enact change, no one is happy. If you feel like you have to avoid eye contact with your neighbors, that ain't living. And of course, no matter how right you are, being in legal trouble is no fun at all.

In this chapter, we address avoiding conflict within our own families and in the larger world outside our home. We strongly believe in actively pursuing harmony through kindness, understanding, and education. Sort of like guerrilla warfare, but with cookies.

Love Thy Family

DON'T THROW THE WII IN THE GARBAGE, OR HOW TO EASE INTO SIMPLE LIVING

You're sold on simple living. You believe having a vegetable garden, maybe a few hens, or a rainwater barrel is awesome. But maybe not everyone in your household is in on the bandwagon. When you want to try something new, eyes start rolling and heels start digging in. How can you turn the tide in your favor?

While standing on a soapbox and preaching the virtues of eco-friendly living is, admittedly, sort of fun, I wouldn't recommend reading the text messages your teenager is sending her friends while you do it. And you probably wouldn't be setting the example you want your kids to emulate if you follow the "it's-easier-to-ask-forgiveness-than-permission" policy, though the look on your husband's face when the postman hands him a surprise box of honeybees would be priceless. So what's the right way?

Because you're reading this book, you've probably been thinking about back to basics for some time now, trying out new things here and there, getting interested in more and more of the types of activities associated with simple living.

It's unlikely you woke up this morning and decided you were going to go from ordering take-out every night to raising all your food from seed, or from sending all your clothes to a laundry service to hanging your underdrawers on a clothesline.

You know about the incremental way you started to flirt with this lifestyle. Maybe you planted an herb garden in containers on the patio and came to love snorting at the four-dollar-a-sprig plastic clamshells of fresh herbs in the produce section. Maybe commercial skin products gave you a horrible rash and you started looking for homemade alternatives. And they worked! The recipe here is: Try something small. It works. You like it. Success!

That's exactly how it works for everybody, including your family members. If you are the major proponent of change in your home (read: troublemaker) and are looking for a way to drag the rest of your household along with you, it makes sense to help them get there the same way you did. Help them try small steps. Watch the steps work. Watch your family members learn to love it.

Begin with a small project like the container herb garden. Make a fabulous Margherita pizza with fresh basil. Let your family's taste buds do the preaching for you. Take whomever you are trying to convince to see a successfully good-looking suburban garden, and discuss how it would fit into your landscape at home. Involve them in the planning and dreaming about the end results. Let them hear your thought processes so they know your motivation and can share in it.

In addition, don't start (or finish) by stripping everyone of their favorite things. Maybe you're serious about getting your family off the fast-food track, but don't go cold turkey. If Friday pizza night is a sacred tradition, let it be. And no, replacing it with whole wheat and tofu pizza is not the same thing.

Start small, include everyone, and remember: Compromise is not a dirty word.

LOVE THY PARTNER

If there are other adults in your household, they have the potential to be your best resources. The other side of that coin, of course, is they can also make things trickier.

Whether it's your spouse, a parent, a roommate, or your colorful Auntie Mame, you share decision-making rights and responsibilities with this person or persons and, most likely, financial ones as well. You can't make unilateral decisions and expect to maintain the peace.

Unless you're a tyrant, and I trust that isn't the case, you'd probably rather have fun than have a fight. But there's a reason bloodless coups are so rare. They require finesse.

Take the decision of whether or not to put a vegetable garden in place of part of the lawn. You're convinced that it will be well worth it. Your significant other has premonitions of an unsightly, high-maintenance disaster area. You say it will look great and produce lots of delicious, organic vegetables. He or she replies that you said the same thing about that upside-down tomato plant on the patio last summer

and it ended up looking like a horticultural torture victim. It's starting to sound like the argument you had with your six-year-old when he begged for a puppy.

This situation presents several good teaching points.

1. Acknowledge the other person's point of view.
   "I can see how after the tomato disaster you wouldn't have much faith in my ability to keep up with a whole garden."
2. Open up.
   "I have a big hankering to grow something useful and I've been reading a lot about how to get started."
3. Suggest compromise.
   "Can you help me think of a solution that both of us would feel good about?"
4. Express appreciation.
   "I really like your ideas about _____. It makes me feel great when we work together like this."

As your partner responds to you, listen carefully. Then, to make sure you've actually understood what he or she is saying, paraphrase what the person just said and ask whether or not you actually got it. If not, ask for clarification until you feel like you're both on the same page.

Now, I know the above sounds stilted and like something out of a filmstrip from 1955. If you did this exactly like I wrote it, people are going to start looking for the battery pack that powers the very lifelike robotic version of you.

Take the gist of this and put it into your own words, your own style of interacting with your loved one.

Ideally, the other adults in your home are already enthusiastic about any changes you plan to make and are just as full of anticipation of that first homegrown tomato or that box of baby chicks as you are. But in case they're not, try to be understanding. Change can be hard. The unknown can be scary. It can also be a lot of fun, so make it easy for the excitement to spread by taking it one step at a time.

LOVE THY OFFSPRING

Adults are one thing. Children are another. Depending on the age and personalities of your kids, they may absolutely love the changes going on around them, or they can have very definite opinions about what they like and what they don't approve of.

Basically, little kids will love it, but once they're older, peer pressure will begin to impact what they find excruciating and what they think is okay.

My teenaged son at one point said he was okay with chickens but that I was *not* allowed to get goats. He had known someone with a goat once and decided goats weren't where it was at. A line had been drawn in his head somewhere between hens and does. And my wistful sighs over the miniature donkey at the zoo prompted a warning look.

That didn't mean it was up to him whether or not goats (or a donkey!) came along, but it was interesting to watch his thought processes. When the chickens arrived, he found them cool enough to show his friends, one of whom remarked that in China, her native country, chickens are everywhere. Case closed.

Some kids are more susceptible to peer pressure than others, but there are measures you can take to moderate the potential impact of being "different."

Make it neat. The less your backyard looks like Pa Clampett's truck, the better. You don't have to break the bank or buy the Taj Mahal of chicken coops, but a decent-looking set-up will go a long way toward keeping your teens and tweens from never wanting to invite friends over. If you've decided to dedicate a big spot in the backyard to a vegetable garden, build your beds so they are easy to weed and water, and keep them tidy.

Educate. Be clear about the reasons you've decided to do something. If your kids know you're doing your small part to combat inhumane conditions in factory chicken farms, they're more likely to see what you're doing as meaningful on a larger scale. Teach them about "slow food" and "eating local" from a young age, and they'll grow up knowing the importance of being conscious of where their food originates.

Make it their own. Give them responsibility over aspects of your simple living. Teach them how to care for the animals, give them their own garden, help them set up a vermicompost bin. My son asked for a blackberry bush at the nursery one day so I let him take it home and plant it. He watered that thing through a long, hot, droughty summer one year and we've all reaped the benefits for years now.

They may think you're a little wacky. But you're used to it. You're a parent.

Like Thy Neighbor

PROBLEM AVOIDANCE

You don't have to be an aspiring urban home-steader to have problems with your neighbor. Wars have been waged over the smallest issues, and it's no wonder you may worry about the potential for trouble when contemplating starting something a little out of the ordinary. For someone like me who hates conflict and pales at the thought that I might be the topic of discussion at a neighborhood gripe-fest, the first step is preparation. It's possible to be unconventional without breaking any rules. This section will show you how.

Research: Before you take any kind of leap, look long and hard. Read books, conduct online investigations, and talk to people who've done what you would like to do in a similar setting. A traditional farmer can teach you a lot about chickens, and I recommend talking to one, but he or she can't tell you much about what it's like to have chickens in the middle of a subdivision. If you have trouble finding someone in your city, search for a website or an online forum, or blog where you can connect with people who've been there and done that in a neighborhood like yours.

Check your city and neighborhood association's laws, covenants, and bylaws to determine whether or not you're allowed to do what you propose. Search the Municipal Code Library on municode.com. Call the city if the laws are ambiguous. A central information line can direct you to the pertinent department, usually code enforcement, animal services, or economic and commercial development.

Do the math: I hate this part. It involves delayed gratification and impulse control. Gross, right? But you'll be glad you did later.

Your research should have yielded information on exactly what you'll need to do the job right. To use our chicken example, if your city

> *Hedges between keep friendships green.*
> —PROVERB

and neighborhood have given you the green light, you will have decided on how many hens, what kind of coop/run you need, and where to get your birds. Add up how much it will cost, including the cost of the birds (plus shipping), if necessary. Factor in monthly feed, periodic bedding replacement, and equipment like feeders and waterers.

You want to be able to have housing where your birds will be comfortable, safe, and healthy—a place that will be easy to keep clean, and of which you can be proud.

The same is true for gardening. Before you till up a big section of your backyard, know the real cost of getting started. If you want raised beds, add in the cost of the materials, soil (not dirt cheap, by the way), soil amendments, etc., as well as equipment. If you know you're going to want irrigation and a row cover set-up in order to make it work for you, get out your calculator.

If it's starting to look like something you should wait on and save up for in order to do properly, then wait.

Experiment: Try it out first. If you've never gardened before, you'll learn so much in one year with a small trial garden. And believe it or not, some areas have a service that will rent you chickens, and the coop, too, to see if it's a good fit for you. If you decide to keep the chickens, you can transform from renter to owner. You may also be able to do this informally if you know someone who would be willing to let you "chicken sit" or "goat sit" a couple of their girls for a trial period.

You can see if the noise level is appropriate for your neighborhood, whether or not you enjoy the experience, and get a good idea of what problems you will have to sort out before you make the arrangement a permanent one.

Communicate: In order to have a good relationship with your neighbors, you first need to have a relationship. Participate in neighborhood association social events. Organize a block party. If you are new to your neighborhood, take the initiative and introduce yourself to your neighbors. Sure, it's technically their move, but you may grow old waiting for them to make it. Welcome new neighbors with something from our new neighbor basket in this chapter.

Educate: One of the main reasons people oppose chickens or goats or honeybees or anything different is the fear of the unknown. Misinformation, myths, and misunderstandings persist in the absence of knowledge. People fear your critters will bring a scourge of disease or danger or noise or odor, bring down property values, and turn the neighborhood into a petting zoo, emphasis on *zoo*. If you have a line of communication with your neighbors, you'll have a means to get the truth out and help calm fears. Copy our Good Neighbor Handouts for goats, chickens and bees (found in the appendix and online at www.littlehouseinthesuburbs.com) to help you get the word out. By the time you've established your flock or your hives or your goats, you'll

> *Sometimes a neighbor whom we have disliked a lifetime for his arrogance and conceit lets fall a single commonplace remark that shows us another side, another man, really; a man uncertain, and puzzled, and in the dark like ourselves.*
>
> —WILLA CATHER

be quite the expert yourself and can answer the questions of curious or fearful neighbors.

PROBLEM RESOLUTION

Being in conflict with your neighbors is a horrible feeling. You may feel threatened, frustrated, just plain angry, or all of the above. Unlike a run-in with a stranger on the subway or a bad experience with a rude salesperson, which are awful enough, you can't easily leave your home. You have roots there. Your family members have roots there. You've invested a lot of money and physical and emotional energy on that piece of property. It's where you're supposed to feel safe and comfortable. Problems with neighbors can eat away at that feeling of security and leave you hypervigilant and anxious.

When all your preparation and planning isn't enough and you find yourself in a struggle with a neighbor, there is hope. There are many tried-and-true approaches to problem resolution. While every situation is different, these general guidelines can improve the chances of success in almost every conflict.

1. *Examine yourself.* This may be the hardest step of all, but there are always at least two people involved in every dispute you have. One of them is you. Not only is it easier to change yourself than it is to get someone else to change, it is conceivable that you're not perfect. A remote possibility, certainly, but one worth entertaining for a good long while. If you find this step particularly difficult, you might try asking a friend to take a look at the situation and ask her to play devil's advocate. Ask her to try and locate some way you may be contributing to the problem and some way you may be able to contribute to the solution. Give her temporary license to be critical. You can rescind it after this exercise.

2. *Ask yourself which is most important: To solve the problem or to win.* Win, of course!

Ideas for a New-Neighbor Basket

- Breakfast Kit: Coffee, tea, homemade or store-bought breakfast bars, fresh fruit.
- Picture-Hanging Kit: Assorted picture-hanging hardware, inexpensive tape measure and hammer, pencil, kneaded eraser.
- Local Emergency Telephone Number List: Include police/fire non-emergency numbers, city hall, electric, gas, waste management, poison control, plus important neighborhood contacts such as the neighborhood association's web address.
- Gifts From the Garden: An assortment of what's growing if it's growing season or a jar of last year's bounty for a winter neighbor, perhaps a few fresh eggs or honey from your supply or a local farmer.
- For the Kids: Dollar-store activity books or puzzles, crayons, bubble solution, sidewalk chalk, jump rope.
- Cookies: Line a basket or cookie tin with a pretty dishcloth, fill with cookies, and tuck in a welcome note along with your phone number.

Vindication at all costs! That's often the perspective we take at first. But remember, it's 110 percent likely that your opponent feels exactly the same way. Something's got to give if the problem is ever going to get better. Because you're reading this, chances are you're the one with the highest probability of being willing to take one for the team. If you were successful with the first step, you've already started thinking about your own contribution to the problem, and this step should be easier. Think about how great it will be to be at peace again once this is resolved, and be determined to do whatever it takes to sort things out, even if you fear you'll have to bite your tongue clear off to keep from saying what you really think.

3. *Put yourself in the other person's shoes.* And house. And yard. Imagine for a moment if all or part of what the neighbor is saying is true. Consider the very strong possibility that there is something going on in that person's life that you know nothing about which is prompting his or her possibly exaggerated response to the situation: an illness, a trauma, a history that left scars. Try to empathize.

4. *Keep it to yourself.* As if I hadn't already made things very unfun, now I'm asking you to remove the last vestige of satisfaction you might have ever gotten out of the situation. With the exception of perhaps your spouse or best friend, don't air your grievances to others, especially neighbors or anyone who is acquainted with the neighbor in question. It can be very vindicating to find a sympathetic ear, but resist the temptation. You may not be able to control what the other party is saying about you, but you can control yourself. If you set an example of keeping your own counsel, people are more likely to return the favor.

5. *Consult with the person face to face.* Letters, e-mails, notes, etc. are impersonal, affronting, and can be misinterpreted. There's a reason the word "nasty" is so often combined with the word "note." It's hard to write a smile or a kind tone into a written message. Letters can also be used against you in a legal proceeding should the person allege harassment. Also, never send an anonymous note, even if it isn't a harshly worded one. Anonymity, by its nature, is intimidating, frightening, and

Tips for a Block Party

1. Organize a committee of interested homeowners to plan the event. It will help divide the work and provide an opportunity for cooperation and communication among neighbors.
2. Call the city to see if your town has a neighborhood coordinator or neighborhood resources office, a department whose job is to help neighborhoods organize. They can provide suggestions and resources for your event.
3. You may need a special-event permit. Check with your city to determine the proper procedures.
4. Invite the local police to stop by and join you. They will welcome the opportunity to establish relationships with the neighbors on their patrol.
5. If you have music, be mindful of your city's noise ordinance. Most refer to "continued and unreasonable noise."
6. A "potluck" format where attendees are asked to contribute a dish and their own lawn chairs will make the event more affordable and foster a sense of ownership of the party among neighbors.
7. Plan for cleanup by providing plenty of trash and recycle bins. Using biodegradable and recyclable plates, cups, and utensils will help set an eco-responsible tone for your gathering.

chicken. If you don't have the confidence to attach your name to it, you shouldn't say it in the first place.

6. *Listen.* It has been said that one of the most basic human needs is the need to be understood. Really hear what the other person is saying. Don't interrupt. Use pauses in the conversation to reiterate in your own words what the person is telling you, as an opportunity to communicate that you really understand his or her perspective, not as an opportunity to slash back; i.e. "So you're saying I'm a jerk?"

7. *Use I-messages.* If you've ever been to counseling, you know the drill. When discussing the problem, describe the issue in terms of how it impacts you. Refrain from making statements about the other person's behavior. "I feel X," rather than, "You're being too sensitive about Y." Reveal to the other person what you have learned about your contribution to the problem.

8. *Don't get historical.* Resist the urge to respond to your neighbor's complaint by bringing out the laundry list of everything he or she has done/is doing that you dislike. Hauling out your own complaints will only move the discussion backwards.

9. *Offer to compromise.* Suggest a compromise based on what you have determined might be fair. If you receive a counter-offer from your neighbor, consider it. Ask for time to think about it, if necessary.

10. *Suggest mediation.* If you can't come to your own agreement, this is the next best step. This can be a mutually agreed upon, neutral third party or a trained mediator. Some cities offer community mediation programs as a part of their government. Contact your local town hall to see if they have such a program or if they can refer you to a local nonprofit or reduced-rate organization with professional and trained volunteers who can help you resolve your conflict. The National Association for Community Mediation (www.nafcm.org) website offers conflict resolution tips and can help you locate a program in your area.

As exhausting and bitter as these experiences can be, try to see them as opportunities to learn something new about yourself. Conflict is often a necessary component of change. Make it a change for the better.

"JUST RIGHT" CHOCOLATE CHIP COOKIES

a.k.a. Drop the Lawsuit Cookies.

Crispy on the outside, chewy on the inside.

Yield: 2 dozen cookies

Ingredients

- 2 cups all-purpose flour
- ½ teaspoon baking soda
- ¼ teaspoon salt
- ¾ cup (1½ sticks) butter, softened
- ¾ cup brown sugar, packed
- ½ cup white sugar
- 2 teaspoon vanilla
- 1 egg plus one egg yolk
- 1 cup chocolate chips (or a mixture of chocolate, peanut butter, or butterscotch chips)
- 1 cup chopped walnuts or pecans, lightly toasted

Directions

1. Preheat oven to 325°F (163°C).
2. In a medium bowl, combine flour, baking soda and salt.
3. Cream together butter and sugars. Add egg and yolk and vanilla and stir to blend thoroughly.
4. Add the wet ingredients to the dry, stirring until combined. Stir in the chocolate chips.
5. Spoon by heaping tablespoonfuls onto lightly greased baking sheet leaving room to spread.
6. Bake at 325°F (163°C) for 12–15 minutes, or until the edges are beginning to brown and the centers are set and no longer glossy.
7. Allow to cool briefly and remove from baking sheet to cool on a wire rack.

Cooperate With Thy Municipality

CHANGING CITY CODES

If you've researched your city's ordinances and find they prohibit something you hope to do on your property, there are actions you can take to change the ordinances. Citizens have overturned and continue to overturn bans on chickens, goats, clotheslines, rainwater barrels, and other homesteading behaviors. The tide seems to be turning, albeit slowly, in favor of actions that help to reduce our carbon footprint. Here's a quick outline of how to initiate change in restrictive ordinances:

1. *Look it up.* Identify the ordinance you want to change. Check www.municode.com or your city's website for this information.

2. *Draft it.* Craft a preliminary proposal for an amendment to that ordinance. You can check online for ordinances in other cities that resemble what you want for your own city. Document these and be prepared to present the reasons you feel your town and its citizens would be well served by making the changes you seek.

3. *Find a friend.* Contact your city administrator or one of the city aldermen concerning the ordinance. You can initiate contact by mail, phone, or e-mail, depending on your and the recipient's preferred means of communication. I suggest you give the official's administrative assistant a call, tell the assistant your intentions, and ask for suggestions concerning the best way for you to communicate this information to his or her boss.

4. *On your way.* Once you find someone in the city government who agrees to present the amendment at the appropriate commission meeting, he or she will draft an amendment and call the city clerk's office and request an ordinance number.

5. *Cross your fingers.* The amendment typically requires three hearings, one of which must be at a public hearing that takes place fourteen days or more after notice of the amendment has been published in a local newspaper. Needless to say, you should be present at these hearings.

6. *Stick with it.* During this process, an amendment often undergoes challenges, and compromises can be suggested. Don't give up. Work with the official proposing the amendment to keep it alive and friendly to your position.

7. *Crack open the champagne.* After an amendment passes the committee during the required number of readings, it becomes official.

WORTH CONSIDERING

Besides finding a city official to take up your cause with you, many cities have a brief period of time during their meetings in which city residents may say their piece. This part of the meeting may be called an "open forum," a "public comment period," or a "citizen presentations." It's an opportunity for the layperson to present concerns and thoughts regarding the city.

You can often find guidelines for how to make presentations during this segment of a meeting on your city's website. It can be a chance for you to bring up your proposed ordinance amendment, and is a good venue in which to present the results of any petitions you have circulated in support of your cause. This may bring to light board members/city officers who support you.

At all times, do your best to remain helpful, cordial, and professional. See yourself as an ambassador for homesteading behavior within your city. It will serve you and others well the next time you have an issue of any sort with your municipal government. And of course,

The Media Can Be Your Friend

Deanna and I have a love-hate relationship with the media. She loves it, I hate it. It isn't personal, some of my favorite people are newspeople, but I turn into the picture of fear at the mere thought of being interviewed. Deanna whips on some lip gloss, checks her bangs in the rear-view mirror, and she's ready to take on Barbara Walters. If you think you're more like Deanna than I am, sometimes a little courtship of the media can be a smart move.

But before you go on camera or sit down with the gal or guy from the paper, do your homework. Try to discover the spin or angle the reporter is aiming for. Better yet, help her along by providing her with the type of information that both makes your cause seem sensible and makes for good copy. Practice some pithy phrases that make great sound bites.

Reporters spend a lot of time trying to talk to people who have no interest in talking to them. A little kindness goes a long way. Deanna was her charming self and sent her reporters home with fresh eggs from her hens. They were enchanted, and it showed in their coverage of her.

Remember, if you are in a skirmish with your city, the goal is to get what you want, not to humiliate the opposition. Focus on the benefits your proposed ordinance amendment will bring to the community, and don't vent your unkind thoughts. If you say something juicy, it *will* end up on camera or in print. Speak in positive terms about your officials and they are less likely to dig in their heels.

it's more effective, too. Flies, honey, you know the old saw. It's true.

CLOSING THE BARN DOOR AFTER THE HORSE HAS BOLTED, OR WHAT TO DO IF YOU GET BUSTED

Not that you ever would . . . but, theoretically, what do you do if you exercised a bit of civil disobedience by being in quiet violation of a city ordinance, and then got caught? Busted. Bagged. Pinched. Riding dirty with forty pounds of lay pellets in the trunk?

Maybe it's not that dramatic, but a letter arrives in the mail or an animal-control or zoning officer knocks at the door.

Sometimes you break the rules unknowingly. You carefully read the ordinance concerning having chickens or goats or whatever it is and interpreted it as allowable, but your city may have a different interpretation of the codes. This is what happened to Deanna with her goats.

She read in her city's code: "It shall be unlawful for any person to keep or maintain one or more horses, mules, cows, or hogs in any residential section of the Town within 300 feet of any residence and without the consent of the owner or occupant of such residence and permission from the Board" and saw no mention of goats.

The title of the ordinance reads: Requirements for Keeping Horses, Cows, Hogs, and the Like. Deanna thought about horses, cows, hogs and imagined her little mini-goats next to them and did not think them "like" at all. Horses, cows, and hogs are full-sized, barn-and-pasture-only, great big, honking creatures that can smother you if they sit on you. She could carry two full-grown mini-goats at one time. They liked to sit in her lap. They could wander around her kitchen without incident. Quite unlike cows, horses, and hogs.

She felt quite within the law when she got Lily and Sylvie. Like the law-abiding citizen she is; however, she got to thinking and decided to call city hall and double-check.

What happened next was the beginning of a confusing back-and-forth between Deanna and her town. She got a crash course in local politics, bureaucracy, red tape, and even television, radio, and news media.

Animal control was fervently against goats in the burbs and threatened to make her remove them from her property. The city interpreted the reference to "and the like" in the ordinance title to mean any animal associated with farming, including goats, despite the practical differences between the animals listed in the ordinance and miniature goats. Deanna countered with the fact that, legally, titles to ordinances are not included within the ordinance, and the ordinance itself made no mention of goats, nor did it refer to "the like" of horses, cows, and hogs. Only horses, cows, and hogs. Period.

Confused yet? It doesn't get much better. It seemed like the board had made up its mind and wasn't willing to give a quarter.

Problem was, neither was Deanna. Somehow, the media got wind of the goat affair. It didn't take much to get a crew around to Deanna's backyard once they had a whiff of a David versus Goliath story complete with cute, fuzzy animals and a progressive aesthetic.

Before the media storm, described by a radio personality as a "buzz saw of controversy," was over, Deanna's goats had well over their fifteen minutes of fame on two local TV networks, in the "big" local paper, and on morning radio shows.

Perhaps, partly as a result of this exposure, the city offered to allow Deanna to keep her goats as long as she got signatures from all her neighbors within three hundred feet as well as permission from the board of aldermen—permission and signatures she was not, in a strictly legal sense, compelled to have. But, she did it anyway.

I would say giving her this option was a way for the city to save face if I thought they were truly aware of how squarely on the wrong side of the law they were, but I don't believe they ever really grasped the situation.

During the whole process, Deanna never got the feeling they were listening. They had their conception of the law and weren't going to be dissuaded by anything as troublesome as facts.

If she wasn't already so exhausted by the process, she would have gone on to try and have the law changed, but for the time being, just having her permission was good enough. None of the neighbors objected, and the majority of the aldermen voted to give her the variance.

So her goats are legal, finally. Getting a personal permit may be one way for an individual to keep goats in a town that prohibits them, and it's an option worth looking into. It may be a particularly good way for people with family members who have an intolerance to cow's milk to obtain special permission to keep milking goats.

In other cases, when you've been caught in violation of an ordinance, the best response is to comply with the ordinance, then work diligently to have the ordinance amended, and then start over once you're in the clear. It can be a tiresome process, but it will help others who follow.

Do your best to remain cordial and respectful despite the distress caused by being subject to ordinances that run contrary to common sense. If you cultivate a reputation as someone who is reasonable and easy to work with, when it comes time for you to engage the city to have a law changed, it will make the process much smoother.

Deanna would say, learn from her mistakes and just don't ask in the first place. But you didn't hear that from us.

HOMEOWNERS' ASSOCIATIONS (HOAS)

You can fight 'em, but it's better for everyone if you join 'em and work for progress in your neighborhood. Public opinion on the national and international level is getting on board with the reality that sustainability is the best response to ecological and economic straits.

If your HOA stands in the way of progressive, sustainable-friendly practices, you may have to jump-start the engine of change.

- Find like-minded members in your neighborhood and form an alliance to assess your HOA's covenants in terms of restrictions on sustainable behaviors. Face it, you're already the neighborhood outlier— you might as well make it official. You'll probably discover you aren't as alone as you thought.
- Propose ways to "green up" your HOA's bylaws. Consider readdressing restrictions on backyard chickens, honeybees, rainwater collection, solar collection, front-yard edible gardening, clotheslines, and compost bins. Discuss the use and maintenance of common areas in terms of community gardening and energy and water usage, as well as landscaping chemical use. Are there changes that can be made to encourage bicycling and walking?
- Set up a website or blog to encourage neighborhood involvement and brainstorming.

APPENDIX

The appendix includes a variety of planting charts and sample garden layouts to help you decide what to grow and when to plant. You'll also find resource lists and good neighbor handouts to help you with keeping chickens, goats, and bees.

Spring Planting Chart

To use this chart, you'll need a calendar and the average dates of the last frost of the winter/spring.

You can find the average frost dates for your area in three ways:

1. Check seed or gardening websites, such as www.victoryseeds.com/frost.
2. Ask a gardener buddy, or find a local master gardener through your county extension office.
3. Ask at the locally owned nursery.

Just plug in your dates and the chart below will tell you what weeks to plant everything your heart desires. It takes about five minutes, and then you never have to think about it again!

FROST-FREE	DATE	SOW OUTDOORS	TRANSPLANT
8 weeks before		spinach	
7 weeks before		spinach	
6 weeks before		kale, kohlrabi, mustard greens, onion sets, potatoes, radishes, turnips, spinach, collards, leeks	
5 weeks before		beets, peas, kale, kohlrabi, mustard greens, onion sets, potatoes, radishes, turnips, spinach, collards, leeks	broccoli, cabbage, cauliflower, leeks, onion, parsley
4 weeks before		chard, beets, peas, kale, kohlrabi, mustard greens, onion sets, potatoes, radishes, turnips, spinach, collards, leeks, lettuces	Chinese cabbage, collards, broccoli, cabbage, cauliflower, leeks, onion, parsely
3 weeks before		carrots, chard, beets, peas, kale, kohlrabi, mustard greens, onion sets, potatoes, radishes, turnips, spinach, collards, lettuces	brussels sprouts, collards, Chinese cabbage, broccoli, cabbage, cauliflower
2 weeks before		carrots, chard, beets, radishes, lettuces	brussels sprouts, leaf lettuce
1 week before		carrots, chard, beets, radishes, lettuces	leaf lettuce

FROST-FREE	DATE	SOW OUTDOORS	TRANSPLANT
Frost-Free!		bush beans, lima beans, pole beans, corn, cucumbers, pumpkins, summer and winter squash, melons, carrots, chard, beets, radishes, okra, lettuces	eggplant, okra, tomatoes, peppers, leaf lettuce, sweet potatoes, melons, pumpkins, summer and winter squash
1 week after		bush beans, lima beans, pole beans, corn, cucumbers, pumpkins, summer and winter squash, melons, carrots, chard, beets, radishes, okra	eggplant, okra, tomatoes, peppers, leaf lettuce, sweet potatoes, melons, pumpkins, summer and winter squash
2 weeks after		bush beans, lima beans, pole beans, corn, cucumbers, pumpkins, summer and winter squash, melons, carrots, chard, beets, radishes, okra	eggplant, okra, tomatoes, peppers, leaf lettuce, sweet potatoes, melons, pumpkins, summer and winter squash
3 weeks after		bush beans, lima beans, corn, cucumbers, summer squash, carrots, chard	leaf lettuce, sweet potatoes, melons, pumpkins, summer and winter squash
4 weeks after		bush beans, lima beans, corn, cucumbers, summer squash, carrots, chard	leaf lettuce, sweet potatoes
5 weeks after		bush beans, lima beans, corn, summer squash, carrots, chard	leaf lettuce, sweet potatoes
6 weeks after		bush beans, leaf lettuce, lima beans, carrots	
7 weeks after		bush beans, leaf lettuce, lima beans, carrots	
8 weeks after		bush beans, leaf lettuce, lima beans, carrots	
9 weeks after		bush beans, leaf lettuce, lima beans, carrots	

Fall Planting Chart

To use this chart, you'll need a calendar and the average dates of the first frost of the fall/winter.

You can find the average frost dates for your area in three ways:

1. Check seed or gardening websites, such as www.victoryseeds.com/frost.
2. Ask a gardener buddy, or find a local master gardener through your county extension office.
3. Ask at the locally owned nursery.

Just plug in your dates and the chart below will tell you what weeks to plant everything your heart desires. It takes about five minutes, and then you never have to think about it again!

FIRST FROST	DATE	SOW OUTDOORS	TRANSPLANT
17 weeks before		bush beans, lima beans	
16 weeks before		bush beans, lima beans, collard, Chinese cabbage	collards, Chinese cabbage
15 weeks before		bush beans, lima beans, collards, Chinese cabbage	collards, Chinese cabbage
14 weeks before		bush beans, lima beans, cabbage, collards, Chinese cabbage	cabbage, collards, Chinese cabbage
13 weeks before		bush beans, lima beans, cabbage, collards, cauliflower	cabbage, collards, cauliflower
12 weeks before		kale, kohlrabi, mustard greens, peas, bush beans, lima beans, cabbage, collards, cauliflower	cabbage, collards, cauliflower
11 weeks before		kale, kohlrabi, mustard greens, peas, cabbage, collards, cauliflower	cabbage, cauliflower, collards
10 weeks before		beets, carrots, turnips, broccoli, kale, kohlrabi, mustard greens, peas, collards, cauliflower	broccoli, cauliflower, collards
9 weeks before		chard, beets, carrots, turnips, broccoli, kale, kohlrabi, mustard greens, cauliflower, head lettuce	broccoli, cauliflower, head lettuce

FIRST FROST	DATE	SOW OUTDOORS	TRANSPLANT
8 weeks before		radishes, chard, beets, carrots, turnips, broccoli, kale, kohlrabi, mustard greens, cauliflower, leaf lettuce, head lettuce	broccoli, cauliflower, head lettuce
7 weeks before		spinach, radishes, chard, beets, carrots, turnips, broccoli, kale, kohlrabi, mustard greens, cauliflower, leaf lettuce, head lettuce	leaf lettuce, head lettuce
6 weeks before		spinach, radishes, chard, beets, carrots, turnips, broccoli, kale, kohlrabi, mustard greens, cauliflower, leaf lettuce, head lettuce	leaf lettuce
5 weeks before		spinach, radishes, chard, kale, kohlrabi, mustard greens, leaf lettuce	leaf lettuce
4 weeks before		spinach, radishes, kale, kohlrabi, mustard greens, leaf lettuce	leaf lettuce
3 weeks before		spinach, radishes	
2 weeks before		radishes	
1 week before			
Frost!			

Companion Planting

According to Daisy, companion planting is just like planning the seating at your wedding reception.

1. Too many members of the same family shouldn't be seated together.
2. Hatfields and McCoys must be kept across the room from each other.
3. Sometimes somebody dated someone else's sister and it ended badly, so those individuals need to be kept apart.

IDENTIFYING PLANT FAMILIES

Members of the same family have the same strengths and weaknesses (remember all that cuckoo and hemophilia running around the royal families?) In the plant world that means that members of the same family attract the same pests and diseases. That, or they just plain hate each other and continually fight.

So, try not to "seat" any two members of the same family together.

Unfamiliar with plant families? Here's a list to help:

Bean Family: beans, peas, peanuts

Carrot Family: carrots, dill, fennel, celery, parsley, cilantro

Cabbage Family: cabbage, brussels, bok choy, cauliflower, kohlrabi, broccoli, collards, turnips, radishes, kale

Corn Family: corn, wheat, oats, rice, other cereal grains

Daisy Family: lettuce, artichokes, sunflowers, daisies, asters, marigolds

Goosefoot Family: spinach, beets, chard

Gourd Family: squashes, melons, cucumbers

Lily Family: asparagus, onion, shallots, garlic, chives

Mint Family: oregano, mint, basil, rosemary, sage, lavender, thyme

Nightshades Family: tomato, petunias, potatoes, peppers

Rose Family: roses, strawberries, blackberries, apples, pears, raspberries

Some plant families just hate each other. It goes way back and they each have a different story for how it all got started, but the point is put 'em together and it's war.

PLANT FAMILIES THAT FEUD

Here's a quick and dirty lowdown on your six major garden feuds (keep them separate):

1. *Tomato Nightshades versus Potato Nightshades:* Tomatoes and peppers hate potatoes and eggplant.
2. *Bean Family versus Lilies and Tomato Nightshades:* No peas with peppers and tomatoes. No peanuts with the onions or garlic.
3. *Cabbage Family verses Nightshades and Roses:* No broccoli with strawberries or potatoes.
4. *Carrot Family verses Potato Nightshades:* No dill with the eggplant.
5. *Corn verses Tomato Nightshades:* Corn hates tomatoes and peppers.
6. *Gourd Family verses Mint and Nightshades:* No seating squash with your peppers and basil.

THE KEEP-SEPARATE LIST

Some plants just don't get along with others. Here are the "trouble-makers."

Fennel: Only plays well with dill. It kills the spirit of anyone else it meets. Keep him isolated from all your other plants.

Parsley: Not nearly as bad as fennel, but still troublesome. Be careful and check your chart (pages 228–229).

Celery and Dill: Pretty much everyone in the Carrot Family, except the carrots, is a total psycho, so again just check the chart.

Pole Beans: I think this one is just a glutton for punishment. He doesn't hurt anyone else, but sunflowers, beets, cabbages, and eggplants do a real number on him, but he just holds on tight regardless. Keep him far away—save him from himself.

PLAYS WELL WITH OTHERS
Just as there are plants that need to be isolated, there are some plants that get along with almost everyone.

Beans and Gourds: Play well with other members of their own families.

Lettuce and Marigolds: Like everyone and everyone likes a goosefoot.

The chart on the next page illustrates which plant families get along with each other and which plant families don't do well together. The smiley-face icon (☺) indicates it is okay to plant these families together. If there are exceptions, they are noted.

Companion Planting Chart

FAMILIES	BEAN	CABBAGE	CARROT	CORN	DAISY	GOOSE	GOURD
BEAN	☺	☺	☺ dill, celery carrot	☺	☺ marigold, lettuce	☺ chard, beets, spinach	☺ cukes, melons
CABBAGE	☺	NO	☺ dill		☺ marigold, lettuce	☺	☺ cuke
CARROT	☺	☺	NO		☺ lettuce		
CORN	☺		yes parsley and dill no celery	N/A	☺ sunflower, lettuce	☺ spinach	☺
LETTUCE	☺	☺	yes dill and carrots, no parsley or celery		☺ sunflower	☺	☺
GOOSE FOOT	☺	☺			☺ lettuce		
GOURD	☺	only radish	☺ dill	☺	☺ sunflower, lettuce, marigold	☺	☺
LILY	NO	☺	yes carrots, celery and dill, no parsley		☺ marigold, lettuce	☺	cuke
POTATO NIGHTSHADE	☺	NO	yes carrots, no dill, parsnips celery	☺	yes marigolds, no sunflowers	☺	NO
TOMATO NIGHTSHADE	NO	NO	yes carrots and celery, no dill	NO	☺ lettuce marigold		☺ cuke
ROSE	☺	NO			☺ lettuce	☺ spinach	

LILY	MINT	POTATO NIGHTSHADE	TOMATO NIGHTSHADE	ROSE	GERANIUM	EXCEPTIONS
NO	☺ rosemary	☺ eggplant, potato	NO	☺ strawberry		pole beans hate sunflowers, beets, eggplant, and cabbage family
☺ alliums	☺	NO	NO	NO	☺	see BEAN exception, radish and cauliflower hate nasturtiums
☺ alliums	☺ sage, mint, rosemary	NO	☺ *may stunt			celery hates corn, daisy, and potato nightshade families
		☺ potato	NO		☺ geraniums	
☺	☺			☺		
☺ alliums	☺ sage, mint	☺ eggplant		☺ strawberry		see BEAN exception
☺	NO	NO	NO		☺ nasturtium	
NO	☺ basil	☺	☺ tomato	☺	☺ nasturtium	asparagus hates potato nightshades, alliums hate parsley
☺ no asparagus	☺	☺	NO			
☺	☺	NO	☺		☺ nasturtium geranium	
☺ onion	☺ oregano thyme	☺ potato			☺ nasturtium geranium	

Fall Garden Plan for Raised Beds

When using this plan, all of your plants should be in seven to ten weeks before the first frost of the fall (use the fall planting chart to determine this date for your area).

I live in an area with a long growing season so I can put this bed in when I clear my summer beds after they've finished producing. If you live in an area with a short season, you may need a separate bed dedicated to fall plants.

This plan can also be used as an early spring garden plan as well, minus the garlic.

Note: If you don't care for broccoli, you can substitute one cabbage or one cauliflower in each broccoli spot. If you don't care for kale, you can substitute four collards beets. If you don't care for beets, you can substitute three chard.

You will need:

2 tomato stakes (any kind)
nylon string
12 flat head nails
2 broccoli plants (see above note)
2 heads of garlic
1 package pea seeds
1 package spinach seeds
1 package beet seeds (see above note)
1 package leaf lettuce seeds
1 package head lettuce seeds
1 package kale seeds (see above note)
1 chrysanthemum plant

1. Build a raised bed, place it in your yard, and fill it with soil following the instructions in chapter 2.
2. Smooth the surface of the soil and, using your finger (or what have you), divide the raised bed in half both ways and do it again on each side to get sixteen squares.
3. Figure out which direction is North. You'll be planting all your tall produce on that side. Use your fingers or a dibble to poke holes ½" (13mm) deep in the pattern shown in the chart.
4. Break apart your garlic and insert one fat clove in each of the nine holes.
5. Open your peas. Pinch out four seeds. Put two in the first hole, and two in the second and cover. Put two seeds in each hole in your garden corresponding to the names on the grid.
6. Put your broccoli plants in the dead center of the corresponding square on the chart.
7. Drive your tomato stakes in deep behind your peas squares. Put a nail in the top of the stake and run string from this nail to nails in the side of your box so it spreads out evenly. The peas may take some coaxing at first, but those bad boys are dying to climb that string.
8. Water every other day for a week, and as needed after that.

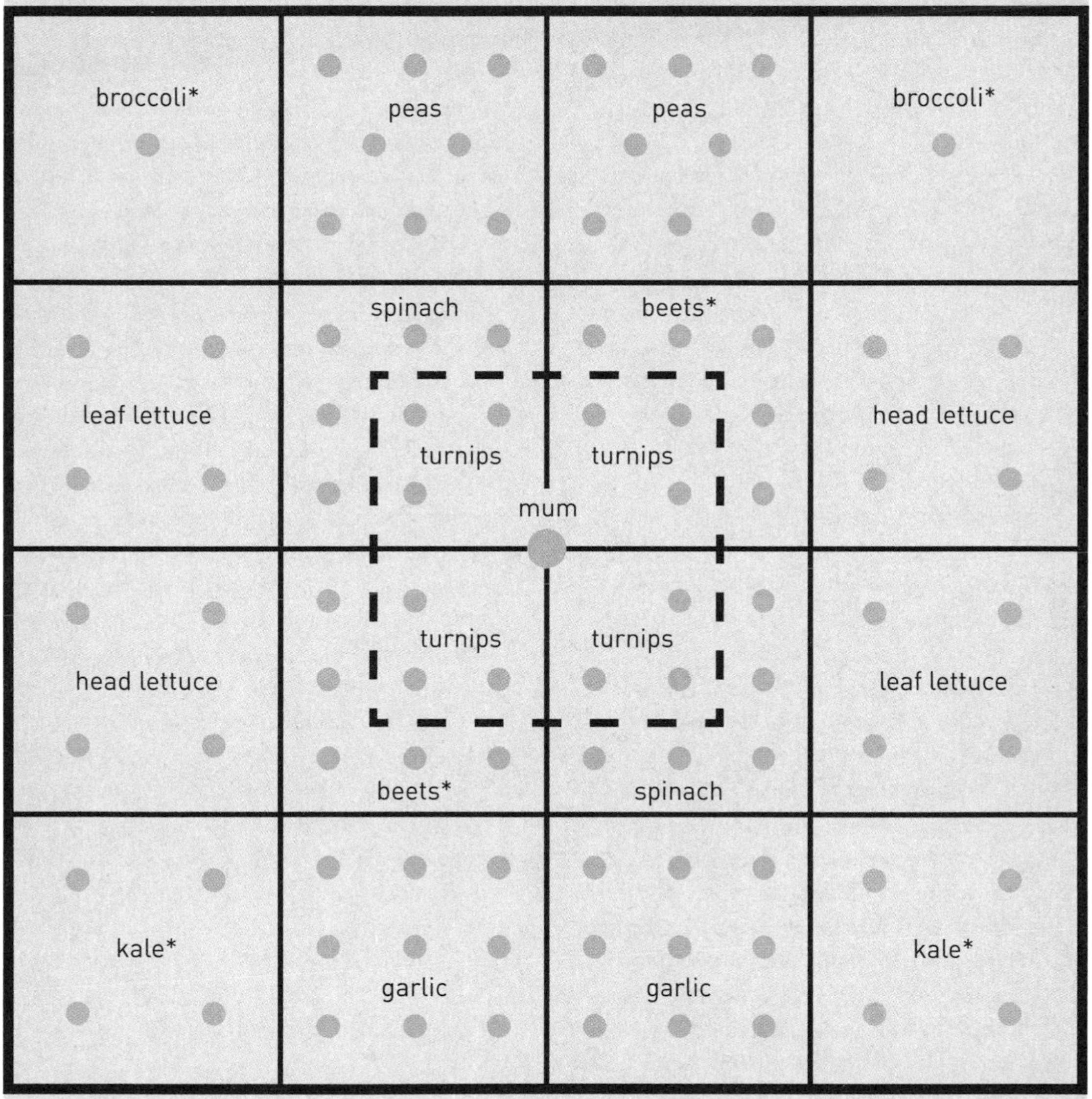

broccoli*

peas

peas

broccoli*

leaf lettuce

spinach

beets*

head lettuce

turnips

turnips

mum

head lettuce

turnips

turnips

leaf lettuce

beets*

spinach

kale*

garlic

garlic

kale*

Root Vegetable Garden Plan for Raised Beds

The cool thing about this plan, other than the companion planting and spacing, is the use of our "tater boxes," which temporarily deepen any raised bed. Build a raised bed, place it in your yard, and fill it with soil following the instructions in chapter 2.

You will need:

> 1 electric drill or hammer
>
> 24 1 × 6 boards, 2' (60cm) long (I used fence pickets cut into thirds)
>
> 48 smaller screws or nails
>
> 8 1' (20cm) bags of potting soil
>
> 8 bags of at least five different composts
>
> 2 red seed potatoes (enough to count four eyes)
>
> 2 white seed potatoes (enough to count four eyes)
>
> 4 sweet potato slips/plants
>
> 1 bunch onion sets
>
> 1 package carrot seeds
>
> 1 package cracker jack *big* marigolds (3ft)
>
> 1 package basil seeds or one basil plant

1. On your driveway, assemble boxes using four of 1×6 boards per box (1 boards per side). Screw (or nail) together your boards in a square (you'll make a total of six). Don't worry about how crooked the screws are or how maimed the heads of the nails end up. Just make the boards stick together in a square-type shape long enough for you to get it to the backyard.
2. With your raised bed properly filled with soil, evenly space two of your tator boxes atop of your freshly damp dirt on the south side of your garden (to make sweet potato and carrot boxes). Fill them with dirt and then water them.
3. With your finger, divide your boxes according to the dotted lines in the plans on the next page.
4. Cut your seed potatoes into chunks with at least one eye each. Bury them in their corresponding spots about an inch deep. Put two marigold seeds in the center of each potato box.
5. Transplant the sweet potatoes.
6. Poke ½" (13mm) deep holes in your carrot/onion box according to the diagram. Put one onion set or two carrot seeds in each hole. Plunk a couple of basil seeds (or a plant) in the center.
7. Water every other day for a week, and as needed after that.

As your potatoes grow (not sweet potatoes, mind you, the other taters), stack on a couple of tater boxes and gradually fill with dirt to keep them buried to the gizzards. When they outgrow those boxes, add the remaining two boxes and fill those with the remaining dirt.

Why, you ask? Potatoes don't grow directly under the plants. They also shoot off the sides, so the more plant you "hill up," the more potatoes you get!

Your marigolds like to root off their big, honkin' stems too, so they should hang pretty well with the burying and keep scaring off those bugs.

Top-left quadrant

baking potato ● | baking potato ●

marigold ⊕

baking potato ● | baking potato ●

Top-right quadrant

red potato ● | red potato ●

marigold ⊕

red potato ● | red potato ●

Bottom-left quadrant

sweet potato ● | sweet potato ●

sweet potato ● | sweet potato ●

Bottom-right quadrant

carrots | onions

basil ●

onions | carrots

Resources for Goat Owners

WEBSITES

Fias Co Farm

fiascofarm.com

This site has a world of information for the beginner goat keeper. It will tell you everything you want to know about raising, breeding, and milking goats. Hands down the best resource on the web.

Goat Justice League

goatjusticeleague.org

This is a Seattle-based site detailing urban/suburban goat care and municipal concerns. Successfully lobbied for pro-goat legislation.

BOOKS

Your Goats by Gail Damerow (written for children, but is perfect for any beginner goat keeper)

The Goat Handbook by Ulrich Jaudas and Seyedmehdi Mobini, DVM

Raising Goats For Dummies by Cheryl K. Smith

Raising Milk Goats Successfully by Gail Luttmann

Barnyard in Your Backyard: A Beginner's Guide to Raising Chickens, Ducks, Geese, Rabbits, Goats, Sheep, and Cattle by Gail Damerow

Storey's Guide to Raising Dairy Goats, 4th Edition: Breeds, Care, Dairying, Marketing by Jerry Belanger

BREED CLUBS AND ASSOCIATIONS:

American Dairy Goat Association

adga.org

American LaMancha Club

lamanchas.com

Oberhasli Breeders International

oberhasli.org

National Saanen Breeders Association

nationalsaanenbreeders.com

Alpines International

alpinesinternationalclub.com

Good Neighbors Handout for Suburban Goat Owners

WHY KEEP GOATS?

The fun: Goats are entertaining, safe, low-maintenance pets. Without top teeth, claws, or the body weight to do anyone any real damage, they are perfect pets for a suburban family.

The lawn care: Goats keep any area they inhabit free of leaves, weeds, and unruly grass. They trim and edge without the noise of machinery.

The milk: Beautiful, best-tasting, and most nutritious ever. Fresh goat's milk cheese is heaven on earth.

Compost magic: Goats consume kitchen waste, weeds, and lawn clippings, reducing stress on landfills and turning household compost into a wonderfully balanced super-fertile soil. Perfect for the best gardening conditions imaginable—without chemical fertilizers.

GOAT FAQS

Q: Is it going to be dirty and/or smelly?
A: A well-maintained goat set-up is a very low- or no-odor environment. Much lower maintenance than keeping cats or dogs.

Q: Am I going to be kept up at night?
A: Goats are very quiet most of the time, particularly during the early morning hours and well before and after sunset. There's no howling at the moon or late night brawls. Goats tuck in for the night before their owners.

Q: Do they carry or spread disease?
A: Zoonoses, or diseases that can be transmitted from animal to human, are almost non-existent in backyard goats. And anything you're likely to catch from a goat, you could just as easily get from a dog or cat.

Q: Is it even legal?
A: Yes, municipal laws in our city permit backyard goats.

Q: Can I bring my children to see your goats?
A: Yes! We love to show them off! And we love introducing our pets to the people who appreciate them the most—kids! Goats are a great teaching tool and there's nothing like the experience of hand-feeding leaves to an eager little goat.

Resources for Backyard Chicken Owners

WEBSITES

My Pet Chicken

mypetchicken.com

Purchase chicks in small batches (as few as four chicks), chick and chicken supplies, coops, feed, hatching eggs, free chicken care e-book, and breed selection tool.

BackyardChickens.com

Comprehensive information including chicken care, coop design, and breed information, plus a helpful forum of online chicken owners

Dave's Garden Poultry and Livestock Discussion Forum

www.davesgarden.com/community/forums/f/animals/all/

Mad City Chickens

madcitychickens.com

Information on getting chicken ordinances passed in your community plus general backyard chicken information.

Sandhill Preservation Center

sandhillpreservation.com

Heirloom chicken breeders dedicated to preserving historic chicken breeds.

CHICKS/HATCHING EGGS

Hoffman Hatchery

hoffmanhatchery.com

Stromberg's Chicks

www.strombergschickens.com

COOPS AND SUPPLIES

Catawba ConvertiCoops

catawbacoops.com

Backyard Pet Structures

backyardpetstructures.com

Omlet

omlet.us

Double R Discount Supply

dblrsupply.com

Tractor Supply Company

tractorsupply.com

Shop the Coop

shopthecoop.com

ORGANIC FEED AND SUPPLEMENTS

Modesto Milling

modestomilling.com

Fertrell

fertrell.com

BOOKS AND MAGAZINES

Backyard Poultry magazine
backyardpoultrymag.com

Storey's Guide to Raising Chickens, 3rd edition by Gail Damerow. Comprehensive guide to just about every aspect of chicken care and keeping.

Raising Chickens For Dummies by Kimberly Willis and Rob Ludlow. Basic, thorough instructions regarding all aspects of chicken care.

Good Neighbors Handout for Backyard Chicken Owners

WHY KEEP CHICKENS?

The eggs: Beautiful, best-tasting, and most nutritious ever. They are higher in omega-3s and lower in cholesterol than commercially produced eggs.

Keeping a few hens reduces the demand for factory-farmed eggs, which are produced under highly undesirable conditions. Plus, as far as eating local is concerned, the backyard is about as local as it gets.

Compost magic: Chickens consume kitchen waste, weeds, and lawn clippings, reducing stress on landfills and turn household compost into a wonderfully balanced super-fertile soil. Perfect for the best gardening conditions imaginable—without chemical fertilizers.

Sustainability: It may be a drop in the bucket, but shopping for eggs in the backyard and enhancing the productivity of a kitchen garden is a tangible step many people can take to reduce reliance on the corporate machinery that has taken a bite out of our independence.

BACKYARD CHICKEN FAQS

Q: Is it going to be dirty and/or smelly?
A: A well-maintained chicken set-up is a very low or no-odor environment. Much lower maintenance than keeping cats and dogs.

Q: Am I going to get a wake-up call at dawn every morning?
A: Few backyard chicken owners keep roosters. Roosters are not necessary for egg production, just for egg fertilization. Some hens intermittently set up an egg-laying cackle in the late morning to early afternoon, but it isn't the penetrating crow of a rooster.

Just a "bawk!, I laid an egg, I laid an egg" announcement.

Hens are very quiet most of the time, particularly during the early morning hours and well before and after sunset. If only all the neighborhood dogs, leaf-blowers, and teenagers would be as considerate!

Q: What about bird flu and other diseases?
A: Bird flu has never been found in domestic flocks in the United States. In fact, experts consider an increase in home egg production to be an answer to the threat of diseases, such as avian influenza, which are aggravated by overcrowded poultry-factory conditions.

Q: Is it even legal?
A: Yes, municipal laws in our city permit backyard fowl.

Q: Can I have some eggs?
A: Yes! We love to share!

Q: Can I bring my children to see your flock?
A: Absolutely! We love introducing our flock to the people who appreciate them the most—kids! Chickens are a great teaching tool and there's nothing like the experience of gathering a warm egg from a nest.

Soapmaking and Skincare Resources

SUPPLIES

Essential Wholesale

essentialwholesale.com

Oils, butters, essential oils and essential oil blends, waxes, natural additives, containers.

Bramble Berry

brambleberry.com

Oils, butters, essential oils, waxes, kits and samplers, plus soapmaking stamps and tools, such as scales and safety goggles.

Camden Grey Essential Oils

camdengrey.com

Oils, butters, essential oils, waxes, additives, plus a wide selection of soap molds.

Majestic Mountain Sage

thesage.com

Home of our favorite online lye calculator, plus supplies and recipes for soap and skincare products. Lots of information about essential oil properties in terms of skincare.

Miller's Homemade Soap Pages

millersoap.com

Friendly, approachable online guide to soap-making, including recipes, methods, helpful links, and troubleshooting help.

Latherings

latheringsforum.com

Online forum with tons of Q&As, recipes, and soap talk.

BOOKS AND ONLINE INFORMATION

The Soapmaker's Companion by Susan Miller Cavitch

The Everything Soapmaking Book by Alicia Grosso

The Complete Idiot's Guide to Making Natural Soaps by Sally W. Trew and Zonella B. Gould

Smart Soapmaking: The Simple Guide to Making Traditional Handmade Soap Quickly, Safely, and Reliably by Anne L. Watson

Milk Soapmaking: The Smart and Simple Guide by Anne L. Watson

Resources for Beekeepers

WEBSITES

American Beekeeping Federation
abfnet.org

Back Yard Beekeepers Association
backyardbeekeepers.com

Bee Source
beesource.com

Beekeeping Forum
beekeepingforums.com

Dave's Garden Beekeeping Discussion Forum
davesgarden.com/community/forums/f/beekeeping/all

Garden Web Bees and Beekeeping
forums.gardenweb.com/forums/bees

Mid-Atlantic Apiculture Research and Extension Consortium (MAAREC)
agdev.anr.udel.edu/maarec

National Honey Board
nhb.org

PERIODICALS

American Bee Journal
americanbeejournal.com

Bee Culture
beeculture.com

BOOKS

The Beekeeper's Bible: Bees, Honey, Recipes & Other Home Uses by Richard A. Jones and Sharon Sweeney-Lynch

Keeping Bees: All You Need to Know to Tend Hives, Harvest Honey & More by Ashley English

Keeping Bees and Making Honey by Alison Benjamin and Brian McCallum

Storey's Guide to Keeping Honey Bees by Malcolm T. Sanford

SUPPLIES

Brushy Mountain Bee Farm
brushymountainbeefarm.com

Dadant and Sons
dadant.com

Mann Lake Limited
mannlakeltd.com

Rossman Apiaries
gabees.com

FIND A BEEKEEPER'S ASSOCIATION NEAR YOU
Bee Culture magazine
online beekeeper's Who's Who:
beeculture.com/content/whoswho

Good Neighbors Handout for Backyard Beekeepers

WHY BACKYARD HONEYBEES?

The honey. Raw, unfiltered honey from local flora is one of the best foods known to mankind. It's incomparably delicious and the nutritional and medicinal qualities of honey are legendary—from boosting resistance to fighting allergens to healing wounds. Home-grown honey is the best.

Pollination perks. Backyard bees travel up to several miles from the home hive, pollinating vegetables, fruit, and ornamental blooms everywhere they go. These terrific pollinators improve fruit set and ornamental beauty as they travel from plant to plant.

The environment and sustainability. Eating local doesn't get any better than this. By fostering honey production in the backyard, we know where our nourishment comes from and are closely connected to its source. No need for honey shipped from questionable sources around the globe when you've got a beehive in your own yard.

The magic. A beehive is a peek into the mystery of nature and a great way to teach children and adults about pollination, honey, and the insect world.

BACKYARD BEES FAQS:

Q: I saw a film about killer bees. It's not going to be like that, is it?

A: Africanized honeybees (AHB), also known as "killer" bees, are a different breed of bees from domesticated honeybees in North American and European hives. Domesticated honeybees are bred for a gentle temperament so they can be easily worked by the beekeeper and are generally docile and avoid conflict. When a honeybee stings, it's the end of that bee, so stinging is literally a last resort for them. Maintaining domesticated honeybee hives is a deterrent to AHB encroachment.

Q: I (or my family member) am (is) allergic to bee stings. Will there be more bees in my yard and the neighborhood?

A: It's unlikely that having bees in a neighbor's yard will increase the number of stinging insects that you come across in your own yard. In fact, the presence of honeybees may even reduce the population of other stinging insects such as wasps and yellow jackets, which are more likely to deliver unprovoked stings. Most people who live near beehives never know the hives are there.

Q: Is it safe to visit your house?

A: Yes. No special precautions are necessary unless we intend to approach the hive area itself.

Q: Is it legal to have backyard beehives?

A: Yes, municipal laws in our city permit backyard beekeeping for personal use.

Q: Can I come look at your hives? Can I taste some honey?

A: Yes! We are happy to share when we have extra. And we love introducing this fascinating hobby to others. Bees are a great teaching tool, and the more we learn about our environment, the better we can take care of it.

Good Neighbors Handout for Backyard Beekeepers (continued)

HONEYBEE IDENTIFICATION

Many insects are commonly mistaken for the honeybee, especially when you know there is a beekeeper nearby. There are a number of flying, stinging insects that act as pollinators, so not every bug you see land on your flowers will be a honeybee.

Other stinging insects commonly mistaken for honeybees are yellow jackets, hornets, and paper wasps.

There are also a number of bees that are not honeybees, such as bumblebees, carpenter bees, digger bees, leafcutter bees, sweat bees, and burrowing bees.

There is even a family of flies (called syrphids) with an appearance that mimics that of bees.

A beehive in the area will not attract additional pollinating insects. In fact, honeybees can help deter other flying insects, such as African honeybees, from invading the neighborhood.

SWARMS

Occasionally, bee colonies decide it's time to split up housekeeping. All or part of a colony will leave the hive to look for a new home. This is known as swarming.

A swarm of honeybees can be an astonishing sight. About the size of a basketball, a clustering swarm, and the resonant hum it emits, is not something you encounter every day. It is a very unusual occurrence.

Rest assured, swarming bees are not interested in attacking or stinging. They are focused on finding a new home.

A bee is most likely to sting when defending its hive and, because a swarm is, by definition, a homeless, hive-less colony, the bees will not be in a defensive mood. They're just waiting in a temporary spot for their scouts to let them know a new home has been selected.

Not all large clusters of insects are honeybees. If the swarm has a nest that looks like it's made of paper, it's probably a cluster of wasps.

If you think you've found a swarm of honeybees, call me, a beekeeper, or your local beekeeper's association.

Stay back and don't try to disturb the swarm. A beekeeper will know how to remove the swarm and provide the bees with a good home.

Purpose and Administration Duties for Baby-sitting Co-Ops

PURPOSE

To provide cost-effective sits to assist families to be more efficient with their time, while simultaneously allowing our kids to have fun and grow new friendships. If the family is truly to come first, then we need to find ways to balance all of the responsibilities without busting the budget, exhausting mom's energy, or neglecting our kids.

CO-OP BOUNDARIES

All of the incorporated township.

PAYMENT REQUIREMENTS FOR SITS

- Between the hours of 7 AM and 5 PM, payment of points will be equal to one more than your amount of children being sat per hour (e.g., 2 children = 3 points/hour.)
- Between the hours of 5 PM and 11 PM, payment of points will be equal to two more than your amount of children being sat per hour (e.g., 2 children = 4 points/hour.)
- Members are to figure sit times to round up to the nearest quarter hour (e.g., 2 hours, 12 minutes earns 2.25 hours of points. One hour and 40 minutes earns 1.75 hours of points. If the child is dropped off early to be acclimated, time does not officially start until the time agreed upon in the sit with the secretary. Please be courteous when dropping off early, and arrange that with the member doing the sit prior to that meeting.
- When sits are done at the home of the member requesting the sit, payment will be an additional one point for each hour.

REQUIREMENTS OF NEW MEMBERS FOR ENTRY INTO THE CO-OP

- Must be recommended by a current co-op member.
- Read, sign, and date bylaws and return to the president for filing.
- Provide directory information to the president.
- Attend one to two playdates as arranged by the president so that all members can meet each other.

ADMINISTRATION DUTIES

The co-op may make bylaw changes if more than 50 percent of the members are present to vote. If a member cannot attend, please provide your vote in writing to the president prior to the meeting.

Duties of the president:

- Serve one calendar year, and receive as payment of duties 5 extra points per month for the duration of that year.
- Oversee the co-op, process new members, and make and distribute member directories, as needed. This information will be kept with the president, as well as in the secretary ledger.
- Create a monthly secretary assignment list and distribute it.
- Update bylaws annually and make necessary changes as agreed upon during the voting process by members.
- Update the member directory as needed and distribute it to current members.
- Meet with current members individually if any complaints or violations have been brought to your attention.
- Notify members of upcoming meetings.

- Upon being notified by the secretary at the end of each month, maintain your own copy of all sit transactions, point counts, and points' forfeited balance. This accounting procedure will be used as a back-up copy, to ensure accurate records on both ends.

Duties of the secretary:

- This position will be served on a monthly rotating basis, with every member taking on the position at least one month during the calendar year. If there are less than twelve current members in any given calendar year, a member may be asked to serve the secretary position for more than one month. The monthly secretary schedule will be created and dispersed by the president. If any member has difficulty serving during any particular month, it will be their responsibility to make arrangements with another member to trade months. Please notify the president if this occurs.
- Fill all day and evening sitting requests as soon as possible by first calling those who have the lowest amount of points, but calling every member, if necessary, to fill the sit. The secretary has to be accountable during her month and needs to return phone calls in a timely manner, especially for emergency/last-minute sits. During her month, she needs to be available for calls, which can be done from home or a cell phone. She must let members know how best to reach her.
- When a sit is requested, record in the call record sheet of the co-op spreadsheet, being sure to note the time and how many children the sit is for. After the sit is filled, record who took the sit and the points used/received on the secretary spreadsheet. Notify members who are involved with that sit.

- In normal circumstances, a member shall sit for no more than four children besides her own. If the occasion arises that two sits are needed and only one member is available, the procedure will be as follows: One person should not be offered two sits at once, unless all other members have been offered it first and all three families are in agreement and comfortable with the arrangement. If this situation arises, another adult will be needed to be available to help and the ages of children are conducive to this agreement. The safety of the children is foremost. If you are not comfortable with an arrangement, please voice your opinion.
- Send one summary e-mail out at the end of the month to the co-op of members. This e-mail will include beginning point balances, sit transactions that occurred that month, any forfeited points, and end-of-the-month point balances. All members will have ten days to review the information for accuracy. If there are any issues with balances, members need to bring that to the president's attention during this ten day window. After these ten days, we will accept that the spreadsheet is accurate for that month.

Baby-sitting Co-Ops Bylaws Agreement

The co-op is stifled if a member accumulates more points than she uses, so please assume your responsibility in helping the co-op run smoothly with the rules set forth.

1. Each member begins with a point balance of 60. Members are required to use at least 9 points per month. If at least 9 points are not used each month, the difference will be forfeited. This process will help ensure that the co-op runs smoothly and that each member is not only sitting for other members' children, but requesting sits as well. Accept your fair share of sits and request your fair share.

2. Call the secretary to request sitting at least twenty-four hours in advance; earlier, if possible.

3. A member shall sit for no more than four children, besides her own, unless prior arrangements have been made with all parties and another adult will be present in the home to help with the children.

4. Sit in your home, unless arrangements have been made with the member requesting the sit.

5. Members requesting the sit will need to make their own arrangements for meals if sit is during eating times (e.g., breakfast, lunch, dinner, or snacks are to be packed when dropping the children off).

6. When dropping off children, parents are to leave an emergency ID card for each child being sat with the member taking the sit.

7. For any emergency or last-minute sits (less than twenty-four hours' notice), the member requesting the sit is responsible for first getting in contact with the secretary to find out the members with the lowest amount of points at that time. It is then your responsibility to contact these members to take your sit. If you are able to fill your requested sit, you must then notify the secretary with all of the sit details, (e.g., member filling the sit, the number of children, the hours of the sit).

8. Whether you are the member who has requested the sit or you are the member taking the sit, and you find that you must cancel plans, you must call the other member involved with the sit, as well as secretary. There are no penalties for canceling; however, mutual respect is necessary if our co-op is to run smoothly. If you are canceling the sit that you have originally taken, it is your responsibility to notify the secretary and try to find a replacement member to take the sit for you. If a member has requested a sit and then forgets to call and cancel, she still owes the sitter the full amount of points agreed upon.

9. Property damage is the responsibility of the family of the child who caused the damages. The two members will mutually agree upon whether the damage will require repair or replacement. If this cannot be resolved among the involved parties, then members may bring it to the attention of the president, who will serve as a mediator to resolve the conflict.

10. No spanking or hitting a child. Any discipline problems should be discussed with the parents. Time out is the preferable method of discipline.

11. Each member is to have homeowners' insurance/liability insurance/renters' insurance to cover the expense of injury or accident to other children in your home.

12. The sitter may not leave home, transport children in a car, or leave children in the

car of another without the permission of the parent, except in an extreme emergency.

13. Procedure for exiting members' point balance: Any remaining points over the initial 60 points granted at joining may be used up within two months after exiting the group. Initial 60 points expire.

14. Notice to secretary on sit requests: All members are to give at least a twenty-four hour notice to the secretary for any requested sits. The only exception to this bylaw will be in the case of a family emergency, if the member has sick children, or if the member is sick herself.

15. Waivers for current members: If a current member moves out of the boundary stated in the bylaws, but wishes to stay in the group, the member will be eligible to apply for a waiver. Granting of this waiver will be voted on by the remainder of the group. A majority vote will determine the granting or denying of this waiver.

Gardening Log

Date: _____

Gardening Week: _____

Outdoor Sowing: _____

_____

_____

_____

Transplanting: _____

_____

_____

_____

Notes: _____

_____

_____

_____

Date: _____

Gardening Week: _____

Outdoor Sowing: _____

_____

_____

_____

Transplanting: _____

_____

_____

_____

Notes: _____

_____

_____

_____

Date: _____

Gardening Week: _____

Outdoor Sowing: _____

_____

_____

_____

Transplanting: _____

_____

_____

_____

Notes: _____

_____

_____

_____

Date: _____

Gardening Week: _____

Outdoor Sowing: _____

_____

_____

_____

Transplanting: _____

_____

_____

_____

Notes: _____

_____

_____

_____

Date: _____   Date: _____

Gardening Week: _____   Gardening Week: _____

Outdoor Sowing: _____   Outdoor Sowing: _____

_____   _____

_____   _____

_____   _____

Transplanting: _____   Transplanting: _____

_____   _____

_____   _____

_____   _____

Notes: _____   Notes: _____

_____   _____

_____   _____

_____   _____

Date: _____   Date: _____

Gardening Week: _____   Gardening Week: _____

Outdoor Sowing: _____   Outdoor Sowing: _____

_____   _____

_____   _____

_____   _____

Transplanting: _____   Transplanting: _____

_____   _____

_____   _____

_____   _____

Notes: _____   Notes: _____

_____   _____

_____   _____

_____   _____

Gardening Log

Date: _____
Gardening Week: _____
Outdoor Sowing: _____
_____
_____
_____

Transplanting: _____
_____
_____
_____

Notes: _____
_____
_____
_____

Date: _____
Gardening Week: _____
Outdoor Sowing: _____
_____
_____
_____

Transplanting: _____
_____
_____
_____

Notes: _____
_____
_____
_____

Date: _____
Gardening Week: _____
Outdoor Sowing: _____
_____
_____
_____

Transplanting: _____
_____
_____
_____

Notes: _____
_____
_____
_____

Date: _____
Gardening Week: _____
Outdoor Sowing: _____
_____
_____
_____

Transplanting: _____
_____
_____
_____

Notes: _____
_____
_____
_____

Date: _____

Gardening Week: _____

Outdoor Sowing: _____

_____

_____

_____

Transplanting: _____

_____

_____

_____

Notes: _____

_____

_____

_____

Date: _____

Gardening Week: _____

Outdoor Sowing: _____

_____

_____

_____

Transplanting: _____

_____

_____

_____

Notes: _____

_____

_____

_____

Date: _____

Gardening Week: _____

Outdoor Sowing: _____

_____

_____

_____

Transplanting: _____

_____

_____

_____

Notes: _____

_____

_____

_____

Date: _____

Gardening Week: _____

Outdoor Sowing: _____

_____

_____

_____

Transplanting: _____

_____

_____

_____

Notes: _____

_____

_____

_____

INDEX

Dedication

Daisy: To Dad
Deanna: To Pop & Gran

About the Authors

Deanna Caswell and Daisy Siskin write the popular blog Little House in the Suburbs, www.littlehouseinthesuburbs.com. The blog had been featured on msn.com, thriftyfun.com, and apartmenttherapy.com.

Deanna is the author of two children's books *First Ballet* (Disney-Hyperion, 2009) and *Train Trip* (Disney-Hyperion, 2011) and is the Practically Green columnist for the *Commercial Appeal*.

Daisy has been gardening and implementing simple lifestyle behaviors for most of her life. Her columns appear in *Birds & Blooms* magazine. She enjoys making her homesteading choices pretty and palatable to the suburban lifestyle. An accomplished cook, she has worked in professional kitchens and bakeries throughout Tennessee. She is a family therapist.

Acknowledgments

Our thanks to the following people:

Our tolerant extended family members, for not batting an eye when we would carry off their various belongings "to take pictures of it in the yard."

Our understanding husbands, for not saying a word about all the weird stuff we bought and did "for the book."

Phil Chandler of biobees.com and Charles Force, for their thoughtful insights on the beekeeping chapter.

Jeff Golladay and Jimmy Gafford for their generous help getting Deanna's yard in shape while she was recovering from baby.

Melissa and Jeff for their generous help getting Daisy's yard in shape.

Jim Rowland, for his beekeeping know-how and the use of his beekeeping gear.

The folks at Hall's Feed & Seed, for their advice and letting us take pictures of their chicks.

Udder Bliss Farms, for the use of their stunt goat and chicken.

Jacqueline Musser, our editor, and Ric Deliantoni, our photographer, for making this book possible and for your expert guidance and support.

And last but not least, our blog reader family, for their helpful comments which appear throughout this book and for being so smart and warm and funny. We love ya.

Other fine Betterway Home books are available from your local bookstore and online suppliers. Visit our website at www.betterwaybooks.com.

16   15   14   13   5   4   3

ISBN 978-1-4403-1024-9

Distributed in Canada by Fraser Direct
100 Armstrong Avenue
Georgetown, Ontario, Canada L7G 5S4
Tel: (905) 877-4411

Distributed in the U.K. and Europe by
F&W Media International, LTD
Brunel House, Newton Abbot, Forde Close, TQ12 4PU, UK
Tel: (+ 44) 1626 323200, Fax: (+ 44) 1626 323319
E-mail: enquiries@fwmedia.com

Distributed in Australia by Capricorn Link
P.O. Box 704, S. Windsor NSW, 2756 Australia
Tel: (02) 4577-3555

Edited by Jacqueline Musser
Designed by Brian Roeth
Photography by Ric Deliantoni and Daisy Siskin
Page 65, White Houdan Bantam photo by Heather Spaet, Rare Feather Farm.
Page 67, Red Sex-Link chicken photo by Rachael Xu;
Buff Orpington photo by Briana R. Bogoski.
Page 89, Oberhasli goat photo by Tangled Roots Farm;
Nigerian Dwarf goat photo © Mark Beers Photography - 2010, rights granted to Smithurmonds Dairy Goats for website use.
Page 90, Alpine goat photo by Goat Milk Stuff.
Page 92, Mini-Nubian goat photo by Gold Ducat Farmette;
Mini-Toggenberg goat photo by Cherry Butte Dairy Goats.
Production coordinated by Mark Griffin

Find More Books on Simple Living

  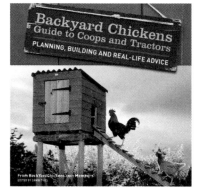

I Garden: Urban Style

by Reggie Solomon
and Michael Nolan

Farm Fresh Flavors

by Randall L. Smith

Backyard Chickens Guide to Coops and Tractors

edited by David Thiel

Available online and in bookstores everywhere!

To get started join our mailing list at betterwaybooks.com

FOLLOW US ON:

Become a fan of our Facebook page: facebook.com/BetterwayHomeBooks

Find more great advice on Twitter: @Betterway_Home